STALIN'S GOLD

STALIN'S GOLD

The Story of *HMS* Edinburgh and Its Treasure

BARRIE PENROSE

GRANADA
London Toronto Sydney New York

Granada Publishing Limited
Frogmore, St Albans, Herts AL2 2NF
and
36 Golden Square, London W1R 4AH
866 United Nations Plaza, New York, NY 10017, USA
117 York Street, Sydney, NSW 2000, Australia
100 Skyway Avenue, Rexdale, Ontario M9W 3A6, Canada
61 Beach Road, Auckland, New Zealand

Published by Granada Publishing 1982

British Library Cataloguing Publication Data

Penrose, Barry
Stalin's Gold: the story of HMS Edinburgh and its treasure.
11. Edinburgh (*Ship*)   2. Salvage—Barents Sea
3. Warships—Great Britain
I. Title
914'0963'24   VK149

ISBN 0-246-11778-8

Made and printed in Great Britain by
Richard Clay (The Chaucer Press) Ltd,
Bungay, Suffolk

Granada ®
Granada Publishing ®

For Edward, Isabelle and Amélie

Contents

Acknowledgements   viii
Introduction   xi

PART I   The Sinking of HMS *Edinburgh*

Chapter 1   The *Edinburgh*'s Last Voyage   3
Chapter 2   Russia and the Bullion Run   41

PART II   The Search

Chapter 3   The Problems   75
Chapter 4   Jessop Lands the Contract   92
Chapter 5   The Wreck is Found   124

PART III   Recovery

Chapter 6   Preparation   143
Chapter 7   Departure   153
Chapter 8   The Dive Begins   169
Chapter 9   Discovery   192
Chapter 10   Gold Fever   197

Index   219

Acknowledgements

I offer warm thanks to the many people who have helped in the research and preparation of this book. I am particularly grateful to HMS *Edinburgh* survivors who were kind enough to let me have their first-hand accounts of their days and experiences with the great warship. Although I cannot name them all on this page, their bravery and deeds emerge forcefully in the story which follows. I am also indebted to survivors from other ships who were prepared to talk about their part in the naval engagement which ended in the sinking of the British cruiser in May 1942. Relatives and friends of survivors, too, were kind enough to send me a wide variety of photographs, newspaper cuttings and other helpful memorabilia.

For Richard Johnson, my editor at Granada, I have nothing but praise for his calm and professional approach to our task. I would also like to thank James Ringrose and David Bona for sparing me so much of their time and for imparting much knowledge of the gold recovery story. To Keith Jessop, without whom there may not have been an *Edinburgh* project, I also extend thanks. For the teams aboard the *Dammtor* and the *Stephaniturm* – especially the divers – no praise is high enough.

At the Ministry of Defence Naval Historical Branch, Captain Beeching, David Brown and Robert Coppock were always kind, efficient and commendably ruthless in their pursuit of accuracy. I would like to thank Gordon Fielden of the Anglo-German Literary Agency for his customary support. And, for their patience and kindness, Brian and June Allen.

I owe a special debt to my researcher Nicole Le Breton. For her no praise again is enough. Without her work, help and encouragement this book would still not be completed.

For permission to reproduce the photographs and the drawing, I would like to thank the *Sunday Times*. Ken Griffiths took the photograph of Ric Wharton and Malcolm Williams.

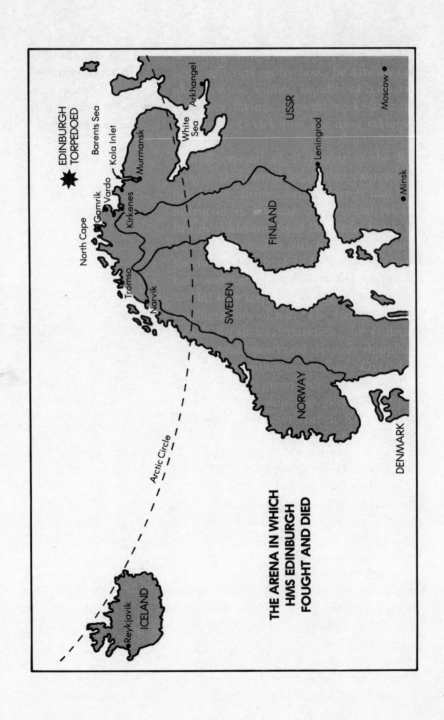

THE ARENA IN WHICH
HMS EDINBURGH
FOUGHT AND DIED

Introduction

On Saturday 25 April 1942, Captain Hugh Faulkner, commanding the cruiser HMS *Edinburgh* anchored near Murmansk in the Kola Inlet of north-west Russia, signed an official receipt for ninety-three smallish, rough wooden boxes delivered to him at the quayside by a party of armed Russian soldiers. What was in those boxes only Faulkner, several of his senior officers, and a few Soviet officials knew in any detail.

In fact, the boxes were packed with five tons of gold bullion, each thick rectangular bar stamped with the Soviet régime's official assay mark and the hammer and sickle. The 465 gold bars were part of Stalin's payment for American weapons and supplies sent to Russia early in the war, supplies carried by Allied convoys above the Arctic circle to Murmansk. The gold the *Edinburgh* was to carry – five 28 lb bars packed in sawdust to each box – was carefully disguised by its Russian packers in Moscow. Secrecy was necessary, not only because of the ordinary risks of transporting valuables but also because Hitler's armies were at that time still deep inside European Russia, with Murmansk well within their military grasp.

Nevertheless, hints were picked up by *Edinburgh*'s crew that they were carrying something unusual. Chief petty officer Levick from Sheffield remembers: 'I was in charge of a working party detailed to stow the cases in the bomb-room amidships. We had a crane for getting our Walrus aircraft back on deck, and we used that to lift them aboard. We had no idea what they contained until the supervising officer, Commander Jeffries, told me: "If any of those fall in the water you'll go down to get them!" I was one of the ship's divers. From that moment we were aware we were carrying something valuable.'

On the outside of the cheap deal boxes were two leaden seals stamped 'Gohran Control' and 'Gohran Section' in Russian Cyrillic: a nondescript Soviet State Bank code which would not, it was thought, attract unusual attention on the 950-mile land journey from Moscow to Murmansk.

'I distinctly remember the boxes being brought to the ship,' says ex-able-seaman Cyril Moore, now a tax inspector in Penzance, Cornwall. 'The boxes were similar to the old lard boxes. I helped secure the boat that brought them alongside us. I think the boxes came on board amidships, almost abreast of the torpedo tubes.'

Reg Levick recalls a flat-bottomed dumb-lighter coming alongside early in the morning. Russian women manned the dumb-lighter while Red Army soldiers carrying automatic rifles guarded the heavy, tightly-packed wooden boxes.

Ex-Royal Marine Bill Miles, now a technical inspector in Ipswich, Suffolk, was also part of the working party. He had heard a rumour that the boxes contained ship's stores, probably beans: 'But then colour-sergeant Quinn said: "When you load this stuff, don't let anybody run off with a box." "Who wants a box of beans?" I remember saying.'

Pat Hughes, who was to spend thirty-four years in the Royal Navy, was servicing a Walrus aircraft on the *Edinburgh* when the lighter arrived with its armed Russian escort. 'The buzz at the time was that the wooden boxes contained two to three million pounds-worth of gold bullion,' he says. 'We understood that it was Polish gold in payment for arms shipments to Russia.'

Despite Captain Faulkner's efforts to keep the matter secret, an accident occurred which ensured that news of the gold would spread rapidly through the ship. When the boxes were being hoisted aboard, one box slipped from its sling. 'It crashed down, just missing me, and there in front of me and the others were the gold bars,' says Bill Miles. 'The box had taken the knuckle of one hand. There was a hell of a panic. This young lieutenant realised we'd seen it was gold and came sliding down the ladder in one go. He tried to grab it away but it was heavier than he thought.'

The lieutenant called for a shipwright quickly to repair the broken wooden box. 'The gold bars were packed in sawdust,' says Miles. 'I remember the chippy being sent for, and the ingots were re-packed. So no doubt my finger-prints were on some of the gold. The bars were bigger than I expected and looked more of a silvery colour than gold. I remember saying to a mate that if we could get a couple of bars to our locker we'd be made!'

Miles was a member of the Royal Marine detachment on board the *Edinburgh*, and one of his duties was to stand guard outside the captain's quarters. The keys for the bomb-room where the gold had been stowed were on a hook outside the captain's cabin.

News that some £2 million-worth of bullion was being kept in the compartment normally reserved for aircraft ammunition had spread quickly through the 10,000-ton cruiser. But the crew had other things to hold their attention at that stage of the war. Reg Levick, who had helped lift the gold, had a strong premonition about the coming voyage. 'I told Commander Jeffries it was going to be a bad trip,' he says. Before he left England Levick had given his wife a gold hunter watch and chain and told her it was for their son. 'There was one really bad omen: water streamed in red rivulets off the decks from those Russian cases. It was only stain from the crimson stencilling on each case, but we were suspicious and apprehensive. I thought to myself: "Russian gold, dripping with blood." '

Such premonitions had a way of fulfilling themselves on the Murmansk convoys, the most dangerous and hellishly uncomfortable of all the epic naval operations of the Second World War. At first *Edinburgh* and the convoys she and her destroyers escorted to Russia had battled against temperatures of 20° to 30°F below zero and against the furious storms that are the natural hazards of Arctic waters, even in spring. Then, when Hitler recognised the importance of the convoys to Russian defences, he attacked them relentlessly with torpedo aircraft, U-boats and warships. Later in the same year that *Edinburgh* left Murmansk at the head of the thirteen-ship convoy QP 11, another convoy, PQ 17, lost twenty-three of its thirty-four-ship strength. The Arctic waters for many ships and men had become a terrible and tragic graveyard.

WEATHER.
Wind from 020°, force 3. Squalls
Mist and Snow
Temp, Air 16°F. Sea 34°F.
Sea and Swell, 22.
Visibility, 2-10 miles, patchy.

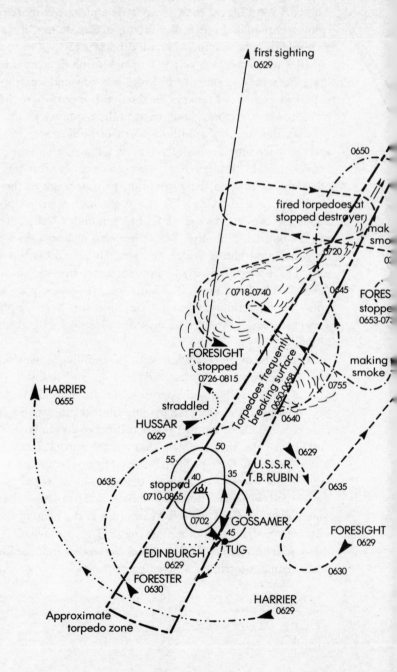

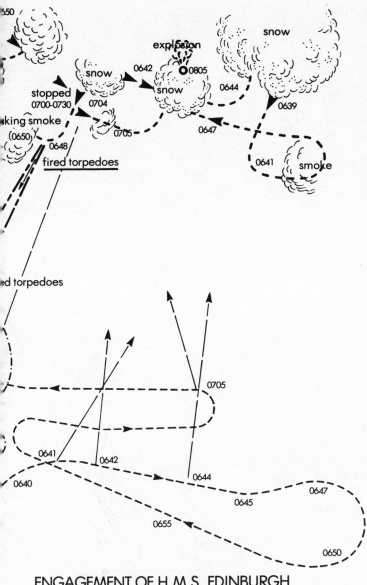

ENGAGEMENT OF H.M.S. EDINBURGH
AND ESCORT WITH 3 GERMAN
DESTROYERS 2nd May 1942
TIMES ARE ZONE MINUS 2
MOVEMENTS ARE APPROXIMATE.

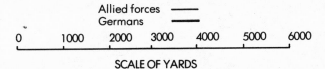

Allied forces ——
Germans ——

| 0 | 1000 | 2000 | 3000 | 4000 | 5000 | 6000 |

SCALE OF YARDS

Based on a map from the Public Record Office

PART I
The Sinking of
HMS *Edinburgh*

I

The *Edinburgh*'s Last Voyage

HMS *Edinburgh*, one of the two 10,000-ton cruisers of the class which bore her name, was launched at Wallsend-on-Tyne in 1938 and completed in the following year. She was a formidable warship with twelve 6-inch and twelve 4-inch anti-aircraft guns plus numerous smaller ones, as well as being fitted with six 21-inch torpedo tubes. With a speed of 32.5 knots, and carrying four Walrus aircraft launched by catapult, the cruiser was one of the most important and modern fighting ships in the fleet. The Germans soon recognised this fact and in October 1939, a month after the outbreak of war, *Edinburgh* was attacked during the first German air raid of the war on Britain, that on the Firth of Forth. Seven men were injured from bomb splinters during the raid, an event witnessed by Thomas Whittle from Frazerburgh. 'I saw that first German bomber descend to drop its load on the Forth bridge, which had no protection so early in the war,' he said. 'The bomber disappeared to the northeast and I think crashed down on a small range of hills known locally as the "Fife Alps".'

HMS *Edinburgh* was by no means new to the work of protecting convoys. She had patrolled in Norwegian waters and had also escorted convoys in the North Sea and on the dangerous run from Gibraltar to Malta. On board, her crew – many of whom had had no leave for almost a year – were well used to the sound of falling bombs and the constant din of shells being fired at attacking aircraft. In other words *Edinburgh* had had its baptism of fire in 1939 and was battle-proven by the beginning of 1942.

Now it was April. High in the forward gun turret, chief petty

3

officer Newman reported to the control office on the bridge that his gun crew were present and correct. Newman settled down to watch several of his men play cards, leaning over the centre gun tray to get a more comfortable view of the game. Outside, a sudden blizzard and the fading afternoon light were reducing visibility. The sea was calm, but it was bitterly cold and the *Edinburgh* was covered from top to bottom in a half-inch-thick crust of ice. The worsening Arctic weather had noticeably worked its way inside 'A' turret; condensation from men laughing and talking had formed icy rivulets above them.

Ordinary-seaman Neville Holt had joined the Royal Navy as a boy and that afternoon was relaxing in the telephone exchange on board the *Edinburgh*. Another boy telegraphist, Alan Higgins, had joined the fast modern cruiser in April 1941. He was perpetually sea-sick and regularly looking for a place to lie down, even when colleagues in his watch sat down for their afternoon tea and bread, butter and jam. The new watch had just gone on duty around the ship, and still there was nothing unusual: only the sway of the cruiser zigzagging at high speed some fifteen miles ahead of the convoy, the whistle of the wind and the biting cold.

Alan Higgins, the boy telegraphist, had found an empty spot on top of some clothes lockers to bed down for the afternoon. There were 850 men on board and space was short. Brown, another telegraphist, shouted at Higgins that he was poaching his billet.

Charles Whitehead had just finished his watch in the foremost 6-inch control tower above the bridge and was making his way down to the canteen for his afternoon tea, when he was waylaid by a mate who wanted to chat. It was nothing important at the time.

In the seamen's mess amidships William Austin arrived to find shipwright Harold Lloyd carrying tins of jam, beans and other provisions. Lloyd carefully placed each tin side-by-side on the mess-room table.

Pat Hughes, senior maintenance rating, was in the store on the port side amidships talking with petty officer McIntyre. The two men could hear the slight shuddering of the cruiser's mighty engines. But it was a constant healthy movement, reassuring to men wanting nothing else but to get back home safely.

Peter Matthews, an electrical mechanic, was on watch with three other ratings in the low-power switch-room. Matthews had often light-heartedly reminded the shipwright, who was in charge of damage control for his section of the ship, not to be over-enthusiastic about shoring up hatches in the event of *Edinburgh* being hit by torpedoes. Matthews wanted the shipwright to make absolutely certain that he had seen the mechanic on deck before he closed any hatches. It was a widespread fear among ratings that they might one day find themselves hopelessly trapped inside a damaged and sinking ship.

Matthews wondered whether Rear-Admiral Stuart Bonham-Carter and Captain Hugh Faulkner shared the same anxieties. On his flagship's bridge that Thursday afternoon, 30 April, Bonham-Carter reflected on the wisdom of moving *Edinburgh* those fifteen miles ahead of QP 11. Theoretically his aim was sound. He was heading as far north as possible in order to find the ice-pack, a solid mass of moving ice that was farthest away from the reach of German aircraft and submarines. The ice-pack was therefore his navigation limit, before the convoy turned to come down the Norwegian coast.

Bonham-Carter was indelibly aware of the danger his convoy faced two hundred miles from the relative safety of Murmansk. The Germans had spotted QP 11 forming at the Russian port forty-eight hours before. But would their reconnaissance aircraft or U-boats scouting this section of the Barents Sea spot the convoy a second time? Visibility was already patchy with welcome mist and snow squalls coming from the north-east. With further mist and thickening cloud QP 11 might possibly steal through the night unnoticed.

While the Rear-Admiral reflected on his decision to zigzag ahead of the convoy, a point he had discussed with *Edinburgh*'s captain, Hugh Faulkner, other naval officers with very different intentions considered their options. One of them, Kapitänleutnant Seibicke, on U-boat 436, had searched without success for the *Edinburgh*, now speeding somewhere well ahead of convoy QP 11. But Kapitän-leutnant Max Teichert, on U-456, struck lucky.

Teichert already had an advantage, as can be seen from an entry in his log-book that morning. At 11.20 a.m. that Thursday he had written tersely: 'Cruiser in sight to the south, definitely *Belfast* class.' Exactly forty minutes later, with his powerful quarry very much in his sights, Teichert added: 'Signal 1142/701: most urgent, square 5582, cruiser type *Belfast* on westerly course at high speed, zigzagging sharply – Teichert.' U-456 moved cautiously closer to HMS *Edinburgh*; stealth and cunning were important against a war machine that, once aroused, could easily despatch the submarine with her awesome array of depth charges and bombs.

In such unpredictable waters Captain Faulkner had kept his ship and its company at battle readiness. In the two engine-rooms, and in the boiler-rooms, the crew had repeatedly practised their emergency drill. In the event of an attack they now knew what to do and how to do it without the need to call for assistance from the damage-control parties. There were other precautions, seemingly mundane but equally important. Z-doors on the upper deck, fitted with manholes, were closed tight to minimise the spread of fire.

While the watch changed on board the *Edinburgh* that grey Thursday afternoon, Kapitänleutnant Teichert estimated his range at 1,000 metres and the British cruiser's speed at fifteen knots. At 4.18 p.m. Teichert noted in his log-book: 'Square 5519 AC, wind NW force 6–7, sea 5–6, visibility 8 miles. Salvo of three torpedoes from tubes I, II and IV. Range = 1,000 metres, target's speed = 15 knots, angle on the bow = 60, torpedo speed = 30 knots, torpedo depth setting = 4 metres, angular spacing = 4, point of aim forward funnel.'

Officers on *Edinburgh*'s bridge, realising from the trails of the torpedoes that they were under attack from a U-boat, immediately sounded the alarm. Nineteen-year-old able-seaman Cyril Moore was on his first ship. 'Normally when off-duty I slept in the ship's telephone exchange because it was one of the warmest spots. That Thursday afternoon, I couldn't sleep there,' he says. 'Then I could hear a voice saying that torpedoes were approaching, in the same calm voice that a station announcer uses to report the arrival of a train.'

Many men aboard the *Edinburgh* did not learn that three German torpedoes were heading in their direction. Some were off-watch and asleep in their hammocks, the officers in their bunks. Others were writing letters home, while the great majority passed the time in unconcerned chatter. 'When the first torpedo struck us,' Cyril Moore recalled, 'the first part of the ship to be cut off was the telephone exchange.' It was the cosy spot where he would normally have been sleeping on such an afternoon.

Max Teichert added to his log record: '2 explosions in quick succession, running time 80 seconds = 1200 metres. Boat dips.' For the U-boat officer it was a considerable triumph and, remarkably, achieved alone; his action would be rewarded with an Iron Cross. For the British cruiser, it was the dull, almost inauspicious, beginnings of an epitaph. 'There was a terrible explosion and a blinding flash, darkness, then cries from the injured and dying in the next compartment, just one steel plate away,' remembered Alan Higgins, who had been accused of poaching another telegraphist's billet above some clothes lockers.

Teichert's first torpedo from tube number one struck the *Edinburgh* on the starboard side, tearing open a mighty hole big enough to take a double-decker London bus, and creating death and destruction inside the heart of the ship. A split-moment later, Teichert's second torpedo struck. 'The whole ship bucked, like a bronco, throwing me up in the air. No sooner had I come down again than there was another explosion,' says Lawrence Newman. 'The first torpedo hit the ship amidships on the starboard side; the second hit the stern and effectively crippled us.'

The lights went off in 'A' turret and elsewhere, followed by an eerie absence of sound, which ended in the loud babble of disorientated and apprehensive seamen. 'It's bombs,' shouted one. 'Bombs, my foot!' countered another; 'that's tin fish.' Tin fish were torpedoes and the second one from U-456 had blown off the cruiser's stern and wrecked her steering gear. Hours later officers established that the first torpedo had struck between stations 70 and 87 and 248 and 260 on the starboard side.

Edinburgh's captain, Hugh Faulkner, wearing his duffle-coat, thick white gloves, woollen scarf, and binoculars around his neck, ordered the starboard torpedoes to be fired to reduce a 7° list to starboard. Luckily, Faulkner and Bonham-Carter soon re-established communication with the engine-room. The two seasoned officers learned that steam pressure was being maintained and that all four shafts were still rotating. But the stern abaft 'Y' turret was fast breaking up from armoured bulkhead no. 238 and broke off two hours later, carrying with it the port inner 'A' bracket and propeller. With the steering gear and both inner shafts gone, the *Edinburgh*'s speed was reduced to under ten knots.

Although her stern had been blown off, *Edinburgh* was still able to steam at slow speed back in the direction of Murmansk. In the Kola Inlet, which leads to Russia's most important northern port, were two heavily armed Russian destroyers, the *Gremyaschi* and the *Sokrushitelni*, which it was hoped would sail to the rescue.

In a letter written at the time to his wife, Rear-Admiral Bonham-Carter recorded: 'We managed to get 60 miles in about 36 hours and then got attacked by German destroyers. The old ship could only steer round and round in a circle at 7 knots.'

While the cruiser steamed helplessly, unable to escape at speed to the safety of Murmansk, some hands below decks saw the damage more dramatically. Alan Higgins says: 'I could see that the quarter-deck had curled up like a sardine tin enveloping the two 6-inch gun turrets so completely that the two sets of triple guns were actually protruding through the quarter-deck itself, making them completely useless.'

Peter Matthews, the naval rating unashamedly fearful he might one day be caught like a rat in a trap below decks, now found himself in exactly that danger. 'I and two or three ratings were on watch in the low-power room when the torpedoes struck. We had to make our way up through a number of decks,' he said, 'hoping that the hatches would still open.' Matthews had escaped with his life – for the moment anyway – but the scene around him reminded him of the danger that still faced the ship and its crew. 'The sudden transformation of a large ship from a powerful fighting force, alive and vibrant, to a dead hulk, silent, cold and dark, needs to be experienced to be appreciated,' Matthews added. Like others aboard the *Edinburgh* at this critical moment he was only too well aware that a German U-boat was still in the vicinity, no doubt preparing for the kill. And how long before the submarine was joined by other deadly predators?

After the first and second torpedoes had chiselled their murderous routes into the warship, water and oil fuel leaked and rushed into vacuums created by the initial explosions. Men in the wireless transmission room close to the bomb-room on the port side had been killed instantly, their bodies sucked into a bomb-room normally used for storing Walrus aircraft ordnance. Others had not been so fortunate. Seventeen-year-old seaman Holt was in the telephone exchange in one of the lower decks when the *Edinburgh* had first been hit. Holt had not been able to fight his way to safety since the compartment he was in was below water. 'The boy's morale was kept up by Captain Faulkner and his divisional officers talking to him through a voice pipe,' recalls Jack Thwaite, an ordinary signalman. 'But eventually he succumbed to the lack of oxygen or to CO_2, which had leaked from the deep-freezer room next to the exchange.'

Former able-bodied seaman James Giddings, from Corsham in Wiltshire, was one of the injured, suffering lacerations and a damaged right shoulder. 'I remember a torch being shone through the buckled door of the mess and a voice calling out to me to come towards the torch. I must have grabbed a pillar,' he recalls, 'because I was still clinging to it when the voice told me to walk towards the torch-light.' Giddings lost consciousness for three days and was one of the few to escape alive from his mess.

Charles Whitehead, from West Yorkshire, was equally fortunate. Just before the first torpedo struck he was heading for the canteen, having finished his afternoon watch. A passing chat with a messmate probably saved his life. Whitehead remembers the lights going out after 'a terrific explosion'. 'I was flung away from the hatch,' he remembers. 'By the time I got my torch the hatch had been closed as the mess deck had become flooded.' Around him Whitehead could hear the groans and pleas for help from injured or dying seamen. Many were his close friends. By using the bomb-room hatch he was able, along with a few others, to lower a rope ladder and escape. 'Many were in a poor way,' he says, 'covered in oil.'

Others were more fortunate. Reg Levick was toasting a slice of bread before a one-bar radiator in the mess when he heard 'a terrible thump'. His pot of tea jumped in the air along with stools and other tables nearby. 'I found myself lying on the deck under a mess table,' he says. 'I scrambled up in the dark trying to decide which was forward and which was aft.' After feeling his way along a line of kit lockers, Levick eventually reached, not before getting caught up in some hammock canvas, the one door out of the mess. When he emerged in a dim light, the secondary lighting system having been switched on by now, he saw an unusual sight. 'The canteen manager was stuffing bundles of bank notes into his pockets, some six weeks' takings.' Several weeks later the canteen manager was to explain to Levick that the mess takings had gone down with the *Edinburgh*.

Staff-sergeant Cyril Jarrett of the Royal Tank Regiment was soon to be grateful to another canteen manager, minutes after the first two torpedoes struck. Jarrett had been serving in Russia as an instructor to Russian officers and NCO's in the maintenance of British 'Valentine' and 'Matilda' battle tanks. He had boarded the *Edinburgh*, bringing with him various parts of captured enemy guns, for the journey back to Britain. After months of privation in Russia he was delighted to be going home.

The first torpedo narrowly missed the area where Jarrett was sipping a cup of tea. 'The hatch was slammed shut and we were locked in, in total darkness,' he remembers. 'The ship had been going at full speed and we were shipping the maximum amount of water in the minimum of time.' Over the intercom he heard orders being rapidly given out and 'fire control', 'fire control' being repeated. The ship was beginning to list heavily and the staff-sergeant from Gravesend in Kent could hear the *Edinburgh*'s own torpedoes being fired. 'The ship's list was getting worse with every passing minute,' he says. 'The port side in which I was locked was going deeper into the water and I remember thinking very danger-ously so. In fact I was quite expecting the ship to turn turtle!'

Jarrett was the last man eventually to clamber out of the compartment where he had been trapped. Gradually the ship righted itself and a hatch was opened to let sailors escape from the real danger of suffocation or drowning. When he saw the daylight he noticed that the gangway was already crowded with sailors who had left the compartment in front of him.

Outside visibility was poor. The ship's canteen, on the same deck from which Jarrett had escaped, had been thrown open. Apart from a few Russian roubles, which were worthless on board, he had no money to buy cigarettes. 'Somehow I summoned the courage to ask for some,' he says. 'The manager who was there threw me a packet of twenty saying: "Here, have these on me;

damned decent of me, isn't it?" They were his exact words.'

William Austin, who had been in the mess with shipwright Harold Lloyd sorting out his collection of jams, beans and other provisions, was left holding the handle of his tea-cup when the explosion occurred. Oddly, in view of most of the other men's experiences, Austin and Lloyd did not realise at first that the *Edinburgh* itself was under attack. One crewman suggested that 'B' turret had opened up on the enemy. But others could smell gas from the mess fridges. Sailors began rushing out of the mess to discover what had happened; several of them clambered over Harold Lloyd, who was still on his hands and knees trying to collect the tins, which were rolling all over the sloping deck.

Nearby men were attempting to bring the injured up from the stoker's mess. Captain Faulkner suddenly appeared and ordered some of the men to go aft. Austin found himself staring at one crewman who was on his knees praying, stark naked, on the aircraft deck, apparently oblivious of the activity going on around him. Austin says he whispered to himself: 'That won't do you much bloody good!' Heading aft, he reached the damage control station but found it wrecked. Shipwright Dicky Bannister was picking himself up from the deck; he told Austin he was not certain what had happened but he had already inspected some of the damage.

The two men picked up tools from the emergency wooden boxes secured near the ammunition housing and gradually began the task of shoring up the deck-head in front of them. Two young shipwrights arrived at the top of the ladder and one of them defiantly called out: 'Hey, you'll cop it. They're only to be used in cases of emergency.' Austin cursed him repeatedly and went on sawing timber as quickly as he could. 'I've laughed about it many times since that day,' says Austin, but there were to be few opportunities for laughing at the time.

Nobody is quite certain how many men died from the first two German torpedoes to hit the British warship. But by the end of a fierce sea-battle which was to continue for almost three days, sixty officers and men had lost their lives, many of them in horrifying circumstances. Some had been trapped inside the ship when the order was given to 'batten hatches'. Unlike those killed outright from the initial blasts, a few men had died slowly; struggling for air, with water rushing around them, they had, in effect, been sac-rificed to save the ship sinking and to help save almost 800 ship's crewmen still facing the possibility of death through drowning or further German attacks.

HMS *Edinburgh* was already carrying wounded seamen when U-boat 456 struck with torpedoes on 30 April and injured dozens more. Charlie from Long Island, New York – nobody knew his sur-name – belonged to a group of some sixteen unlucky Americans whose merchant ships had been repeatedly attacked and damaged, and who had finally ended up on *Edinburgh*'s last voyage.

These Americans, and particularly Charlie, had had a rough time by March 1942, having first been rescued that month from the Panamanian merchant ship SS *Ballet*. The *Ballet* had been bombed during an air raid and the Americans had transferred to a small craft named *Sylla* which in turn also came under attack shortly afterwards within the Arctic circle.

Charlie and his group were now taken on board the SS *Induna*, a merchant-ship sailing with convoy PQ 13 bound for Murmansk. On the *Induna*, Charlie met Yorkshireman Austin Byrne, a twenty-year-old naval gunner. The two seamen got on well together. Then on 30 March, exactly a month before the *Edinburgh* was hit, the *Induna* was torpedoed and the New Yorker and the Yorkshireman found themselves in the same lifeboat.

'We were adrift for four days and three nights about ninety miles north of Murmansk,' recalls Austin Byrne. 'It was very cold and most got frost-bite very badly and several lost limbs later. Fortun-ately, I was lucky.' Eventually Charlie and the other survivors reached Murmansk. At the makeshift British hospital in the Russian port Charlie had to have all his toes amputated; others were even more unlucky. But his comparative luck would not last long.

On 26 April, less than a month after the *Induna* was torpedoed, Charlie was taken on board the *Edinburgh*, then anchored close to Murmansk in the Kola Inlet. Two days later, the American had his right foot amputated in the ship's hospital. Frost-bite had caused greater damage than naval doctors examining him had first suspec-ted.

Charlie finally got back to his wife and grown-up family in New York later that year, but not before further misfortune had befallen him. In a short but touching letter to Austin Byrne, written in New York on 9 November 1942, Charlie signposted without any bitterness his catalogue of catastrophe. Perhaps he was well aware that others had suffered far worse disasters, and he was, after all, alive and still in good heart.

'Hello Pal,' he wrote to Byrne, in handwriting that had a confident flourish and style. 'You probably are wondering what happened to me since we parted. Well, a lot has happened to me ... my toes were amputated, my right foot was amputated, the *Edinburgh* on April 30 was torpedoed as you probably remember.'

Charlie had survived the *Edinburgh* disaster and had been taken back to Murmansk where he received more medical attention. 'I was in Russia until the 26 of August when the SS *Tuscaloosa* took us over to Scotland,' he told Byrne in his letter. 'We were there for ten days and then brought back to New York on the *Queen Elizabeth* ... I had further amputation on my right leg and tomorrow I am to have a piece of bone taken off. I hope you are all right ... I often wondered when I was over there if I would ever see home again. I am in a Marine hospital now and I'll have to stay for a few months before they can fix me with an artificial leg ... In conclusion I wish you lots of luck and best wishes to you pal through this war.' Charlie ended his letter cheerfully: 'Sincerely, your lifeboat pal, Charlie.'

Before the war was over Austin Byrne was to meet Charlie at his home in New York. 'He told me about the day the *Edinburgh* was first attacked,' says Byrne. 'The wounded were put in lines on stretchers and Charlie said he didn't think he had much chance. He said he could see the enemy destroyers coming out of the mist. *Edinburgh* was still firing at them and in all this battle a man came round with tea and a cigarette to keep the cold out. He thought the British Navy was the greatest thing in the world. I felt ten foot tall.'

Almost as if nothing calamitous had happened that Thursday afternoon, the first day of the battle, Commander Eric George could watch calmly as the ship's crew slipped back into a disciplined routine. In the circumstances there had been no real panic on board the *Edinburgh* when she had been hit. And many officers and ratings were aware that this had not been the case in every instance when a British warship had been torpedoed and started to sink.

Despite their deadly situation some officers relaxed the rules with the sensible aim of minimising fuss and maximising the efficiency of *Edinburgh*'s crew as a formidable, if almost stationary, fighting force. After all, the cruiser still had guns which could be turned against the enemy: her two forward turrets 'A' and 'B' were undamaged. Food and beverages were handed out at any time to anybody who wanted them. 'Warrant officers' baths were scrubbed clean and filled with hot soup and cocoa,' says Commander George, who now lives in London. 'Sausage rolls were baked. Anyone who wanted something to eat or drink could get it without red tape.'

But as Rear-Admiral Bonham-Carter later observed to his wife: 'The old ship could only steam round and round in a circle at 7 knots.' And U-456 was still shadowing the *Edinburgh*; Kapitän-leutnant Teichert had radioed for reinforcements but still wished to finish off the cruiser single-handed. Soon he wouldn't have to worry: other submarines from the Strauchritter pack were already on their way from their base at Narvik in Norway.

While the British on board the crippled warship waited for the Germans to choose their moment to attack again, one or two lighter incidents occurred which in retrospect seem wholly out of keeping with the *Edinburgh*'s dire position. Alan Higgins recalls that after the first explosions the ship 'felt as though it had been clasped in a trembling hand which was turning it over to its starboard side at a steep angle'. He adds: 'Oil had spilled on to the cork lino and I remember being last in a queue of Royal Marines and communication ratings, unable to keep my feet on the slippery deck. You can imagine how slowly the queue moved as the men squeezed through the single small hatch one by one.'

Skating uneasily on the oily lino, as though on a crowded ice-rink, Higgins says 'a very funny incident' occurred. The Admiralty in London had issued a standing order that, in the event of a warship like the *Edinburgh* listing to one side, her crew should muster on the opposite side, thereby righting the balance. With the ship now listing heavily to port, men began scurrying as best they could towards the starboard side of the damaged ship. 'I had emerged on the side nearest the water and was urged in no uncertain manner that my eight stone was urgently needed on the high side of the ship,' says Higgins. 'The list was so steep that I had to crawl across

and up the catapult deck where a number of men had thrown a
Carley float [or raft] over the side.'

In their haste the seamen had forgotten to hold the line securing
it to the ship and the float had drifted away from the *Edinburgh*. But
Higgins was well aware that a man could only survive for a few
minutes in the icy Barents Sea, especially when clinging to a raft.
Higgins reflected that it was just as well that the Carley float had
broken away from its line. For the time being the boy telegraphist
preferred to remain in the dry and relative warmth of the stricken
ship.

Despite being torpedoed *Edinburgh* was not alone in that remote
part of the Barents Sea. When the convoy she led, QP 11, had left
Kola Inlet on 28 April, the close escort consisted of six destroyers,
the *Bulldog*, *Beagle*, *Beverley*, *Amazon*, *Foresight* and *Forester*, four
corvettes and a trawler. The *Edinburgh*, wearing the flag of Rear-
Admiral Bonham-Carter, was detailed to provide the close cover for
the convoy. It had been zigzagging at high speed some fifteen miles
ahead of the convoy when it had been attacked by U-456, and its
position so far in front of the rest of QP 11 was eventually to be a
matter of controversy and enquiry at the Admiralty.

For the first twenty-four hours of the journey from Murmansk
minesweepers from the Kola Inlet accompanied the *Edinburgh* and
the rest of the British convoy, with the Russian destroyers *Gremyaschi*
and *Sokrushitelni* standing by to reinforce the escort as far as longitude 30° East, potentially the most dangerous part of the convoy's
voyage. The fact that the Russian warships arrived for their vital
rendezvous only to disappear again shortly afterwards, would have
serious consequences for the *Edinburgh* and would later lead to an
important and hitherto secret diplomatic incident between Russia
and Britain. But the details of that squabble would only surface
after the *Edinburgh* had been sent to the bottom.

By early evening of 30 April there was still plenty of fight left in
the *Edinburgh* and a real possibility that the cruiser might be able to
limp back slowly to Murmansk. The explosion that afternoon had
been seen by QP 11, and the *Foresight* and *Forester* had been urgently
sent to give *Edinburgh* much-needed protection from the marauding
German submarine. The two Russian destroyers, *Gremyaschi* and
Sokrushitelni, had also arrived shortly afterwards, reminding Teichert

in U-456 to keep his distance. But the U-boat kept shadowing and reporting *Edinburgh*'s movements, and at Kirkenes, in Norway, the German flag officer for Northern Waters decided to send three destroyers to attack Convoy QP 11. The plan was a curious one because earlier, owing to the lack of a supporting escort, the decision had been taken not to operate destroyers against the convoy. At exactly 0100 that night, the *Hermann Schoemann*, Z24 and Z25 steamed menacingly towards the scene of battle some thirty hours away to the north.

On the *Edinburgh* the crew awaited the arrival of a Russian tug to tow the cruiser to Murmansk. By now the weather had worsened slightly with increasing snow squalls making the visibility patchy. The *Edinburgh*'s own log-book recorded the visibility as varying between two and ten miles. Lieutenant-Commander Howe, who was to play a significant role in the battle, looked anxiously at *Edinburgh*'s extensive damage. 'The torpedo that had hit us in the stern took away our rudder and the two rearmost propellers,' he says, 'leaving us with two propellers capable of being used. We had a big hole under the bridge, and this part of the ship filled with water; and with the stern missing, what was left of that part of the ship rose, so that the two propellers that we had left weren't really very much use because they were too close to the surface of the sea.'

Petty officer Bettridge, from Romford in Essex, was on the British minesweeper *Harrier* when he heard that *Edinburgh* had been torpedoed. The *Harrier*, along with the other Murmansk-based minesweepers *Hussar*, *Gossamer* and *Niger*, were ordered to race to *Edinburgh*'s assistance. With them steamed the Russian escort vessel *Rubin* and the much-needed Russian tug.

Harry Bettridge had joined the *Harrier* on his twenty-first birthday, 6 August 1940. The war with Germany had almost reached its first anniversary. At the beginning the *Harrier* had served on Atlantic convoys, but when Hitler attacked Russia, in June 1941, the *Harrier* had joined the first convoy to Murmansk, which was made up of almost as many escort vessels as merchant ships.

Bettridge, like other seamen, found the Atlantic harsh enough. But conditions on the Arctic run to Murmansk were worse. 'Thick ice, ships not built for the purpose, and inadequate clothing,' says Bettridge, recalling those years. 'On my first convoy I remember I had an old second-hand naval great-coat, a pair of 1914 vintage leather naval boots and some motor-cycle gauntlets over a pair of knitted gloves.' Later in the war proper sheepskin clothing and boots were issued. 'But the gentle old ladies of my church did not realise how useless their painstaking work was in that severe wet and cold. Two, sometimes three balaclavas and untold layers of clothing were worn underneath.' Apart from the freezing temperatures excessive clothing was another hazard in itself, especially if a seaman found himself in the water.

By mid-day on Friday 1 May, the *Harrier* and its companions were nearing *Edinburgh*'s position. Convoy QP 11, meanwhile, continued steaming towards Bear Island and the escape route to the relatively safe haven of Reykjavik in Iceland.

Understandably, the Germans were trying to press home their advantage. While the *Hermann Schoemann* and the accompanying Narvik-class destroyers Z24 and Z25 sailed in *Edinburgh*'s direction, four torpedo aircraft attacked the escaping convoy. At precisely 0540, with the convoy some 150 miles east-south-east of Bear Island, the German air force introduced a new fighting tactic in its tussles with allied convoys. Until the autumn of 1941, the German fleet air arm had some twenty-four torpedo-carrying seaplanes, but their performance had been poor. Goering persuaded Hitler in December 1941 that the Luftwaffe should develop torpedo aircraft. By April 1942 twelve crews had been trained to fly converted HE-111's and JU-88's. Fortunately for the convoy the four Luftwaffe aircraft attacking at dawn with torpedoes all missed their targets. Close by four U-boats were keeping pace with QP 11, one of them being spotted by the British destroyer *Amazon* and forced to make an emergency dive.

For Harry Bettridge on the *Harrier* it was to be his first taste of surface action and he would not enjoy the experience at all. 'We were involved daily with the elements, and many U-boats, but I remember that the feeling of shells flying overhead frightened me more.'

While Bettridge experienced bombing by the Luftwaffe, another British rating, Charles Whitehead, on the *Edinburgh*, waited for the Germans to attack his ship again. The cruiser was by now escorted, and to some extent protected, by *Foresight* and *Forester*. The two

British destroyers had reached the *Edinburgh* an hour after she had been hit. Shortly afterwards the two Russian destroyers arrived, but they were not to stay for very long.

For Whitehead, the emergency work on board the damaged cruiser had become routine. 'There was still this heavy list to starboard,' he says, 'so we had a big job in moving anything moveable to the port side. We were kept busy doing routine work and watches. But the cold was intense; it was numbing the mind as well as the body.' The question that troubled everybody was: when would the Germans renew their attack? 'As we were still in a danger area I thought we were rather like the blushing bride. We knew we had it to come but when and how or from where we didn't know. Things continued on a knife-edge.'

Jocelyn Salter, later Vice-Admiral, commanded the destroyer *Foresight.* 'When we arrived at the scene the after-part of the *Edinburgh* looked rather like that of an alerted scorpion,' he says. The accompanying destroyer *Forester* threw a tow-line to the cruiser, but the attempt failed dismally. With no stern and several feet down by the bow, she came 'rapidly into the wind as soon as she gathered headway, and parted the tow,' as an official report said later. 'Further attempts to aid her were then delayed while the destroyers hunted a U-boat that was sighted on the surface four miles away.'

'So *Edinburgh* then took *Foresight* in tow,' says Salter, 'the object being that *Foresight* should act simply as a rudder. If *Edinburgh* sheered to starboard *Foresight* would do likewise and so pull *Edinburgh*'s stern back, and vice versa if the sheer were to port.' During the cold uncertain night of 30 April/1 May, the *Edinburgh* made its unorthodox and halting way towards Murmansk. 'By the *Edinburgh* taking the *Foresight* in tow, this did work,' says Salter, 'and a speed of about three knots was maintained in roughly the desired direction.'

With the German U-boat pack still close-by, the four destroyers, two British and two Russian, formed an anti-submarine screen. But at 6 a.m. on May Day, *Sokrushitelni* and *Gremyaschi* reported that they were running short of fuel and must return to harbour. 'This left *Edinburgh* and *Foresight* as virtually sitting targets for any U-boats,' explains Salter. 'With *Forester* as the sole anti-submarine screen Admiral Bonham-Carter wisely decided that such a state was unacceptable and the tow was cast off. We on *Foresight* then joined *Forester* screening.'

While the ship at the centre of this unfolding drama, the *Edinburgh*, waited for the Russian tug to arrive and take over from the *Foresight*, convoy QP 11 was now in imminent danger from the fast-approaching German destroyers which had left Kirkenes the night before. On board Z24, under Fregattenkapitan Saltzwedel, seaman Hermann Galewsky helped prepare battle stations for the action that would come soon enough. Nearby the reassuring sight of the *Hermann Schoemann*, with its powerful 5.5-inch guns, and Z25 with, like Z24, 5.5-inch guns, steered towards their prey.

Because the ships were within the Arctic circle there was almost full daylight, although the weather affected the visibility. The sun scarcely dropped below the horizon. 'The temperature was − 10° Centigrade (ten degrees below zero),' says Salter, 'and altogether it was a most uncomfortable experience, especially for those whose duties kept them in exposed positions. A fresh wind from the north caused a lot of sea spray which froze as soon as it touched anything, adding an undesirable top weight to the destroyers if not removed at once.'

In the early hours of Saturday morning the weather was moderate, although snow squalls interfered with visibility. At 12.45 that morning QP 11 was on a northward course, avoiding heavy drift ice to starboard. The corvette ship *Snowflake* reported three radar contacts several miles away. Then the destroyer *Beverley*, screening on the port bow, reported enemy vessels in sight. The *Hermann Schoemann*, Z24 and Z25, larger than their adversaries, repeatedly attempted to reach and attack the convoy, but failed on each occasion.

Commander Richmond on the *Bulldog* turned towards the three German destroyers on a south-westerly course, with the destroyers in line ahead in the order *Beagle, Amazon, Beverley*. The German warships steered towards the convoy and just after two o'clock both sides opened fire with torpedoes. The engagement was brief, but *Amazon* was hit, her steering gear, telegraphs and one gun being put out of action. Fifteen minutes later QP 11 suffered its only loss: a Russian ship which had straggled behind the rest of the convoy was hit by a torpedo and rapidly sank; survivors were rescued by the trawler *Lord Middleton*.

Richmond's aim was to keep his destroyers between the convoy and the estimated position of the enemy. Just before mid-afternoon, the Germans were spotted again; at 12,000 yards the Germans opened fire once more. The British warship returned the fire, but no hits were obtained. An hour later shells fell close to the *Bulldog*, damaging her slightly. The British convoy now spread out over a distance of some seven miles, picking its way through the heavy drift ice in single-line formation. The Germans attacked the convoy again later: their fifth and final attack came just after eight o'clock. The last German destroyer disappeared into the smoke to the southeast. Shortly afterwards they were ordered to attack the *Edinburgh*, then some two hundred miles eastward, and changed course accordingly. Convoy QP 11, at least, was out of immediate danger, although Commander Richmond on the *Bulldog* was not to know this until he reached Reykjavik a week later. As QP 11 had headed steadily northwards, one of its escort destroyers narrowly escaped being hit by U-251; close-by, another marauding German submarine, U-589, attacked a steamer, but the merchant vessel continued unscathed. Eventually, the German U-boats had given up the chase and hurried back to their base in Norway. Before arriving in Iceland, Richmond sent a congratulatory signal to the accompanying British destroyers, one of which replied: 'I should hate to play poker with you.'

QP 11 would survive, but *Edinburgh*'s fate was to turn out very differently. When Rear-Admiral Bonham-Carter learned from the *Bulldog*'s reports about the German destroyer attacks he realised the likelihood of their turning to attack him. Bonham-Carter gave the following instruction: 'In event of attack by German destroyers, *Foresight* and *Forester* are to act independently, taking every opportunity to defeat the enemy without taking undue risks to themselves in defending *Edinburgh*. *Edinburgh* is to proceed wherever the wind permits, probably straight into the wind. If minesweepers are present they will also be told to act independently retiring under smoke screen as necessary. *Edinburgh* has no RDF [radio direction finder] or Director working.'

At 6 p.m. on 1 May, the Russian escort vessel *Rubin* came close to the *Edinburgh*. Then the Russian tug, along with the minesweepers *Hussar*, *Harrier*, *Gossamer* and *Niger*, arrived. But the

tug was not powerful enough to tow the 10,000-ton British cruiser.

By the next morning *Edinburgh* was making a steady three knots
under her own power. There was still a chance she would make it
back to Murmansk. Steered by the tug line on the starboard bow,
and with the *Gossamer* acting as a drogue on the port quarter,
Bonham-Carter knew he had one extra trump card besides luck:
the two Russian destroyers, which were supposed to have refuelled
at Murmansk and then returned to *Edinburgh*'s assistance. Bonham-
Carter had sent the minesweeper *Niger* to meet them. But their
failure to sail on time was to prove critical to the outcome of the
ensuing battle.

At 0627 gunfire from the *Hussar*, then on the starboard quarter,
signalled the approach of the three German destroyers. 'On the
morning of Saturday, 2 May, three German destroyers came out of
the mist,' recalls Lieutenant-Commander Howe. 'I rushed to the
two forward turrets, "A" and "B", which were in good working
order. But communication was only by word of mouth. Captain
Faulkner leaned over the bridge and gave me the order: "Engage
the enemy." '

Seamen on the three German destroyers also faced the extreme
cold and the regular task of knocking ice off their vessels. Heavy ice
could affect the steering of a ship and, importantly, the efficiency of
its fire-power. 'Suddenly the men in the listening room below us
reported loud engine noise and the sound of screws,' says Hermann
Galewsky. 'Then the British ship came in view. We could see the
Edinburgh quite clearly on the horizon. Our own U-boats were
already out of sight under water, ready for action.'

As the opposing ships prepared for the fight, seamen on both
sides waited apprehensively for the sound of shell-fire and reports of
torpedoes heading in their direction. 'The cooks were kept busy
brewing scalding coffee,' says Lawrence Newman. 'I know I drank
gallons of the stuff without ever feeling it.' Men on board had been
on their feet since the *Edinburgh* was first attacked and many were
beginning to feel the strain. The ship was covered in a coating of
ice, which made work on the upper deck extremely tricky. 'Many
of the company took a tumble,' adds Newman.

Bonham-Carter had ordered the ship's company to spend the

night at action stations, largely to disperse the crew in case of further attack. *Edinburgh* was by now in a very bad way, listing and weighing heavily from the water inside her. With her main control damaged, the only part of the ship which could fight was the foremost section.

While Galewsky busied himself on Z24, Newman and his watch were resting below decks when the German destroyers were first sighted, ominously appearing and vanishing in the indifferent grey light. 'My eyes were heavy for want of sleep and my thoughts were: "I'm going to have a sleep and if the ship goes down, well, she goes down",' says Newman. 'My head was just about to touch the cushion when I heard the bosun's mate piping, "Hands to action stations, surface action!" '

As Newman and the rest of his watch raced towards the forward turret guns and his action station they were being attacked by German destroyers. Altogether the enemy had thirty 5.5- and 5.9-inch guns trained on the *Edinburgh* and the other British ships. *Edinburgh* had only six 6-inch guns remaining. Despite the presence of minesweepers, with their one 4-inch gun apiece, and *Foresight* and *Fearless*, the British found themselves out-gunned and out-distanced.

'The Germans were coming in on our quarters, firing as they came,' says Newman.

'We were ordered to give covering fire to the *Hermann Schoemann*,' says Galewsky.

At the first sight of this new danger the *Edinburgh* cast off her tows and went into her maximum speed, some eight knots. Unable to steer the cruiser circled round to port, sometimes rapidly, sometimes on a wider curve, firing with 'B' turret whenever it could be directed from the bridge on to a fleeting target. Meanwhile the minesweepers, *Hussar*, *Harrier* and *Gossamer*, kept close to *Edinburgh*, firing at the Germans with their one-gun salvoes whenever they appeared on the horizon and always looking out for the deadly U-boats which they knew were in the vicinity. 'The minesweepers arrived and came tearing in,' says Charles Whitehead, 'and it made you feel proud to be British to see these little ships with their one 4-inch gun firing away at the larger ships.'

Below decks medical officers continued treating the wounded, some of whom were very ill indeed; many had lost limbs and were in pain from acute frost-bite. 'On 1 May the Admiral had it in mind to transfer the casualties, those of the *Edinburgh* plus forty-five very severely disabled survivors of previous convoys,' says Dr Douglas Lillie, who was then one of the junior medical officers on board. 'But he did not proceed with the idea of transferring men to the destroyers.' Bonham-Carter had no choice in the circumstances. The *Edinburgh* had to fight first and deal with the plight of the wounded later, *if* they survived the German onslaught.

Charles Whitehead watched the battle unfold with growing concern. 'We were able to return fire and as far as I know we were hitting them, setting at least one of them on fire.' He was right. 'Suddenly, there was a big burst of flame and shouts from the deck of the *Hermann Schoemann* opposite us,' says Galewsky, who was on the receiving end of the British shells. 'Rubber dinghies started plopping off the side with seamen leaping after them. The *Schoemann* had been hit by a broadside from the *Edinburgh*, and shells had gone straight through engine-rooms one and two.'

Lt.-Commander Howe was later awarded the DSC for hitting and sinking the *Schoemann*. Bob Howe had been having breakfast when the battle alarm had been raised: ' "A" and "B" turrets were all on top line for action so I didn't take very long to get them into action. I gave the necessary orders to get the guns round and trained in the right direction. Then we opened rapid broadsides with these two turrets. The *Schoemann*, a large destroyer and the leader, was hit. The other two German destroyers then disappeared back into the gloom. But during this action torpedoes were being fired at us: some were visible and some were not.'

The British attempted to strike the torpedoes before they reached their intended target. Although *Edinburgh* could continue firing, she was by this time making hardly any way in the water. On the *Hermann Schoemann*, now badly damaged by a direct hit from the *Edinburgh*, Captain Schulze-Hinrichs decided to transfer his crew to Z24 and Z25. Reluctantly he then gave orders that the sinking *Schoemann* should be scuttled to prevent its being captured by the British. Howe had hit the *Schoemann* by visual spotting and word-of-mouth control. It was a remarkable piece of shooting, as the Germans were forced to acknowledge.

Z24, under Commander Saltzwedel, and Z25, under Commander

Peters, began picking up the survivors from the sinking *Schoemann*. According to Galewsky: 'By the time our first survivors were starting to come on board we and the other undamaged destroyer were pounding away with our guns and the air was full of the scream of enemy shells dropping around us.' With as many survivors as they could find on board, the two remaining German warships returned to the attack. 'We made what we used to call a torpedo fan, firing three torpedoes simultaneously, every thirty or forty yards or so for optimum effect.'

The torpedo fan was the one seen by Lt.-Commander Howe. 'Unfortunately, one of the torpedoes hit us on the other side of the bridge,' says Howe. *Edinburgh* had now been hit by three torpedoes in as many days: two of them on either side of the bridge. Howe adds: 'It was extremely fortunate that the magazines of the two turrets were not affected.'

'You see,' says Galewsky, 'one of our torpedoes found her weakest spot. It was one of ours from Z24 and it put her in all sorts of trouble. Her firing pretty well stopped and huge clouds of smoke started to pour out of her rear end. The British were trying to set up a smokescreen to make it more difficult for us to hit her.'

Commander Eric George was at action stations on the upper deck at the time and had the impression that the sea was full of torpedoes. 'In actual fact I suppose there were three or four torpedoes coming towards us. One of them hit us under the bridge on the port side; of course it sent up a large column of water, a lot of which came down on me.' George says he immediately felt round his neck and shoulders to see if he were wet. 'In fact, to my surprise I was not at all wet. I was simply covered with little spangles of ice.'

Other men carried different memories of that third torpedo. Pat Hughes says: 'It was just a dull thud.' Alan Higgins was below decks when an explosion threw him 'among the dust, falling pipes, vent shafts' and other débris scattered around. 'After gathering my wits,' he says, 'I found I was alone; the deck outside the galley had collapsed and the hatch above me was battened down.'

Higgins was suffering from mild shock, but his memory of what he felt at the time remains clear. 'I remember thinking, what silly bugger closed the hatch?' he says. But it was not long before the hatch opened and he was asked what he was doing down below. 'With hindsight I've thought of dozens of answers, but at the time all I wanted was to get out in the open!'

Some 300 German sailors had clambered aboard Z24 and Z25. 'We had to rescue our buddies from the *Schoemann*,' says a German survivor. 'Every man of us on board the two destroyers was intent on saving men floundering in the water.' Remarkably every survivor was successfully hauled on board.

Edinburgh was hit just after 7 a.m. on 2 May, in the port side amidships, next to the bomb-room that was later to create worldwide interest. 'The Germans had hit us opposite to where the first torpedo had struck, so the ship immediately listed to port very badly,' says Charles Whitehead. 'We thought that it was going right over, but it stopped at a nasty angle.'

A growing number of men on the *Edinburgh* realised that the order to 'abandon ship' might be given at any time. Others hoped that Bonham-Carter would continue firing at the enemy until the very last possible moment. 'There was still a good deal of fight in her,' says Reg Levick.

Alan Higgins decided to take a few precautions in case the order to leave the sinking *Edinburgh* was given. 'After the fashion of Channel swimmers I went to the hangers and applied liberal dollops of thick grease about my ears and hands. I thought I would have a better chance of surviving if I did go into the water.' Staff-sergeant Jarrett remembers the fact that it was 'perpetually daylight' during the battle. 'One didn't know if it were morning, noon, afternoon or midnight,' he says. 'But when the weather cleared, "Faithful Freddy", our nickname for a German spotter plane, was always hovering on the horizon, just safely out of gunfire reach.'

The *Edinburgh*, said Rear-Admiral Bonham-Carter, was 'open from side to side'. He believed she might break in two and sink at any moment. But as he noted in a letter to his wife: 'We went on firing at the blighters until the end.' In fact, this was no empty British boast. The cruiser continued to engage the enemy whenever a German destroyer appeared; her shooting was later described by Fregattenkapitan Saltzwedel on Z24 as 'extraordinarily good'. Saltzwedel had every reason to offer compliments about Bob Howe's accuracy from 'A' and 'B' turrets, for on two occasions heavy fire from the *Edinburgh* had prevented him from going to the *Hermann Schoemann*'s assistance. But her list had now reached 17° and Bonham-Carter considered, for reasons soon to be made clear, that not only was his ship in danger but it was also a liability. Whatever else happened the *Edinburgh* must not fall into the hands of the enemy.

Meanwhile, the two destroyers *Foresight* and *Forester* were engaging Z24 and Z25 at virtually point-blank range; the two warships at one stage were skirmishing just 4,000 yards apart. Commander Salter's aim was to finish off the *Hermann Schoemann* with a salvo of torpedoes. But these went wide of their mark and *Foresight* was hit four times as she attempted to escape at full speed under a heavy self-created smokescreen. *Forester* too had been stopped and put on fire, with her sole remaining gun firing in the direction of the stationary, and now sinking, *Hermann Schoemann*.

The British ships feared the worst. There seemed little to prevent the Germans pressing home their advantage and picking off *Edinburgh*, *Foresight* and *Forester* at their leisure. The last two had been hit in their boiler-rooms and stopped. 'For a short time, both destroyers and the *Edinburgh* were immobile,' says Salter, 'but this most unpleasant situation lasted only for ten minutes before *Forester* was under way again. When *Forester* was stopped *Foresight* increased speed to twenty-eight knots and made smoke to screen her and to draw the enemy's fire. Providentially *Foresight* was not hit again and when *Forester* got going she was able to take over the smoke-screening.' But the two ships had not escaped losses. *Forester*'s captain and ten other men had been killed. Two more were to die later. On the *Foresight* a first lieutenant and eight seamen had been killed in the fierce and lengthy action which had stretched over three days.

Foresight and *Forester* had brilliantly held the German destroyers at bay and convoy QP 11 had escaped to the safety of an Icelandic port. But, equally, the poorly armed minesweepers *Harrier*, *Gossamer* and *Hussar* had earned very considerable battle honours, even from their adversaries. During and after the action the Germans, as the naval records show, believed that the minesweepers were destroyers. 'They were only armed with a "pop gun", but they charged the three German destroyers,' says Alan Higgins. To men watching the scene it seemed like suicide, the hopeless charge of the light brigade.

'It was an incident which made me feel very proud. The minesweepers survived a welter of German salvoes, miraculously it
seemed, always emerging to pop away at the Germans again.'

HMS *Harrier* was leader of the British minesweeping force in
north Russia at the time of *Edinburgh*'s last voyage. By 1942 it was
based in the Kola Inlet and given the task of reinforcing the warships and convoys then visiting and leaving the ice-free port of
Murmansk. Although they were fitted with the very latest minesweeping gear and with the new 10-cm wavelength surface warning
radar, the minesweepers' maximum speed was only fourteen knots
and they each had only one 4-inch gun and two light Oerlikon
anti-aircraft guns. But they had sonar and depth charges, and in
the words of one of *Harrier*'s officers, David Moore, 'every little
helped when the shortage of escorts was so desperate'.

Harrier's captain, Commander Eric Hinton, was a 'fine seaman,
expert in shiphandling', according to Moore. He added: 'Beneath
Hinton's unassuming and humorous manner, there was an irredu-
cible core of courage. The minesweepers were never intended to
engage enemy surface ships, but all knew that our Captain would
never entertain the thought of running away, even from a German
battleship.'

Fortunately, *Harrier* and the other minesweepers, *Gossamer*, *Hussar*
and *Niger*, were up against destroyers and U-boats, not battleships,
but the odds were still formidable. From the *Edinburgh* Bonham-
Carter had the day before signalled to the senior officer, sixth
minesweeping flotilla, that in the event of meeting enemy surface
forces the sweepers should 'retire under a smokescreen'. But
according to official reports later that signal did not reach the
minesweepers. In the event many lives may have been saved because Hinton either did not receive the signal or else chose to ignore
it in an almost Nelsonian gesture.

'German destroyers came in sight intermittently,' describes
Moore, 'dodging in and out of the snowstorms and making smoke
that increased the haze. In such poor visibility the Germans could
see gun flashes coming from five separate directions and probably
imagined that they were confronting a superior force.' Luckily
Harrier and the other 'fleet' minesweepers could be mistaken for
destroyers at a distance, especially when seen end-on.

'The minesweepers were like three young terriers going in and firing when they could,' Bonham-Carter told the Admiralty afterwards. But fearing the *Edinburgh* might break in two, he gave the order to abandon ship. He was the third officer that day to give such an order. Earlier, one of the German destroyers had hit a Russian ship belonging to QP 11: the convoy's only loss apart from *Edinburgh*. Russian survivors had been rescued by the trawler *Lord Middleton*. Then the *Schoemann*'s captain had given the order to abandon ship, shortly before Bonham-Carter did likewise.

Hermann Galewsky had gained the mistaken impression that every seaman had been rescued from the *Hermann Schoemann*. In fact some sixty men had been left behind and only two hundred reached Z24 and Z25. But fortunately the remaining sixty had scrambled into boats and onto rafts and were later picked up by U-boat 88.

By eight o'clock on Saturday morning the *Edinburgh* had been abandoned; the *Gossamer* rescued about 440 men, and the *Harrier*, in which Rear-Admiral Bonham-Carter hoisted his flag, about 350. But there was considerable drama in the way that several hundred men transferred to comparative safety on the two minesweepers.

Bonham-Carter told his wife simply: 'I managed to get two ships alongside under very difficult conditions and got everybody away who was alive, including about 80 wounded . . . I am thankful I managed to get all the officers except two away who were killed and about 800 men out of 850.'

Gradually the heavy sea had become almost flat calm, and this helped the escape of several hundred men from the *Edinburgh*. But others saw the escape in far more dramatic terms than the Admiral did. Some had seen the Russian ship *Rubin*, her skipper having misunderstood a signal, crash into the *Harrier* as Commander Hinton was attempting to take off survivors from the stricken cruiser.

Giddings had narrowly escaped death from the first torpedo to hit the *Edinburgh*. For three days, he says, 'I lost consciousness and my mind was blank.' He had been placed on a stretcher and laid down in the officers' passageway at the end of the ship. 'When I did come to I was taken on the stretcher to the side of the ship and put over to HMS *Harrier*.' Peter Matthews recalls that 'transferring our passengers, some of them injured merchant seamen and stretcher cases, was no easy task. But having got them away, it was with some urgency that the crew dropped onto the minesweepers' decks to be stowed away like sardines.'

Alan Higgins, as we have seen, had already smeared thick grease on himself in case he should fall in the water. Meanwhile, the Welshman assisted by off-loading some of the wounded to the *Gossamer*. 'I remember a coder by the name of Kneebone helping me with one stretcher case, a seaman who couldn't move,' he says. 'The *Edinburgh* and the *Gossamer* were moving apart and I could imagine the poor chap's feelings as he passed over the gap between the two ships.'

In fact, not one man was lost during this tricky operation, a source of surprise for many who took part in it. 'At one stage, Kneebone and myself were carrying a stretcher across the flight deck and our forward 6-inch gun opened up,' says Higgins. 'The shock was such, I almost dropped the stretcher.' Fine on the port bow Higgins could see the *Hermann Schoemann* firing its last rounds. A few moments later Higgins and Kneebone saw it hit and set on fire.

While men made their way as best they could to the rescue ships, others waited somewhat apprehensively on the *Edinburgh*. Petty officer Bettridge says: 'I remember the moment well, worried that the "big ship" would roll over and take us with it, yet knowing we must get these people off first. Looking up at the large battle ensign I felt a mixture of pride and fear. The urgency of the task was with us all, but there was no panic. Hundreds of men were scrambling over the full length of the ship . . . Everybody wanted to get away but felt bound to stay until the job was done.'

Master-sergeant Jarrett watched from the *Edinburgh* as survivors slipped down safety nets and onto the *Gossamer*. 'I leaped from the turret of a high-angle gun and landed halfway up the rigging of the rear mast,' he says. There were moments of remarkable heroism. One merchant seaman had been paralysed from the waist down. His stretcher-bearers carried him as far as the side of the *Edinburgh*, ready to hand him over to men on the *Gossamer*. 'The movement of the two ships was very much like that of a concertina,' says Lawrence Newman. 'One moment they could be close together and the next some distance apart.' The stretcher-bearers waited for a favourable moment. 'It must have tried the patience of that cot case,' adds Newman, 'for as the two ships did come together he scrambled from his stretcher and clambered onto the *Gossamer* where he collapsed on the deck.'

The minesweepers had complements of eighty and were by no means meant to carry several hundred men. Soon the small ships were packed to overflowing with survivors. Bonham-Carter watched the *Edinburgh* slowly, almost imperceptibly, list further to port. The fact that the cruiser was agonisingly slow to sink was ironically to become a nightmare for the Admiral.

Alner Hember, a boy musician of the Royal Marine Band, had been helping to keep the cruiser afloat by manning the pumps. Chief petty officer Lewis had earlier been sent to see the damage control officer. He reported back that the situation was hopeless: no repairs could be done. Lewis's report helped Bonham-Carter and Captain Faulkner make up their minds to abandon ship.

'When all surviving members of the crew had been transferred,' says Lewis, 'the Admiral requested me to go to his sea cabin just below the bridge to collect his children's photographs. As I was crossing the deck I slipped on the surface and went through the guardrails. Fortunately, I was able to grab the rails, but the photos regretfully slipped from my grasp.' Lewis was hauled to safety on one of the minesweepers, having almost risked a ducking and perhaps his life too in the icy waters. On board he was immediately given food and a hot drink. Along with other survivors his thoughts then turned to the perilous return journey they had to make to Murmansk.

Alner Hember remembers being asked to go to Admiral Bonham-Carter at the last moment. 'I helped to get his clothes,' he says. Somehow in the understandable confusion Bonham-Carter ended up with very few clothes. He told his wife later: 'I am sorry to say I have lost everything I had in the world as regards clothes, address book, papers, etc . . . Unfortunately I was wearing my very oldest suit and I must say I look pretty awful.'

But Bonham-Carter had more pressing problems during *Edinburgh*'s final hours. The 10,000-ton cruiser, now empty of the living, was not sinking fast enough for the Admiral's liking. With enemy destroyers in the distance he feared his ship could fall into German hands. Because of the cargo he was carrying and the possibility that the *Edinburgh* might later be towed to Kirkenes by the enemy, Bonham-Carter decided to sink the warship himself.

'As the German destroyers were still about, I told one of our destroyers to sink her quickly with a torpedo,' he wrote to his wife afterwards. But this was more easily ordered than executed. At first Commander Hinton attempted to sink the *Edinburgh*, or as the Admiralty prefer it, to 'hasten her end', with gunfire and depth charges. The cruiser took such an attack without noticeable damage. (The commanding officer on the *Hermann Schoemann* had little trouble finishing off his own ship a little while later.) Some of the depth charges landed on the *Edinburgh*, only to become lodged in the deck equipment. And supplies of explosives on board the escort minesweepers were running short. 'It meant a high-speed run alongside the *Edinburgh* with depth charges set at a low depth, and this was a hazardous operation,' says Harry Bettridge, who was on the *Harrier*. 'The *Edinburgh* didn't seem in a hurry to go,' recalls Lawrence Newman. 'And we didn't know whether the German destroyers had cleared completely off.'

By no means everybody wanted to abandon the *Edinburgh*. Reg Levick remembers a group of men who wanted permission to re-board their ship. They discussed approaching the Admiral but thought better of it at the last moment. Alan Higgins has similar memories of that special moment. 'A few of us were going to ask the Admiral if we could go back aboard as the old *Edinburgh* seemed almost unsinkable,' he says. 'After all, a sailor gets very attached to his ship. However, the thought of a humble ordinary telegraphist daring to approach a rear-admiral was too great to contemplate, so I stayed on the stern and watched whilst one of the destroyers delivered what might only be described as the *coup de grâce*.'

Fowells, on the *Foresight*, knew the destroyer had one misfired torpedo which could be used against the *Edinburgh*. 'She had to be sunk, but how?' says Fowells. 'We steamed slowly past the *Edinburgh* while I took my sight. "If you miss, I'll never speak to you again!" said the Captain, and I think for the moment he meant it. He took out his watch to time the run of the torpedo and after the allotted time put it away with as grim an expression on his face as I have

ever seen. Then there was the noise of an explosion and a great
cascade of water. The *Edinburgh* slowly sank.' Fowells adds that he
then turned to *Foresight*'s Captain and said: 'I think your watch
needs adjusting, Sir. It must be all these explosions.'

At one stage Bonham-Carter had considered going back to the
Edinburgh with a skeleton crew. But the *Foresight*'s arrival changed
his mind. On the *Harrier* David Moore was by his side: 'We watched
the *Foresight* position herself at point-blank range, 1,500 yards,
abeam of the cruiser and saw the torpedo dive into the sea. There
followed the longest two minutes that I can remember, towards the
end of which the Admiral was saying: "She's missed!" But just at
that moment the torpedo struck and exploded and we witnessed
the sad end of this fine cruiser.' *Edinburgh*, says Moore, simply 'rolled
over and sank'.

But even that moment is remembered in slow motion by some of
the onlookers. 'We had a constructor commander on board at the
time and he was quite delighted to see her sink stern first on an
even keel,' says Commander Eric George. 'He thought it was a
masterpiece of design and construction.' Bob Howe, who had been
firing at the enemy that day, says: 'As the ship was finally on her
beam ends, I could look straight down the funnel and see the ex-
haust, which comes up the funnel, still popping away. The diesel
engine which had been supplying me with electric power for my
turrets was still running. Then she sank.'

The action had stretched over three days and the participants
had collected a variety of memories and impressions. 'I suppose the
thought of dying affects people in different ways,' says Alan Higgins,
'but all I could think of at the time was how my parents would take
the news.' Viktor Gernhard, who was on Z25 from the day she was
commissioned in December 1940, witnessed *Edinburgh* sinking.
'Naturally, our officers had a better overall view of the battle,' said
Gernhard, who kept a diary throughout the war. 'We lower ranks
didn't see very much apart from the grenades in the water but we
felt the direct hit on our radio room.' Nonetheless the German
sailor, whose battle station was on a 2-cm gun forward of the bridge,
did see the British cruiser disappear beneath the waves.

Many survivors were realistic enough to realise that their escape
was hardly a victory. One of the Royal Navy's largest and best-

known ships had been lost. Bonham-Carter said afterwards that he 'shall not get the thanks of the Admiralty but we could not have done more. I must be a bit of a Jonah though as I have not told you before [that] the *Sheffield* was mined two months ago when I was in her.' Before the month was out Bonham-Carter would be rescued from another ship, this time the cruiser HMS *Trinidad*. In his letter to his wife he was somewhat disparaging about the enemy's performance. 'I don't quite know why the German destroyers didn't sink every one of my little force. They showed a lack of guts and it was grand to see the old *Edinburgh* firing away with a 17° list and not a man moving away from his work until I gave the order . . . I am now longing to have another go at the blighters.'

Captain Faulkner turned his mind to the official report he would have to submit to the Admiralty in London. In time he was to end that report: 'Throughout the three days the work of all men below decks . . . was beyond praise and their behaviour and bearing were in the highest traditions of the service . . . An efficient, well-trained ship's company has been saved for further service.'

In an earlier reply to pressing Admiralty questions about the loss of the *Edinburgh*, Bonham-Carter said somewhat tartly: 'No. Nothing saved except personnel. Gold was in compartment flooded by first torpedo.' The Admiralty, and members of Winston Churchill's Cabinet, were relieved that a British warship had not been captured, but they could hardly be pleased with the news that a vast fortune in gold bullion had also sunk to the sea-bed.

Many survivors huddled inside the rescue ships which had taken them off the *Edinburgh* were not to witness the cruiser's final moments. 'A red sheet of flame leapt in the air as the fourth torpedo (from *Foresight*) struck, this time our own,' says Lawrence Newman. 'Slowly and what seemed leisurely, the *Edinburgh* sank beneath the waves. But suddenly her bows reappeared, shooting up almost vertically; then, gradually, she slid beneath the waves again. We turned sadly away, never realising until then how good a stout and strong ship we had beneath us.'

Some survivors even detected a certain poetic moment in the manner in which she finally disappeared. 'She went very quickly, in seconds, stern first, vertically until the bows were perpendicular,' says Alan Higgins, who was to pass out on the *Gossamer* shortly afterwards. 'She curtsied when the water level reached her forward gun turrets and then slid quietly out of sight.'

James Doyle remembers toasting the *Edinburgh* with a tot of rum. 'It was tot-time in *Harrier* and her Cox'n broke out a few kegs of "Nelson's blood",' says Doyle, who now lives in Canada. 'We each, boys included, though it was against regulations, were issued a full mug of the heavy, dark, navy rum. We "spliced the main brace" and stood on *Harrier*'s upper deck and toasted our ship as we watched her go down by the stern. Her bows rose magnificently above the turbid surface of the Barents Sea.' Nearby stood Bonham-Carter and several other officers. '*Edinburgh* paused briefly and taking our cue from Admiral Stuart Bonham-Carter we saluted and the cruiser slid swiftly down, down, down forever, taking with her some sixty of our shipmates . . . A giant vortex boiled and shuddered over her grave briefly and it was over.' Doyle added that he felt 'a sort of deep emptiness within me'.

Such experiences that day appear in retrospect to have been almost commonplace. Other seamen, like Harry Bettridge, are still surprised that there were so many survivors. 'How they got off the *Edinburgh* I shall never know,' he says. 'And I believe all who could make it, did, when the skipper gave the order to cast off. But one pitiful memory (on the *Harrier*) was of these poor wounded trying to contend with the sloping deck, wrapped only in a blanket in that terrible climate.' Many would carry such chilling memories for years. Bettridge remembers one survivor's experience a few moments before *Edinburgh* had gone down: 'A movement was seen in a pile of disregarded blankets and a couple of lads jumped across to discover a man with no legs,' he says. 'That man was, to everyone's relief, helped safely on board.'

Lieutenant-Commander Fowells on *Foresight* saw the sea battle and his continuing survival as nothing short of a miracle. At one stage enemy gunfire had stopped both *Forester* and *Foresight*, the latter's remaining gun becoming jammed and useless. Fowells wondered why the Germans did not finish their task and sink the two British destroyers. He went to the chart house to collect the secret books and codes which were to be dumped overboard the moment a ship seemed doomed. 'A leaden feeling of dread replaced the exhilaration of the fight. I thought to myself that for the third time in my war unless a miracle happened I was dead. I also couldn't understand how the Captain could still smile and look happy in the circumstances.'

But both *Forester* and *Foresight* somehow got underway once more. *Forester* had managed to make one of her guns fire again, throwing up smoke to screen *Foresight* at the same time. 'Blanketed by the smoke a great calm descended,' says Joseph Fowells, 'as though the battle had suddenly moved to a great distance. We could no longer see the flashes of the enemies' guns or the splashes of their shells.'

Unbeknown to the British and German participants in the battle over the convoy QP 11, hostilities for that day at least were over. Z24 and Z25 steamed away in the distance, allowing the British force to straggle back in the direction of Murmansk. Commander Hinton on *Harrier* believed that the Germans had mistaken the minesweepers for destroyers: range and poor visibility had therefore helped to save them from almost certain annihilation. At the end of the war he was to be proved right. According to the log-book of Z24 the Germans believed they had been facing five destroyers 'of the Tribal, Jarvis and F or H classes, and one American'.

For men like Hermann Galewsky there had been enough fighting that day in May. He had seen the *Hermann Schoemann* go down and had wondered if Z24's turn might be next. Galewsky had spotted an old schoolfriend aboard the *Schoemann* and he now wondered whether the friend from his hometown of Sarstedt near Hanover had survived. 'During the rescue I had tried to find him, but the dinghy he was in had disappeared,' he says. 'Funnily enough, I came across him again in Hanover about six months later. He'd been picked up by a U-boat. But then he bought it next time out, up on the Norwegian coast.'

Fowells, like Galewsky and countless other survivors of the battle, thanked God, luck or whatever stars they believed in for their deliverance that first Saturday in May, 1942. Fowells recalls *Foresight*'s chief engineer arriving on the bridge and telling Commander Hinton: 'Ready to go ahead, Sir,' saluting in 'the less than military way that engineers affect'. Hinton ordered half-speed ahead, 140 revolutions, and *Foresight* was on her way back to Murmansk. 'When the Germans saw both destroyers on the move they retired in the mist and we saw no more of them,' says Fowells. 'I remember thinking to myself: Who said "miracles hardly ever happen"? I've had three! And then thought: Oh dear, that's a misquote, it's hurricanes, not miracles!'

On board the returning destroyers and minesweepers there was much to be done. Men, many of them badly injured and in pain, had to be given what medical attention was available. Food and hot drinks had to be provided; men had to be kept alive and got back to the relative safety of the Russian mainland.

Edwin Dennerley, a sick-berth attendant on the *Edinburgh*, vividly remembers survivors covered in fuel oil, unable to stand. His last task had been to transfer a rheumatic fever case to one of the minesweepers. 'Somehow or other, he got up on my back wearing only a vest and pants and covered with a blanket. I must have slipped down the deck and my sick rider had gone straight into the net. His blanket had gone. He had then been hoisted aboard literally by his vest, amid hearty cheers from his shipmates.'

Such stories, with their varied mixture of pitiful, dramatic and even risqué moments, would help sustain survivors during their journey to Murmansk. James Giddings, on board HMS *Harrier*, added one light moment of his own. He had had his money-belt round his waist when *Edinburgh* was first hit three days before. It contained seven pounds, a goodly sum on board in those days. He handed his money to the master-at-arms while he was being treated after the first torpedo had struck. 'Later he told me it had been put in the office safe which had gone down with the ship,' he says. Years later, he added, 'it crossed my mind that if anybody ever did attempt to get the gold from the *Edinburgh* they might even bring the safe up. Wouldn't that be something if I got my belt and money back!' Giddings said it would be easy to identify because it had his name sewn on it.

Captain Hugh Faulkner did not disguise his feelings about what had happened. 'It had been thirty-six hours of absolute hell,' he said. He comforted himself with the thought that despite the loss of *Edinburgh* the Germans had not scored further success. 'I shall never understand why they didn't come and finish us off. I think they had to acknowledge defeat. They had been so heavily shot at.' For the time being he put the fact that fifteen torpedoes had been fired at *Edinburgh* during the action to the back of his mind. His official report would be written later.

Harrier was steering in the direction of the Kola Inlet in company with *Hussar*. The Russian escort ship *Rubin* and the tug had already been sent back to Murmansk. Before *Rubin* left the battle she had inadvertently crashed into *Harrier*, causing some slight damage. The commanding officer of the *Rubin* tried to make amends by sending the following curiously worded message to Rear-Admiral Bonham-Carter: 'Dear Sir: Soviets seamens was witness of heroic battle English seamen with predominants power of enemy. English did observe their sacred duty before Fatherland. We are proudings of staunchness and courage English seaman's, our allies. I am very sorry what injured your ship by approach to board for what I must beg pardon.' Signed: 'Commander of Division.'

Meanwhile, on the *Harrier*, Bonham-Carter sought reasons for the failure of the two Russian destroyers, *Sokrushitelni* and *Gremyaschi*, to return to the battle which had ended in *Edinburgh*'s destruction. The only plain facts he knew at this time were that the Soviet warships had not left harbour in Murmansk for hours after they were expected. HMS *Niger*, which Bonham-Carter had sent to rendezvous with the Russian ships, never did find them. So the British were left to fight on their own. For some survivors the Russians had in real terms helped contribute to the sinking of the cruiser. For the more cynical the Russians had simply chosen to stay at Murmansk to celebrate May Day. Such thoughts would soon be incorporated in 'most secret' reports to the Admiralty in London and would lead to a growing distrust between the Allies.

On board the *Foresight*, Joseph Fowells had more urgent matters to settle. Damaged guns and communications had to be examined and, if possible, repaired. The dead had to be buried at sea and a heavy list to starboard corrected quickly. There was a large hole in *Foresight*'s side and the chief engineer ordered the starboard tanks to be emptied and oil and water pumped to the port side until the hole, which was about ten feet square, could be seen above the water-line. 'Hammocks and bedding were then stuffed into the hole, after which fresh boiling water was poured over it,' he says. 'The whole contraption froze solid in seconds and was quite watertight.' There were other holes to see to and many leads, circuits, gun receivers and telephones to be repaired. 'The Germans had fired many shrapnel shells into *Foresight* and these had been mainly responsible for this sort of damage, as well as for the many casualties.'

The wounded survivors were also suffering from cold and frostbite. 'Once we started Russian convoy duties our living conditions had become frightful,' says Bill Daley, a survivor from the *Edinburgh*. 'Now they were worse.' Ice bit into seamen and endangered the ships they were in. 'The ice on a ship was everywhere: above deck and below,' says Frank Hodges, another *Edinburgh* survivor. 'It even caused problems below deck because of condensation. I remember having forty ledgers in my office on the *Edinburgh* and the condensation was so heavy that one day I found them all covered in water.'

Doctors on the Arctic runs were continually treating men for accidents sustained because of the ice. Radar aerials had to be kept turning in case they became frozen solid. 'Men used to chip out pictures in ice on the mess deck wall,' says Harry Cook. 'Once when we dropped a potato it was so cold the potato broke in half.'

In spite of such harsh climatic conditions, even in early May, the dead from the battle had to be buried. On the *Foresight*, for example, eleven men had died. 'The burial ceremony was the simple navy one,' says Fowells. 'Each body was sewn in canvas with a 50-lb. shell at its feet. A few prayers were said and then the body slid into the sea.' And so the men who had died aboard *Foresight* were slipped into the water from beneath a White Ensign. Watching the ceremony, says Fowells, 'were a bunch of frozen, grimy, unshaven spectators . . . all eyes remained fixed on the swirl of water where the body had sunk until the last ripple had gone.'

Once the service was over, men went back to their different duties around the warship. Fowells adds: 'All that remains of a seaman is the little pile of possessions in the coxwain's office, a few letters, a knife, a little clothing, a few shillings, a photograph of his girl and perhaps that pair of nylons he bought for her in the little store in Hvalfjord before his ship left Iceland, soon to be auctioned for the next-of-kin.'

Such were some of the thoughts and impressions of men returning on the ships to the Kola Inlet. Pat Hughes on the *Harrier* remembers being served a good helping of rum on the short voyage. Others were especially grateful for the rum because they slept for most of that uncomfortable journey. Even now, men could make light of their predicament, sometimes cracking the most awful jokes. Commander Hinton on *Harrier* proudly pointed out to Admiral Bonham-Carter how his flag with two red balls had been correctly improvised and hoisted. According to David Moore, Bonham-Carter replied: 'Two balls! That's more than I expected to have this afternoon!'

Few seem to have given any thought to the fortune in gold which had gone down with the *Edinburgh*. News of the bullion consignment had not reached many crew members from the rest of the thirteen-strong QP 11 convoy. 'I didn't know until almost forty years later that there was gold aboard the *Edinburgh* when she went down,' says Harry Bettridge. 'I wonder what I would have felt at that moment had I known.'

Hermann Galewsky on Z24 did not know he had helped sink the *Edinburgh* until the end of May: 'It was only from news reports weeks afterwards that we found out what had finally happened to the *Edinburgh*. And I never knew at all about the gold she'd had on board until just a few days ago.' Others who knew about the bullion, now 800 feet down in the Barents Sea, could hardly care less about its fate, safe as it was from both Allies and Germans alike. The War Risks Insurance Office in London had insured £500,000-worth of the gold for a premium of £14,625, while Gosstrakh, then the state insurance house in Moscow, had insured the rest. As far as the Americans were concerned the gold might go to the bottom of the ocean, but their money was safe enough because it had been backed by insurance and the British and Soviet governments.

Survivors from HMS *Edinburgh* turned their thoughts gradually to what lay before them in Russia. Some men worried about their lack of proper clothing; a few pulled around them coats that they had taken from the officers' quarters on board *Edinburgh* shortly before she sank.

Slowly the evening passed. Towards midnight, while still daylight, the first rescue ships drew closer to Murmansk. Commander George had taken possession of *Edinburgh*'s ledgers and had already suggested to Captain Faulkner that the ship's company be mustered by 'open list' at the Russian port.

'I explained to the ship's company that the object in doing this was to get an accurate record of the number and names of the

casualties,' says George. 'I knew that the Admiralty in London
would say, in making a statement to the press, "the next-of-kin of
casualties will be informed". This would mean that relatives would
be in a panic wondering if their loved ones were dead or alive. I
felt it most desirable that the Admiralty should have immediate
information about the casualties.' On Sunday evening, 3 May, a
wireless message giving the names of casualties was sent to London.
However, some families in Britain were not to learn about the fate
of their men for more than a fortnight.

Not only British sailors had died that terrible day. Andrzei Pow-
ierza, First Secretary at the Polish Embassy in Moscow, was returning to England to join the RAF. He was killed in the first
torpedo attack.

2

Russia and the Bullion Run

Edinburgh's crew were returning to Murmansk in very different circumstances from those surrounding their previous visits. On earlier
occasions few ratings or officers had been allowed ashore. 'This was
because there was little amusement and the ship had always to be
ready for sea at an hour's notice,' says Lawrence Newman. Others
took a less charitable view of their being confined on board during
their visits to the Russian port. They came to the probably correct
conclusion that the Russians actively discouraged contact between
themselves and their visiting allies.

'We didn't mix with them and they didn't mix with us,' says
Norman Cosser, from Aylesbury in Buckinghamshire. 'I have
always believed the commissars had a lot to do with this.' Harry
Bettridge, who served on a minesweeper based in Murmansk, agrees
that the Russians seemed to discourage real contact. 'They didn't
seem to relish our presence in their harbours,' he says. 'After the
first convoy which had the usual official welcome and shore leave
in Murmansk I have memories of feeling isolated. We were moored
on the far side of the river on a vast wooden jetty and the whole
area was stacked high with wood, acres of it.'

Murmansk, even today, is hardly an attractive town. Built up
around the Czar's naval base shortly before the Bolshevik revolution
of 1917, it was largely destroyed by the Germans during the Second
World War. Many seamen who visited the port in 1941 and 1942
remember it as a drab and depressing place. There was very little
food and every encouragement to stay on board in the comparative
comfort of a warship. 'The town consisted mainly of wooden shacks,'

says Fowells, 'although one beautiful building remained from pre-revolutionary days. It was decked out in gorgeous red plush-and-gold furniture and was in striking contrast with the depressed Mongolian-featured inhabitants sludging along the dirt track roads in their coarse and often tattered clothes. They were friendly if not exuberant in their friendship, and it seemed as if a general order had been issued to preserve a reserved correctness.'

Charles Whitehead had clambered on board a minesweeper from the crippled, sinking *Edinburgh*. He remembers his arrival in Russia with a certain initial gratitude: 'I was so cold I didn't know much about it until it was time to go ashore. We were given a meal and it was the best meal we had for days. In fact, it was the best we were to get for a couple of months.'

Many survivors arriving at Murmansk remember their first impressions vividly. Some men were billeted in Murmansk; others were sent to Polyarnoe and Vaenga, two bases further along the Kola Inlet.

Edward Lewis had been coxswain to Bonham-Carter on the *Edinburgh*. He had been rescued by a destroyer and then taken to Murmansk. 'We disembarked and were taken to some barracks, which were virtually windowless. Inside were rows of bunks, one above the other down one side, on which were palliasses filled with straw and a rough blanket.' He and his mates were told not to move too far from the huts as there was a risk that 'the sentries would shoot us.' Washing facilities were almost non-existent in the camps. The toilets were about a hundred yards away and consisted of a trench over which a plank had been placed. 'In sub-zero conditions this wasn't very pleasant,' says Lewis without a trace of humour. 'And no paper was supplied.'

Charles Whitehead was sent to Polyarnoe, where conditions were much the same. He ended up sleeping in a school where some Russians were also billeted. 'We had to go to a Russian camp to eat, some two miles away,' he says. 'The food was poor and rough but we were glad to get it.'

Lewis did not have to walk far for his meals. 'We were assembled outside our huts and marched to the dining-hut. I'm afraid that none of us were very happy with the food which was served. It was a form of very thin soup with a few pieces of fat yak meat and a small piece of black rye bread. For tea we were given a very muddy-looking drink containing a few berries.' Everybody complained that it was completely tasteless, and for the first few days many refused to eat anything. 'But after that hunger pains got the better of most of us and we began to eat.'

Many survivors were well aware that the Russians themselves were even worse off. 'We were billeted with the Russian army and they did the best they could for us,' explains Peter Matthews, an electrical mechanic 4th-class on the *Edinburgh*. 'But so many extra mouths to feed must have caused them some embarrassment when they were short of food themselves.' For Matthews there were lighter moments, even in those harsh conditions. Clothing was short but 'the Russians managed to supply us with a set of army under-wear and a towel, all beautifully stamped with a hammer and sickle.'

Cyril Moore was billeted at Vaenga, where living conditions were primitive and the food especially spartan. 'The daily rations provided by the Russians consisted of three bowls of gruel, one bowl of soup, three cups of berries in hot water and three blocks of very coarse bread. But occasionally a supply of corn-beef and biscuits would arrive, and almost everyone in the camp had one visit to a Royal Navy ship in the harbour for 'one real meal'.

Commander Graeme Ogden arrived at Polyarnoe with convoy PQ 16, almost a month after *Edinburgh* had been sunk. Ogden con-tacted Rear-Admiral Bevan, who was the commanding officer in charge of British naval personnel in the Murmansk area. 'I found Bevan to be a very worried man because our naval base was crowded with survivors from HMS *Edinburgh* for whom little provi-sion could be made,' says Ogden.

Relations between the British and the Russians were gradually souring. 'The Admiral was in a rage because a hospital ship had been rushed to the scene, and believe it or not, the Russians had refused her entrance to the port, sending her away. Hence the panic,' Ogden adds. With Admiral Bevan's approval Ogden says he spent days 'scrounging anywhere I could to collect food, medical supplies, clothing and berths for the *Edinburgh*'s crew.'

Some survivors were quickly found berths on ships leaving Mur-mansk. Rear-Admiral Bonham-Carter was transferred to HMS

Trinidad, a cruiser, lighter than the *Edinburgh*, though not wholly unlike it in appearance at least. On 13 May 1942, Bonham-Carter sat down on board *Trinidad* and wrote a four-page letter to his wife. 'I have been through an exciting and sad time, but the old bad half-penny always turns up again and I am feeling very fit.' He went on: 'I didn't realise before what a large man your husband was as I can neither get boots, shirts or pyjamas to fit me where I am at present. I have managed to pinch a razor, tooth brush, tooth powder and hair brush.' But the Admiral admitted that he had managed to 'borrow a pair of pyjamas and towels etc.'

At Polyarnoe Charles Whitehead remembers that everybody seemed to wear different dress. Few men had brought any clothing with them from the *Edinburgh*: 'All we had was what we stood up in,' recalls Whitehead, 'so we were kitted out in Russian sailors' uniforms. Their sailors were very friendly and gave us cap ribbons with Russian names to wear on our caps.'

But *Edinburgh* survivors risked their lives wearing Russian caps with name ribbons on them. The Soviet guards could not tell whom they were challenging and there was a danger of British sailors getting shot. 'We looked so alike we had to remove the ribbons,' says Whitehead. 'The sentries used to challenge us and we'd reply: "Niet rusky, matros englisky." '

In spite of the odd amusing moment, the majority of survivors remember the real horror they were to witness. Edwin Donnerley, the medical attendant, was sent to help at the makeshift hospital in Murmansk, where some of *Edinburgh*'s doctors were already working. 'Beds were touching side by side and in them were men from previous convoys and of many nationalities,' he says. 'The operating theatre had six tables, and the sterile dishes and trays were saucers and plates. I don't remember seeing any anaesthetic machines of any kind, and the only anaesthetics the Russians had was a solution they sluiced into the wounds.'

The hospital at Murmansk treated many *Edinburgh* survivors, but it was a frontline hospital and many of its patients were Red Army soldiers. According to one survivor, a hundred wounded might sometimes turn up together, producing an inevitable strain and confusion. 'There would be two wounded at a time to a bed,' he says, 'one Russian with his head alongside the other's feet. Another

Russian, with a shattered face, just sat in his bed with nothing being done for him. He was as patient as a dog.'

Sometimes the British fared little better. 'The hospital conditions were bloody horrible,' said a survivor. 'I had a chipped bone in my leg and I could feel it festering but nothing was done. The Russians just said "da, da, da".' Later, at Polyarnoe, the man was given a piece of plaster to put over his leg.

Percy Jefford, chief stoker, remembers sleeping at Polyarnoe on a long bench 'on which we all slept side by side like sardines'. He adds: 'We had one blanket and a straw palliasse but you kept warm because so many were packed together. I lost twenty-eight lbs in twenty-eight days.' Jefford was comparatively lucky; many other survivors lost more weight far more rapidly.

In fact, one naval official described the conditions at Vaenga as 'sub-human'. But he agrees with survivors that, as far as food went, they were no worse off than the Russians themselves.

The bases were made worse by bad organisation and the overall impression that the Russians were running prisoner-of-war camps. At Polyarnoe, the dining-hall, which was shared with the Russians, was miles away. Some survivors thought it hardly worth the walk. 'We only got black bread and pine-needle tea and by the time we got back we were even hungrier,' said one. Many resented the camp being guarded by armed Russian women soldiers, but Russia was at war and the Germans were still fighting close to Murmansk. There was always the danger that the Russians would be overrun and the bases turned into real prisoner-of-war camps: this time by the Nazis.

Eric Grenfell, later Commander Grenfell, had joined the *Edinburgh* in September 1940. He was on the cruiser when she helped chase the German battleship *Bismark*, and he had served with her on the Arctic convoys to Murmansk. In early 1942, Grenfell joined the 11,000-ton merchant ship *Empire Lawrence*. Shortly afterwards he sailed with convoy PQ 16 and en route to Murmansk heard that *Edinburgh* had been sunk. On 27 May, the *Empire Lawrence* was attacked and sunk by JU-88 dive-bombers; several days later Grenfell arrived in Murmansk, and soon he would meet many of the survivors from the *Edinburgh*. 'When we arrived at the Russian port all the dead, dying and wounded were placed in a bomb-damaged warehouse on a jetty,' he says. His description of that first day in Murmansk paints a vivid sketch of events at the time: 'As the ambulances collected us and drove through bomb-pitted streets, sometimes on the pavements to skirt a crater, an aerial attack on Murmansk began.' After a brief spell in a Russian military hospital the young naval rating was sent to a camp opposite Murmansk, from where he watched countless German attacks against the town. 'Every day Murmansk was attacked by planes. The town was plastered, but never have I seen so many planes shot down by ack-ack fire. As the attacks developed the tremendously long barrels of the Russian guns could be seen rising from well-concealed sites in the woods.'

Grenfell did not care for the camp in which he had been placed. Most of the men there were merchant seamen. During German attacks, says Grenfell, 'some of these seamen would push and fight to get into the crowded 1914-type slit trenches.' Grenfell, then the senior naval rating in the camp, ordered his men into the woods during the fighting. 'Often we would see an elderly American merchant seaman calmly clearing twigs and rubbish from a stream.' The man was trying to make the stream flow freely and took no notice of the shelling. 'He said he had no fear of bombs. He'd had a long life and after his experiences during attacks on Arctic convoys he would never be frightened again.'

Grenfell asked Admiral Bevan, who was visiting his camp, for permission to be transferred with his men to another camp, this time under Royal Navy discipline. Grenfell was moved to Vaenga, which was near a large Russian and RAF airfield. 'I met up with many of my pals from the *Edinburgh*,' says Grenfell. 'Our living conditions were no better than at our previous camp, but at least there was discipline. Naval officers ordered everything as if we were in the barracks at Portsmouth.'

Among *Edinburgh* survivors who soon found new ships, Rear-Admiral Bonham-Carter went on board HMS *Trinidad*, only to be sunk by torpedoes a few days later. Thus he found himself being rescued twice from his flagship in less than a fortnight. When he wrote to his wife on the Fiji-class cruiser he headed the paper 'HMS *Trinidad*, 13th May'. Little did he suspect when he described himself as a 'bit of a Jonah' that two days later his new ship would go down too.

For those left behind in the camps time passed slowly. Gradually the days grew warmer. Men made sedan chairs out of dining chairs so that badly wounded comrades could be carried on walks close to the huts where they lived. Cricket bats were made and some of the Russians joined in the matches played on an improvised ground between rival teams.

Despite daily German bombardments, the Russians managed to organise concerts and film shows. The day after *Edinburgh*'s survivors had arrived in Murmansk, on 4 May, the Red Navy put on a special evening of songs and dances. A programme was printed, several copies of which have survived. The programme for Monday 4 May was headed and underlined: '*Down with Hitler*', and then went on: 'Long live the combined forces of the USSR, Great Britain, US and other free Nations waging the War of Freedom against German and Italian Barbaric Imperialism.'

After this propaganda opening the Red Navy singers sang 'Song of the Party', followed by less obviously political songs like 'Kalinka'. By the second half, the Russians were singing 'Three little pigs', 'On the Prairies of Texas' and, more appropriately perhaps, 'A Sailor on a Rock'.

As the evening wore on the Russians produced some vodka and the atmosphere relaxed. The problem was that the Red Navy wanted the Royal Navy to respond with some of their own songs. 'We rather lacked talent,' remembers Joseph Fowells, 'but we did a few parlour tricks with matches, handkerchiefs and glasses which seemed to impress the rather fuddled guests.' Eventually the British began singing 'Tipperary', but nobody could remember all the words. So a little conference was held which concluded that since none of the Russians understood English the words were of no importance. 'We each chose some poem or song we knew and went through the words to the tune of "Tipperary", which is no easy thing to do.'

While the Russians entertained their allies, they also started repairs aboard the British warships which had brought the survivors to Murmansk. Work on the HMS *Trinidad*, which had been damaged in an earlier convoy, was almost completed. Soviet welders and riveters turned to patching up *Foresight* and *Forester* in readiness for another convoy.

In the camps the men talked most of all about getting home. Letters were rare; outgoing mail stood the same chance of going to the bottom as the ships that carried it. Nerves in the bleak wooden huts were understandably frayed at times. Many survivors got used to the rats which ran around them at night; even the food, such as there was, became almost palatable as the days turned into weeks.

Russian women made an especially strong impression on the survivors. Most behaved, and some even looked, like men. 'The women in the forces were well and truly liberated in Murmansk,' recalls James Doyle. 'Some flew Stormoviks and Yaks in combat patrols against the Stukas and Junker-88s. Some suicidally crashed their aircraft into oncoming waves of German bombers when they ran out of ammunition. They drank Red Army-issue vodka straight from the bottle, rolled coarse-grained "mahorka" tobacco in yesterday's issue of *Pravda* and *Isvestia*, then twisted the ends of the cigarette and flashed up.'

Soviet discipline and control were invariably severe, occasionally chilling. Eric Grenfell, at the camp in Vaenga, remembers being invited by some Russians to a naval friend's home nearby. On the way Grenfell saw a well-guarded camp for German prisoners-of-war. 'Never have I seen human beings living more like pigs as the poor sods behind the high barbed-wire fence. The ground was sodden and muddy, and a few of them, in rags, squatted in the mud by a wooden pot, something like a trough, from which they scooped out food with their hands.' He adds that he would have felt less concern if the prisoners had been members of the Gestapo or the SS. But the Germans were ordinary soldiers captured in battle.

Minutes later, the British rating found himself drinking vodka inside a Russian house. The host, in bed wearing a striped sailor's shirt, hurriedly pulled a blanket over the young girl by his side. Soon the Russians and British sailor were drinking endless toasts to Churchill and Stalin. In time Grenfell and the other naval rating made their way back past the prisoner-of-war camp and into their wooden huts.

Not long afterwards a Russian petty officer arrived at Grenfell's camp late at night. 'He was roaring drunk and wanted to visit his

Angliski friends,' says Grenfell. 'He was then roughly led away by
Russian sentries outside our hut.' Later that night the survivors
heard a volley of shots. The next morning a Soviet commissar
arrived and apologised to the British for the petty officer's 'dreadful
behaviour'. The Russian, he said, had been executed.

But lighter moments did occur, and genuine friendships were
struck up. George Daniels, a Royal Marines corporal and *Edinburgh*
survivor billeted at Polyarnoe, describes the electrifying effect on a
Russian audience of *Tin Pan Alley*, the American film starring Betty
Grable and Alice Faye.

At the hospital in Murmansk, meanwhile, countless casualties
were arriving from the German front. The Russians had tried to
push against enemy forces in the north but had been repeatedly
driven back, suffering enormous losses in lives and equipment. Even
in Murmansk the Russian survivors from the front were still not
safe. The Germans had recently intensified their dropping of in-
cendiary bombs in a town that was largely built of wood.

Able-seaman Norman Cosser was at Vaenga and has clear
memories of Russian soldiers returning from the front. 'They were
brought to our camp for a rest before moving back again to the
front. We didn't mix with them and they didn't mix with us.' Despite Russian aloofness Stalin continued to press the British and
Americans for more war supplies. Already Soviet production of
planes and tanks was rising rapidly in the east, replenishing what
Hitler had destroyed in such numbers the previous year, but the
Russians still wanted more convoys, more equipment. Survivors
from HMS *Edinburgh* at Vaenga, which was close to the main airfield, could actually see British-made fighter planes in dog-fights
with the Germans. 'Aircraft often flew low over us,' says Cosser,
'and Spitfires, no less. The ones we had brought up.'

But the Allies could not afford to leave the survivors languishing
in Russia, often no better off than POW's in Germany. They were
needed urgently to fight elsewhere, and there was always the additional risk that hundreds of them might fall at any moment into
enemy hands. Slowly, British and American ships began taking
home survivors, ensuring that wounded men were among the first
to go, especially if they were stretcher cases. Those who were told
they were leaving Russia were usually delighted, but those left

behind often felt bitterly angry. Ironically some survivors who remained in Murmansk found they were better off than their erstwhile colleagues who fell victim to renewed German bomb and torpedo attacks on the voyage home from the Kola Inlet.

On 22 June 1941, Winston Churchill was not surprised to learn that Hitler had invaded the Soviet Union and he reflected on the implications against the background of recent Anglo-Russian relations which for many years had been characterised by hostility and suspicion. In 1939 Britain had altered its policy of appeasement of Nazi Germany and attempted too late in the day to conclude a treaty with Russia. But instead a Russo-German pact was signed by Molotov and Ribbentrop on 23 August 1939.

Nine days later Germany invaded Poland. On 3 September, Britain and France declared war on Germany and the Second World War had begun. Stalin took advantage of his pact with Hitler and on 17 September 1939 Russian troops entered Poland from the east. Poland, the diplomatic excuse for Britain fighting the Germans again, suddenly found itself partitioned by two totalitarian powers ideologically at loggerheads with each other. Nazi and Red Army soldiers were photographed together at the newly-drawn frontiers in occupied Poland: an irony that was not wasted on the world at large.

Now it was Russia's turn to feel the wrath of German occupation. At exactly 3 a.m. on 22 June, a Sunday, German aircraft crossed the border into European Russia. In fifteen minutes some thirty planes would 'blitz' the fighter bases behind the Soviet central front, just three German bombers per airfield. Numerically, the Russian air force was twice the size of the Luftwaffe and Hitler wanted it destroyed before it could strike back at his land forces.

Stalin sent out a warning that a German attack was expected less than two hours before the first Stukas made their attack. He had ordered: 'Before dawn on 22 June all aircraft are to be dispersed on their airfields and camouflaged. All units will come to immediate readiness . . .' But the dictator's orders arrived too late. Longer-range Luftwaffe bombers struck at more distant Soviet bases, while low-flying fighters attacked at will without opposition.

By midnight on 22 June, almost 2,000 Soviet warplanes had been destroyed, three-quarters of them on the ground. Behind the onslaught from the air came the rapidly advancing German army formations. Hitler now demonstrated on land the same destructive ability as the Luftwaffe had shown in the air. The Red Army was decimated and its equipment captured intact or destroyed. Soon Soviet tanks and guns were being turned against the Russians by the victorious German armies.

In London Churchill had no second thoughts about coming to Stalin's aid. Whatever qualms the Cabinet may have felt, individual members were well aware that Britain and Russia now needed each other in the fight with Hitler. (The United States would not declare war on Germany for another six months.)

Hitler estimated that there were almost two hundred Soviet divisions massed behind the Russian borders, of which just over half faced the German front. As German troops pushed forward effortlessly inside the Soviet Union, they found no evidence of offensive preparations in the advance zone, and the Russian troops they did find were rapidly overcome.

Stalin had been warned consistently by Britain and the United States that the Nazi régime would in time turn against him. In Moscow the British Ambassador, Stafford Cripps, found not only an unwillingness to listen among the Russian leadership but also a barely-veiled contempt and hostility at such warnings. Stalin also ignored information from Soviet agents like Sorge in Japan that Russia was in danger of imminent attack by Germany.

Winston Churchill related after the war how he drove down to Chequers, his official home in Buckinghamshire, on the evening of Friday, 20 June. 'I knew that the German onslaught upon Russia was a matter of days, or it might be hours,' he said. 'I had arranged to deliver a broadcast on Saturday night dealing with this event . . . the Soviet government, at once haughty and purblind, regarded every warning we gave as a mere attempt of beaten men to drag others into ruin.'

Ironically Churchill decided to put off his broadcast until Sunday evening, 22 June – the very day Hitler was to launch his attack on Russia. On 15 June, Churchill had cabled to President Roosevelt: 'From every source at my disposal, including some most trustworthy, it looks as if a vast German onslaught on Russia was imminent. . . . Should this new war break out we shall of course give all encouragement and any help we can spare to the Russians following the principle that Hitler is the foe we have to beat. I do not expect any class political reactions here and trust a German-Russian conflict will not cause you any embarrassment.'

The American Ambassador, John Winant, was Churchill's guest at Chequers that weekend and the two men discussed the implications of Britain accepting Stalin as an ally. Roosevelt had said boldly that he would publicly support 'any announcement that the Prime Minister might make welcoming Russia as an ally'.

Sir John Colville, Churchill's private secretary, kept an account of the conversation he heard at Chequers over dinner on Saturday evening. The British Foreign Secretary, Anthony Eden, and the American Ambassador heard Churchill state that a German attack 'on Russia was now certain, and he thought that Hitler was counting on enlisting capitalist and right-wing sympathies in this country and the USA. Hitler was however wrong and we should go all out to help Russia. Winant said the same would be true of the USA.'

While they were walking on the croquet lawn after dinner Colville asked Churchill if this was 'not bowing down in the House of Commons'. But Churchill had replied: 'Not at all. I have only one purpose, the destruction of Hitler, and my life is much simplified thereby. If Hitler invaded Hell, I would make at least a favourable reference to the Devil in the House of Commons.'

Colville learned from the Foreign Office at 4 a.m. the following morning that Hitler had attacked Russia. 'The Prime Minister had always said that he was never to be woken up for anything but the invasion of England,' says Colville. Churchill was not told the startling, if not unexpected, news until four hours after it had reached Chequers.

Despite Churchill's willingness from the outset to give Russia 'any help we can spare' he at once made clear in a broadcast that Sunday evening his strong dislike for Stalin's régime. 'The Nazi régime is indistinguishable from the worst features of Communism,' he said over the air. 'It excels all forms of human wickedness in the efficiency of its cruelty and ferocious aggression. No one has been a more consistent opponent of Communism than I have for the last twenty-five years.'

But Churchill on this occasion was a happy realist and well understood the advantage for Britain of the war being extended. He went on to say in his broadcast: 'The past, with its crimes, its follies and its tragedies, flashes away. I see the Russian soldiers standing on the threshold of their native land, guarding the fields which their fathers have tilled from time immemorial. I see them guarding their homes where mothers and wives pray – ah, yes, for there are times when all pray – for the safety of their loved ones . . . I see the ten thousand villages of Russia where the means of existence is wrung so hardly from the soil, but where there are still primordial human joys, where maidens and children play. . . . I see also the dull, drilled, docile, brutish masses of the Hun soldiery plodding on like swarms of crawling locusts. I see the German bombers and fighters in the sky, still smarting from many a British whipping, delighted to find what they believe is an easier and a safer prey . . . His invasion of Russia is no more than a prelude to an attempted invasion of the British Isles. He hopes, no doubt, that all this may be accomplished before the winter comes, and that he can overwhelm Great Britain before the Fleet and air-power of the United States may intervene . . . the Russian danger is therefore our danger, and the danger of the United States, just as the cause of any Russian fighting for his earth and home is the cause of free men and free peoples in every quarter of the globe.'

Churchill's throaty roar of approval for Russia's entry into the conflict had not been checked with the War Cabinet. 'There was no time,' wrote Churchill later, 'nor was it necessary. I knew that we all felt the same on this issue. Mr Eden, Lord Beaverbrook and Sir Stafford Cripps – he had left Moscow on the 10th – were also with me during the day.'

Three days after Hitler's onslaught on the Soviet Union a British naval liaison mission, under Rear-Admiral Miles, was on its way to Moscow. Geoffrey Miles was told that his primary brief was to ensure 'the prolongation of Russian resistance as this is obviously of very great importance to British interests'. But Miles, with a staff of six, including the naval attaché from the British embassy in Moscow, was under no illusions about the task in hand. The Germans had made rapid military advances inside Russia, and many believed the early defeat of European Russia a distinct possibility.

Churchill wanted to prevent Soviet naval ports and port facilities falling into the hands of the victorious Germans.

Stalin immediately asked Britain and the Royal Navy to strike at German warships and supply vessels supporting the German advance from northern Norway to Murmansk. Murmansk was Russia's only major ice-free port and naval base on the Soviet Arctic coast and therefore vital to Russia's northern defences.

Hitler's advancing forces, some 164 divisions all told, stretched along the whole boundary from the Baltic to the Black Sea. Stalin on the first day of the attack could match the Germans division for division and still have twenty-two to spare. But just as the invaders had outmanoeuvred the French and British in 1940, so now they ran rings around the Russians. But although Stalin was to lose huge quantities of equipment and countless thousands of men, he still had in reserve the vast expanse of Mother Russia where his armies could regroup and in time fight back. Time therefore became the crucial factor and Stalin recognised that war materials from his new allies would play a significant part in his country's defence.

Britain herself was desperately short of munitions, but this did not hinder Russia from making demands for urgent assistance. Stalin demanded British landings in Europe by July 1941, a call which British Communists, who had earlier denounced 'the capitalist and imperialist war', eagerly echoed. In towns and cities around Britain appeared the slogan 'Second Front Now', soon to be added to Stalin's other appeal: 'Help Russia'. 'Uncle Joe', as Stalin soon became known in Britain, was not just asking for slogans. He wanted tanks, planes and guns, and much else besides, and he needed them immediately.

Britain had no landing-craft to invade a heavily-guarded European coast and did not enjoy air or sea superiority in the summer of 1941. Since she was also unable to supply her own demands for war supplies, Stalin was soon compelled to turn to the United States for vital help. After all, Stalin argued from the Kremlin, Roosevelt had proposed as early as December 1940 that lend-lease should be arranged for Britain. After legislation was passed in March 1941 Britain was able to buy airplanes, tanks, ships and machinery for dollars. Why, Stalin suggested, could not Roosevelt arrange a similar deal for Russia?

Stalin's first request was for 20,000 anti-aircraft guns; a million rifles; high-octane gasoline for his Red Air Force; and aluminium to build new aircraft. Another list soon followed, on 8 July, this time for a staggering $2 billion-worth of equipment, including large numbers of pursuit planes and 3,000 bombers.

By 30 October, Roosevelt told Stalin that he could approve shipments worth $1 billion. On 7 November, the American President said that the Soviet Union had been added to the list of countries now eligible, like Britain, for lend-lease assistance, formally declaring that 'the defence of the Soviet Union is vital to the defence of the USA.' Roosevelt explained that shipments of war material up to the value of $1 billion would be financed under the lend-lease act and no interest would be charged. Russia would be granted ten years to repay the debt, beginning five years after the end of the war.

Stalin was delighted at such an arrangement. 'Your decision,' he wrote, 'is accepted with sincere gratitude by the Soviet government as unusually substantial aid in its difficult and great struggle against our common enemy, bloodthirsty Hitlerism.'

On 7 July 1941, Churchill sent Stalin a cable, telling him that he had 'ordered a serious operation to come off in the near future in the Arctic, after which I hope contact will be established between the British and Russian navies. Meanwhile by sweeps along the Norwegian coast we have intercepted various supply ships which were moving against you. We welcome arrival of Russian Military Mission in order to concert future plans. We have only got to go on fighting to beat the life out of these villains.' Churchill wanted to stiffen Stalin's resolve and to ensure that the Russians did not conclude an early, and separate, peace with the Germans. He told the Admiralty that the arrival of a 'British fleet in the Arctic' would have an enormous effect on the Russian armed forces and could 'spare a lot of English blood'.

On 10 July, Stafford Cripps told Stalin formally in Moscow the terms of a proposed Anglo-Soviet agreed declaration under two heads, namely:

(1) mutual help without any precision as to quantity or quality;
(2) neither country to conclude a separate peace.

The following day the proposed agreement was signed in Moscow. But the Russians continued badgering for a Second Front against Germany in the West. Stalin cabled Churchill on 18 July: 'It seems to me that the military situation of the Soviet Union, as well as of Great Britain, would be considerably improved if there could be established a front against Hitler in the West-Northern France, and in the North, the Arctic . . . the front just mentioned would be popular with the British Army as well as with the whole population of southern England.'

Churchill replied that the Germans had forty divisions in France alone and therefore an attempt to invade Europe could only lead to military fiascos. But he did promise a large northern operation by the Royal Navy against German shipping which could transport enemy troops to attack Stalin's Arctic flank.

At the end of June 1941 the Germans occupied Minsk; by the end of July they were entering the Ukraine. Rear-Admiral Philip Vian had arrived in Moscow in early July to see if a Royal Navy base could be established at Murmansk. But Vian told the Admiralty in London that British naval units could not be sent there until local defences had been strengthened, especially against German air bombardments. In late July Churchill's northern operation consisted of an air attack against the two ports of Kirkenes in Norway and Petsamo (now Pechenga – formerly in Finland). Losses were high; sixteen aircraft out of fifty-two failed to return. The Germans lost only four planes, but their daily air attacks on Murmansk were affected for several days.

Churchill had moved quickly in arranging the first war supplies for Russia. On 25 July the British Prime Minister told Stalin that his War Cabinet had agreed to send 200 Tomahawk fighters to Archangel: 140 from Britain and the rest from British supplies in the United States. Churchill added in the cable that he was sending 'up to two to three million pairs of ankle boots' and large quantities of 'rubber, tin, wool and woollen cloth, jute, lead and shellac'.

Meanwhile, on 30 July, the first British support party arrived by air in Polyarnoe, the Russian naval base close to Murmansk. By mid-August the first Royal Navy submarines were patrolling waters close to the Kola Inlet and the entrance to Murmansk. By the end of September five German-controlled vessels had been sunk and Germany began to feel the growing bite of Churchill's embryonic cooperation with Stalin.

In Britain the Government launched 'Russian Tank Week' on 22 September and arms factories throughout the country were urged to 'produce more for Uncle Joe'. A week later, Lord Beaverbrook, then a member of Churchill's War Cabinet, and Averell Harriman, representing the United States, flew to Moscow to discuss war material in greater detail.

But already supplies were reaching Russia. The first convoy carrying forty-eight RAF Hurricanes was nicknamed 'Operation Dervish' and arrived off the Russian coast in early September. On 7 September 1941, HMS *Argus* flew off twenty-four of the Hurricanes to help in the desperate defence of the Murmansk area. The other twenty-four fighters, with their ground crew and stores, were sent overland to Archangel.

While British fighter aircraft reached northern Russia, the Germans had advanced to the outskirts of Leningrad. A fortnight later they had captured Kiev. By the end of September, seemingly invincible, their armies were leaving Smolensk for Moscow. The Soviet capital was within striking distance of Hitler's forces and likely to fall. From the United States President Roosevelt, his country not yet at war with Germany, declared that the Russian front would hold and that Moscow would not be captured.

Churchill discovered that Stalin's entry into the war was a mixed blessing. Hitler's lurch to the East had eased the threat of an immediate invasion of Britain, but vital supplies and equipment from America were now having to be diverted to Russia. Not only did Britain have to send tanks, planes, oil, rubber and other essential supplies, she also had to organise convoys to get them there. Churchill was happy to have Stalin as an ally, but as he said after the war: 'For more than a year after Russia was involved in the war she presented herself to our minds as a burden and not as a help.'

Whatever reservations Churchill held in September 1941 he knew that Russia, with its vast land mass and enormous manpower, could in time break the back of the German army. With the Anglo-Russian Protocol signed by Beaverbrook and Harriman in Moscow, the Admiralty in London planned the first convoy schedule. On 29 September 1941, convoy PQ 1, made up of ten ships, left Iceland, arriving safely in Archangel twelve days later.

British and American supplies to Russia were not free, of course, a fact which many did not then, or later, properly appreciate. Stalin was under no illusions that his allies wanted anything else but hard cash for their weapons, and he agreed to pay in dollars and in gold. Britain, too, was in an identical position with her own lend-lease arrangements with the United States. Guns cost dollars, and Britain was fast running out of dollars; Stalin was financially in an even more perilous position in September 1941, with the Germans close to his capital and no sea to give him additional protection against invasion and occupation.

In a cable to Churchill on 4 September, Stalin began, perhaps unconscious of a certain irony: 'I express thanks for promise *to sell* [emphasis added] to Soviet Union a further 200 fighters in addition to the 200 previously promised.' The Russian dictator, who had recently appointed himself a full field-marshal of the Red Army, then catalogued Soviet misfortunes in the wake of the German advances. After demanding a Second Front 'somewhere in the Balkans or France', Stalin requested '30,000 tons of aluminium by the beginning of October next and a monthly minimum of aid amounting to 400 aircraft and 500 tanks (of small or medium size).' Stalin did not mince words, particularly as Russia faced almost imminent defeat. He admitted to Churchill: 'Without these two forms of help the Soviet Union will either suffer defeat or be weakened ... for a long period ... on the fronts of the struggle against Hitlerism.'

Churchill now promised the Russians one-half of Britain's monthly production of tanks and aircraft. The Americans, hoped Churchill, would supply the same numbers from their own production lines. But towards the end of his lengthy cabled reply to Stalin on 4 September, the British Prime Minister said tersely: 'In your first paragraph you use the word "sell". We had not viewed the matter in such terms and have never thought of payment. Any assistance we can give you would better be upon the same basis of comradeship as the American lend-lease bill, of which no formal account is kept in money.'

Churchill was being slightly disingenuous. Russia would have to pay Britain and America, the question was *when* and *how much*. Even so, Stalin, in a cable to Churchill on 15 September, seems to take the British Prime Minister at his word. 'I can only welcome the intention of the British Government to render the assistance in aluminium, tanks and aircraft not on the usual commercial basis [but] of comradeship and collaboration.'

From President Roosevelt in Washington Stalin learned at the beginning of October about American aims for future aircraft and tank production. From July 1942 until January 1943 Russia and Britain would be allocated 1,200 tanks together each month. With mounting American production the monthly figure would then grow to 2,000 tanks every month. Combined with Roosevelt's promise to supply the Soviet airforce with 3,600 front-line fighters and bombers between 1 July 1942 and 1 July 1943, Stalin's dangerous military plight was slightly easing.

Britain and America had also agreed, however reluctantly, to help transport these vital war supplies to Russia. The Harriman-Beaverbrook Protocol, worked out with Stalin in Moscow in September 1941, ended with the words: 'Great Britain and the United States will give aid to the transportation of these materials to the Soviet Union, and will help with the delivery.'

Churchill was as good as his word and gave instructions that the convoys would become what amounted to a regular, though dangerous, ferry service between the new allies. On 6 October 1941, Churchill cabled Stalin the following message:

I am glad to learn from Lord Beaverbrook of the success of the Tripartite Conference at Moscow. We intend to run a continuous cycle of convoys, leaving every ten days. Following are on the way and arrive Archangel October 12:
  20 heavy tanks – 193 fighters (pre-October quota).
Following will sail October 12 arriving October 29:
  140 heavy tanks – 100 Hurricanes – 200 Bren carriers – 200 anti-tank rifles and ammunition – 50 2-pounder guns and ammunition.
Following will sail October 22nd:
  200 fighters – 100 heavy tanks.
Above shows the total of the October quota of aircraft, and 280 tanks will arrive Russia by November 6. The October quota of Bren carriers, anti-tank

rifles, and 2-pounder anti-tank guns will all arrive in October. Twenty tanks have been shipped to go via Persia, and fifteen are about to be shipped from Canada via Vladivostok. The total tanks shipped will therefore be three hundred and fifteen, which is nineteen short of our full quota. This number will be made up in November. The above programme does not take into account supplies from the United States.

In arranging this regular cycle of convoys we are counting on Archangel to handle the bulk of deliveries. I presume this part of the job is in hand. Good wishes.

With their massive attack along the whole Russian front moving ahead rapidly, the Germans at first paid little attention to the convoys sailing from Britain. Although the routes to north Russia were constrained by narrow seas already controlled by German naval and air bases, Hitler initially ignored his advantage and let the Allied convoys battle with icy conditions rather than with his own forces. He chose, from Berlin, to direct his land armies as they drew steadily closer to Moscow.

By the end of 1941 a third of a million tons of war material had been sent to Murmansk and Archangel, for the loss of only one merchant ship and a destroyer. Eighty-six eastbound merchant ships had got through waters where marauding U-boats and other German warships had yet to strike in earnest. But the pattern changed when convoy PQ 13 left Britain for Russia in March 1942. Out of the nineteen-strong convoy five ships were sunk and the cruiser HMS *Trinidad* was badly damaged while sinking the German destroyer Z26 on 29 March 1942. An official Admiralty account after the war starkly catalogues the havoc wreaked by the Germans upon the Allied convoys. After recording the losses sustained by PQ 13, the report continues: 'PQ 14 ran into bad weather, which drove back all but eight of the 24 ships, and lost one of those which continued, while the next two convoys lost ten out of 60 ships to aircraft and U-boats. PQ 16 arrived at Archangel on 1 June 1942, bringing the total safe arrivals of merchant ships to 179, compared with 17 ships lost and 18 turned back for various reasons. Of the 145 ships in the 12 westbound convoys, six had been sunk and six returned to Russia.'

Far worse was yet to come. PQ 11, of course, had ended with the destruction of HMS *Edinburgh* in May 1942, but the rest of the convoy steered safely through to Iceland. Commander Eric Grenfell, who had been on *Edinburgh* until early that year, was transferred to the merchant ship *Empire Lawrence*. His experience on convoy PQ 16 would become commonplace for seamen carried on such transport vessels. The *Empire Lawrence*, loaded with ammunition, and with its decks stacked with tanks, planes and lorries, left Hvalfjord in Norway in the same month that *Edinburgh* had been sunk. (Grenfell heard about the loss of the two British cruisers, *Edinburgh* and *Trinidad*, before leaving Iceland with PQ 16.) On the 11,000-ton *Empire Lawrence*, Grenfell was in charge of the RDF (radio direction finder) crew. Unlike many smaller merchant ships the *Lawrence* carried some armaments and a Hurricane fighter which could be launched by rocket catapult. For four days Grenfell watched seemingly unending attacks from submarines, torpedo bombers and dive bombers. 'There was an almost stand-up fight between the two RAF pilots about who would take up the Hurricane,' he recalls. 'There was no landing back on the ship. Anyhow, the Hurricane brought down two attacking aircraft before being shot down himself.' The pilot, Flight-Lieutenant Hay, was badly wounded, rescued by HMS *Volunteer*, and later decorated with the DFC.

The merchant ship, however, was destined for the sea-bed. On 27 May, it was attacked by waves of JU-88s. Bombs struck the ammunition on board and the ship disintegrated and quickly sank. Grenfell was hurled into the icy water and then watched one of the JU-88s return to machine-gun the floating remains of the ship, killing several survivors floundering in the sea. Grenfell was fortunate in the circumstances, for he found a wrecked lifeboat, scrambled into it, and was rescued by the corvette *Hyderabad* less than an hour later. 'There were few survivors that day,' says Grenfell. 'Our captain and, as far as I know, all our officers had been killed. Many then died on the *Hyderabad* on our way to Murmansk.'

Such grim scenes and experiences became common on the Arctic run. The following convoy, PQ 17, suffered far greater destruction. German submarines and aircraft destroyed twenty-three of the thirty-four ships which left the Denmark Strait on 28 June 1942. And PQ 17 had an exceedingly strong escort and cover: a combined force of two battleships, a Fleet carrier, eight cruisers, twenty-six destroyers, sixteen escorts and rescue ships, three oilers, and a formidable force of eleven submarines. In addition three Russian submarines, assisted by nine of the British, were positioned close to the expected path of the enemy's surface squadron: a force made up of the battleship *Tirpitz*, two pocket battleships, a cruiser and ten destroyers.

In the event the *Tirpitz* did not even need to take part in a battle which seriously damaged the Royal Navy's prestige. The United States, which had declared war on Germany and Italy in December 1941, now felt the destruction and hardship of the Arctic convoys at first hand. No less than twenty-two of the ships in convoy PQ 17 were American, and many merchant seamen were forced to wonder why the apparently well-protected convoy should have scattered and suffered such devastating losses.

For Stalin the ill-fated outcome of PQ 17 spelled a different kind of disaster, not just in terms of the missing tanks and planes so vital for his depleted defences inside Russia. PQ 17 would soon mean something more; it would become almost synonymous with an impending diplomatic rift between the Soviet Union and its Western allies.

The failure of PQ 17 meant that Stalin would not get another eastbound convoy until mid-September 1942. That convoy, PQ 18, reached Murmansk with twenty-seven out of the forty cargoes sent, and it represented the final delivery that year. Britain was also hard-pressed to supply Malta, then in the throes of incessant Axis attacks, and for the time being British convoys headed for the beleaguered Mediterranean island.

Yet as early as the summer of 1941, weeks after Stalin had been forced into war with Germany, cries came to 'Help Russia' from all shades of political opinion. The British Communist Party now turned its earlier, somewhat puny, efforts to sabotage the war effort into a wailing catcall to produce more arms for 'Uncle Joe'. And there was a widespread impression in Britain, shared by some people in the United States, that not enough was being produced and sent to Russia. Churchill's wife, Clementine, told her husband that money should be raised to help buy medical supplies. Later she would tell him that the temporary cessation of war supplies, whatever the cause, was not popular in the country. As early as October

1941, Mrs Churchill urged her husband to renew his efforts to start a Second Front. Churchill had to disappoint his wife just as he had dismayed Stalin.

In fact, the British Red Cross and St John's had already been fund-raising for Russia, and Churchill encouraged his wife to head an appeal for more much-needed cash. Clementine Churchill agreed to lead a combined appeal called 'Aid to Russia'. In her first public call for money she declared: 'There is no one in this country whose heart has not been deeply stirred by the appalling drama now going on in Russia . . . We have been moved to profound admiration for the valour, the tenacity and the patriotic self-sacrifice of the Russian people.' She told the public that already '53 emergency operating outfits, 30 blood-transfusion sets, 70,000 surgical needles of various kinds, and 1,000,000 tablets of M. and B. 693' had been sent. This drug, she went on, is the 'wonderful new antiseptic which has revolutionised the treatment of many diseases caused by germs'. Other drugs had been sent in considerable quantities.

Mrs Churchill ended by appealing for £1 million. Already the King and Queen, she said, had sent a further cheque for £3,000 to the Red Cross, saying that £1,000 should be given to the Aid to Russia Fund. 'Thus, from the King and Queen to the humblest wage-earner and cottage-dweller,' she said, catching the combination of feeling and rhetoric in the air, 'we can all take part in this message of goodwill and compassion. Between the cottage and the palace, between those who can spare only pennies and a great imaginative benefactor like Lord Nuffield, who can send a cheque for £50,000, there are millions of people who would like to share in this tribute to the Russian people.'

In four years the Aid to Russia Fund collected £8 million. Churchill valued such fund-raising both in itself and for the propaganda and morale-boost it contributed to the overall Allied war effort. Stalin too, a Communist who would not look a capitalist gift horse in the mouth, was pleased to accept such genuinely unencumbered charity.

'In spite of heavy losses in the Arctic convoys,' wrote Churchill, 'medical and surgical supplies and all kinds of comforts and special appliances found their way in unbroken flow through the icy and

deadly seas to the valiant Russian armies and people.' When Churchill and Roosevelt, and perhaps even Stalin, looked at the figures
for supplies reaching Russia they would probably have agreed that
such sacrifices had been worthwhile. Examined coldly and critically
the gross tonnage of war material getting to Russia was impressive.
In 1942, the year when the Arctic convoys took the brunt of their
losses, 1,350,000 tons from Britain and America arrived safely.
270,000 tons had been despatched to the sea-bed, along with valiant
ships like the *Edinburgh* and the men who served with her.

But in the intermittently chilly relations between the western
Allies and Stalin, years later to turn into cold war, the loss of the
Edinburgh with her gold did not escape controversy and Russian
criticism and comment. When the Russian admiral, Arseni
Golovko, who was in charge of the Murmansk naval region, learned
that HMS *Edinburgh* had been sunk he ordered a secret inquiry into
the circumstances surrounding her loss. His conclusion was that
Rear-Admiral Bonham-Carter should not have abandoned and
then sunk his flagship.

Unusually some of the findings of Golovko's confidential inquiry
have become known. In his war memoirs entitled *With the Red Fleet*
Golovko gives his own controversial and critical views of *Edinburgh*'s
final hours. He describes the initial German submarine attack, stat-
ing factually that '*Edinburgh* received a torpedo hit in the stern and
lost her propellers and rudders'. But the Russian admiral then
observes: 'However, *Edinburgh* remained not only capable of staying
afloat, but even of being towed to one of our ports. Everything in
the cruiser was in working order except the rudder and propellers.
Possessing, as she did, a solid armament and being protected by
other ships, she was quite capable of standing up for herself.'

Golovko and the Soviet government were well aware that certain
high-ranking Royal Navy officers laid much of the blame for *Edinburgh*'s destruction on the Russians. Some of their information came
from conversations with British naval personnel after *Edinburgh*'s
survivors had been rescued by accompanying Royal Navy warships
and taken back to Murmansk. Far more significant was the fact
that information in Admiralty documents marked 'secret' had been
passed clandestinely at the height of the war to the Russian
authorities. In spite of Stalin's enforced espousal of the anti-Hitler

cause, he still remained deeply distrustful of Britain's underlying long-term motives and objectives.

The Soviet Union had been humiliated by the dexterity and power of the German attack in June 1941, but in one arena, espionage, she remained supreme. Stalin's appetite for covertly-obtained information about his allies remained constant throughout the war. In London the Russians were well served by the spy network which had been prompted by certain Soviet diplomats and included such zealous Marxist converts as Guy Burgess and Anthony Blunt. During the war, the flow of information would be passed by NKVD agents such as Blunt, then a serving MI 5 officer, to Soviet NKVD officers posing as diplomats at the Russian embassy in London.

So it was that one snippet of secrecy, about the loss of HMS *Edinburgh*, may well have found its way via the Burgess-Blunt espionage network back to Moscow. And perhaps the Russians were not surprised to learn that Rear-Admiral R.H.L. Bevan, the British senior officer in command of Royal Navy personnel in north Russia in 1942, was highly critical of the Red Navy's performance at the height of the engagement which had resulted in the loss of the British cruiser and sixty of her crew.

One document classified as 'Secret' by the Admiralty was written six days after *Edinburgh* had been sunk. In it Rear-Admiral Bevan discusses the peculiar behaviour of the two Russian destroyers, *Sokrushitelni* and *Gremyaschi*. Both ships had signalled to *Edinburgh* at the height of the fierce battle with the Germans that they were short of fuel and needed to return urgently to the Kola Inlet. The untimely and unexpected exit from the engagement surprised and gladdened the Germans but seriously weakened the protecting screen of allied ships around *Edinburgh*. But the Soviet captains in command of the two destroyers both signalled 'that they would return to escort *Edinburgh as soon as they had fuelled*', a fact included in the secret Bevan memorandum of 8 May.

Bevan goes on to state that 'supposing them to be 500 tons short, they could have completed with fuel from Rosta Fuelling Jetty and the tanker *Scottish American* in about six hours. The *Edinburgh* was then about 200 miles distant.' Bevan added that he had been asked in Murmansk if the Soviet destroyers should remain in harbour or return to bring *Edinburgh* safely back to Murmansk. The Admiral's reply had been unequivocal: 'I said the only thing that mattered at the moment was to bring *Edinburgh* safely into port and that (further) attacks were certain, once she had been reported as damaged. That additional escort was essential as quickly as they could reach her.'

Oddly, the Russians then claimed that faults had developed in one of the destroyers, the *Gremyaschi*, and that this was preventing her from leaving Murmansk at once. Bevan suggested that the *Sokrushitelni* might go alone to *Edinburgh*'s rescue. In turn the Soviet chief-of-staff then claimed that the weather might hinder the destroyer's speed, reducing it to some twelve knots. But as Bevan stated icily in his report: 'It has since been reported that there was no sea and wind force.'

At 0100 Bevan asked the Russians what the destroyers were doing and was told they would be leaving seven hours later to help the crippled British cruiser. But when the Soviet warships did finally sail, two hours after *Edinburgh* had been attacked again, it was too late.

The Royal Navy and the Admiralty in London were both perplexed and furious at their ally's almost perfidious casualness at a moment when help was critical. Bevan gave London his opinion about the destroyers' failure to return to the fight: 'The fact remains that an excellent chance of meeting the enemy with a superior force, or, if they had arrived too late for that, of chasing a damaged enemy back to port, was lost through lack of willingness to leave harbour.' Such a top-level condemnation from Rear-Admiral Bevan in Murmansk, implying bad faith, even cowardice, on the part of the Red Navy, had obvious implications for Anglo-Russian relations, particularly as Bevan had also told the Admiralty in his secret memorandum: 'Personally, I believe that the May Day celebrations proved too strong an attraction and that the defects were unimportant, since they [*Sokrushitelni* and *Gremyaschi*] returned at high speed [to Murmansk] on Sunday 3 May.'

Combined with Golovko's disparaging remarks about Bonham-Carter's handling of the cruiser came testy references, also, to the lost gold bullion. Golovko was not slow to make his feelings known in May 1942, later publishing his opinions in his memoirs. 'No sooner was the *Edinburgh* damaged than her crew abandoned ship and boarded a destroyer which came alongside without taking anything with them, either personal belongings or the crates of gold slabs which the ship was carrying to England as payment to that country by the Soviet Union for deliveries of war materials.' He went on to say that 'the cruiser was despatched by the English ships and went to the bottom with her cargo of gold, weighing about ten tons and equivalent to a sum of one hundred million roubles.'

Golovko was not correct in saying that the gold represented payment to England for war materials: rather, it was payment for the United States, transported in a British convoy. But the Russian Admiral's reference to *ten tons* of gold, rather than the five tons signed for by *Edinburgh*'s captain in April 1942, would years later have puzzling repercussions and intrude a further element of mistrust in talks between the British and Soviet governments.

In 1942, Stalin was naturally more concerned with getting tanks and planes to Russia than troubling to argue about Soviet gold bars on the sea-bed. In any case London and Moscow had taken the precaution of insuring the bullion which had sunk with the *Edinburgh*, and the United States would therefore get her money. The gold bars had not fallen into enemy hands and, now that they were 800 feet down in the Barents Sea, there seemed nothing to do but forget them.

Meanwhile, with Hitler directing his naval forces increasingly against the convoys travelling from America to Britain in the North Atlantic, the Arctic route gradually became safer. In the first two months of 1943 two convoys with thirty-five ships reached the Kola Inlet without losing a single vessel. Later in 1943 preparations for the Allied invasion of Sicily, and the need for heavy escort warships, stopped convoys to Russia altogether. Now the only war material to arrive in the Soviet Union had to be taken to the Persian Gulf and then overland into Russia.

Stalin showed his displeasure by imposing additional restrictions on Allied personnel stationed in the Kola Inlet. Soviet officials began exercising their right to search the personal belongings of seamen on warships and merchant ships. On one occasion customs officials confiscated a British jammer which was employed against enemy homing beacons, giving the excuse that it had been imported illegally. Soon afterwards the Russians asked their allies to close down the wireless stations they ran at Polyarnoe and Archangel. Even seamen's letters were seized in June 1943 and sent to the Russian capital to be censored; many of them never reached their destination.

Some of the restrictions imposed on orders from Moscow were undoubtedly brought on themselves by the British. In the aftermath of the PQ 17 débâcle Rear-Admiral Bevan began, without Russian permission, to set up Royal Navy hospital units in Vaenga and Archangel to treat Allied seamen who were sick or wounded. When the request to land naval personnel was denied by the Russians in August 1942, making the medical units virtually inoperable for the time being, the British had to turn to 'the highest level' for the necessary permission. Even then only half of the Vaenga group was allowed to land.

Such pettiness inevitably affected men who had been wounded on the *Edinburgh* and in subsequent actions and who looked forward to more sophisticated medical treatment at Vaenga. They now suffered because the convoys were slowing down and because Anglo-Russian relations were steadily worsening. In Murmansk Russian civilians openly repeated their own government's incessant demand for a Second Front. Stalin would not accept that the invasions of North Africa or Sicily amounted to such; he wanted an immediate landing by Allied soldiers in France, and nothing less was acceptable in diplomatic terms.

By May 1943 British naval strength in north Russia stood at 202 officers and ratings divided between Murmansk and the other bases along the Kola Inlet. In addition there were the crews of two mine-sweepers and a trawler berthed at Polyarnoe and eight naval members of the British Military Mission. The Russians wanted the British contingent reduced and demanded the right to select personnel coming to Russia. In London the Soviet embassy refused to issue visas to men wanted in Murmansk to replace 153 Britons long overdue for leave.

Unaccountably American personnel were not treated as poorly as the British. But the United States had no mission in Moscow in mid-1943, and despite US Navy units, including battleships, being used on the convoy runs there 'were no Americans,' as an Admiralty historian put it later, 'on the naval staffs in north Russia to provoke Soviet xenophobia. The distinction between Allies was not lost on the British, who clearly resented it.'

In 1943 two Royal Navy ratings were arrested by the Russian authorities in Murmansk and sentenced for what their officers considered to be 'trivial offences'. Trivial or not, Churchill decided that the moment had come to intervene. His suggestion that the British should ostentatiously withdraw from north Russia was not popular with the British chiefs-of-staff. In spite of the *Edinburgh* incident and the diplomatic sparring which had gradually deteriorated into half-open hostility, British military experts recognised that Britain still needed Russian facilities. In London the Admiralty was actively planning an imminent Midget submarine attack on the German battleship *Tirpitz*, then a powerful force in waters close to the Kola Inlet. And along the waterway to Murmansk were twenty-four merchant ships at anchor, waiting for a convoy to return to Britain. British naval chiefs argued with Churchill that the two minesweepers and trawlers based at Polyarnoe should stay where they were in order to give protection to any new convoys which might be sent to north Russia.

Churchill lost his argument with the chiefs-of-staff, and British naval personnel remained in the Kola Inlet. The operation against the *Tirpitz* succeeded brilliantly on 22 September 1943, and the battleship was put out of operation until the following spring.

Stalin then learned from London that the convoys would resume in October 1943. That same month the British Foreign Secretary, Anthony Eden, and his Soviet counterpart, Vyacheslav Molotov, talked about the promised convoys in detail. Eden told Molotov that the next British convoy would leave Scotland in mid-November. On 15 November the convoy left Loch Ewe, arriving two weeks later without loss. By the end of 1943, seventy merchant ships in four convoys had reached north Russia, again without loss.

Molotov, however, had complained to Eden that British sailors were not treating the Russians 'as equals' and claimed that this was primarily responsible for frictions which had arisen in Murmansk. Nevertheless, relations with the Soviet government had by now slowly improved, partly because the convoys had resumed deliveries of war supplies and partly because of a more impressive British naval presence. On Boxing Day 1943 the Royal Navy's Home Fleet sank the German battlecruiser *Scharnhorst* in Arctic waters; the next day the battleship *Duke of York* arrived at Murmansk to celebrate her triumph and to show the Russians that Britain had renewed her mastery of the Arctic convoy routes.

In the final phase of the war, between 12 January 1944 and 22 May 1945, thirteen convoys reached the White Sea. And of 379 ships which left Britain for Arctic waters, only five were sunk by U-boats, another six turning back. Stalin and Churchill had much to be pleased about. In this period alone almost two million tons of vital war material were sent, compared with under half a million in 1943.

But the harsh statistics behind such successes look cruelly stark when they are set out like cricket scores in official accounts of convoy losses inside the Arctic circle. 'Eighty-seven out of the 1,528 merchant ships which sailed in either direction were sunk, with the loss of 829 merchant seamen,' states one official report. 'The Royal Navy lost eighteen ships and 1,956 men; [but] the personnel losses do not seem to have impressed the Russians, whose Army casualties were of such staggering proportions and whose manpower resources were such that such figures seemed trifling.' Nevertheless, Molotov did concede at the time of the final convoy that the 'Russian convoys are a northern saga of heroism, bravery and endurance.'

In the spring of 1945, with Germany defeated, the British and other Allied naval staff left the Kola Inlet and Archangel with the last convoy. The wartime Anglo-Russian cooperation was at an end. Soon the victory celebrations, the exhilaration and the memory of having survived such rigours would slowly fade on both sides. Later, when such thoughts and impressions were revived, it would not be for the scent of battle victories at sea but the lure of what the icy Arctic waters held deep down below the waves: gold, tons of the stuff, which had been quietly beckoning those who remembered its presence on board *Edinburgh*. In time the treasure on the sea-bed, worth much more than a mere king's ransom, would bring back some of the spirit, and suspicions, of those perilous wartime years: and at least some of the dangers.

Edinburgh was not the only British cruiser to sail from Russia carrying gold destined for her allies in the West. The first shipment, ten tons of bullion, left Archangel on HMS *Suffolk* in October 1941, arriving safely at Scapa Flow in Scotland thirteen days later.

Four months afterwards, HMS *Cairo* sailed from the Kola Inlet with 200 cases of gold addressed to the Bank of England in London. Stalin was proving with his bullion what he had already stressed in his cables to Churchill and Roosevelt: Russia *was* paying for war materials.

Not all the gold, of course, was payment to Britain. In late March 1942, HMS *Kenya*, carrying ten tons of bullion, left Russia with convoy QP 9, reaching Scapa Flow with her precious cargo before the month was out. By mid-April, this consignment of gold had been landed at Halifax in Canada by HMS *Churchill* and the Polish destroyer *Piorum*. Days later the gold crossed over the Canadian border and into the custody of the United States government.

But the mounting German attacks on convoys and the disastrous loss of *Edinburgh* and the five tons of bullion she carried had halted, at least temporarily, the flow of Soviet gold to the West. Yet Stalin needed war materials throughout his country's fight to the death with Hitler, and he needed to go on paying for them. In March 1944, the dictator paid for a few more tanks and planes with the $10\frac{1}{2}$ tons of bullion which left Russia on HMS *Black Prince*. The convoy RA 57, the Royal Navy cruiser and the gold bars got through to Scapa safely in six days.

There had, of course, been a certain amount of official tidying-up to do after the sinking of *Edinburgh*. Captain Faulkner had returned from Russia to stay briefly at his family home at Hawick in Scotland, from where he wrote sympathetically to the relatives of men who had died on his ship a few weeks before. Necessarily he couched the condolence letters in similar phrases, just as the German captain did when writing to the relatives of men who had died on the *Hermann Schoemann*. 'Your son was a fine member of our very fine ship's company,' Faulkner wrote to the mother of twenty-year-old ordinary seaman James Yates. 'As far as I can ascertain your boy was killed outright by the first torpedo to strike the ship and I am thankful to say that he was spared all suffering.' Yates had genuinely enjoyed serving on the *Edinburgh*. In letter after letter to his mother the young seaman praised his life on board, even the food. Now he was dead; in April 1947 his mother received a war gratuity of £4 10 shillings and naval prize-money of £4 4 shillings.

Bonham-Carter, too, had done a fair amount of writing that year.

After all he had given the orders which finally sank the *Edinburgh*. 'She rolled over on her side and the fore part broke off where the first and third torpedoes had hit, the bows rising vertically and then sliding down into the water,' he wrote in his report to the Admiralty. In notes he made on the *Harrier* he described *Edinburgh*'s last moments more graphically: '*Edinburgh* had had all she could take. She rolled over to port, her back broke, and the last seen of her was her bows rising vertically in the air and then disappearing. The after part just rolled over.' Apart from extensive reports about the sinking of the *Edinburgh* he had also drawn up a list of survivors whom he recommended for awards. Top of his list, marked 'Secret', was Hugh Faulkner, whom he praised for displaying 'utmost coolness, calmness and leadership'. There followed the names of men like Salter, Bitmead, Crease and Biggs, all of whom had served bravely on ships accompanying *Edinburgh* and all of whom would be awarded the DSO.

Faulkner at the time was given the more modest award of MID (Mention in Despatches), an award that Bonham-Carter took as a personal slight. In a note written on 2 August 1942, Bonham-Carter, now a Vice-Admiral, told Faulkner: 'Have you seen the *Times* of July 31st . . . it has made me so angry . . . there is a heading "Naval Awards [for] service in Convoys to Russia" . . . Every captain gets a DSO except you who deserves it as much if not more than any of them. I have just looked up my list of recommendations and I am just astounded that your name is not down.'

Bonham-Carter went to the Admiralty and spoke to the Commander-in-Chief about Faulkner's 'missing' award for his part in the battle around *Edinburgh*. The Vice-Admiral learned that the cruiser's captain had got a 'Mention in Despatches'. Bonham-Carter was furious and said so in a letter to Faulkner. 'If, because a captain loses his ship after having done all the world could expect to keep her afloat, the Admiralty policy is not to decorate them, it is time we packed up.'

Fortunately Hugh Faulkner's naval career was not to suffer from any controversy surrounding the sinking of the *Edinburgh* or the minor setback of his temporarily missing award. Later in 1942 Faulkner got his DSO and ended his distinguished career a decade later as a rear-admiral. In turn Stuart Bonham-Carter was knighted and became a full admiral before retiring from the service in 1944.

PART II
The Search

3

The Problems

With the end of hostilities in 1945 the *Edinburgh* and its lost gold became for many another blurred wartime memory, just as the loss of the British cruiser *Hampshire*, with its valuable bullion cargo, off the west coast of Scotland had largely been forgotten after the First World War. Some men who had survived the sinking of the *Edinburgh* died on other ships in subsequent sea battles; others had returned after the war to more mundane jobs in civvy street, while a good few stayed behind in the Navy. As for the *Edinburgh*, it had sunk, rather like the *Titanic* before it, to a depth far beyond the reach of man and his technology. The gold bullion, it seemed, would stay on the sea-bed for ever.

Or would it? For despite *Edinburgh*'s fading memory some men believed that the gold could one day be recovered. Tantalisingly it sat there *somewhere* in the Barents Sea, that inhospitable stretch of international waters now claimed both by the Soviet Union and by the West. Whether the three German torpedoes and the single British one had spread the gold bars like ninepins inside the wreck nobody could tell. Anybody who had access to Admiral Bonham-Carter's secret reports could only speculate on whether the cruiser, its back apparently broken, had landed in one piece on the bottom. If the ship *had* broken apart, the gold could be anywhere: countless ingots hidden in the silt, sludge and torn wreckage of the spread-eagled ship lying on the sea-bottom.

The first salvors to show discreet interest in the *Edinburgh* were a British firm, based in Southampton, called Risdon Beazley. In 1954, just nine years after the end of the war, Risdon Beazley, who had been Admiralty salvors since the 1930s, inquired about the Royal Navy wreck. In a letter written that year the Admiralty made no objection to Beazley attempting to salvage the *Edinburgh*, a decision many inside the Ministry of Defence were later to regret.

But the truth was that in 1954, as later, no salvage company actually needed permission to search and recover the gold, because the wreck lay in international waters. In inter-departmental letters at the Admiralty lawyers pointed out that nothing could be done to stop a company trying to salvage the bullion. However, for the time being Risdon Beazley forgot about the *Edinburgh* and its cargo; around the British Isles and farther afield there were other wrecks that, if not as rich, were certainly more readily accessible.

Risdon Beazley had originally asked one of their researchers, Tom Pickford, to examine whether it was possible to find the *Edinburgh* and to recover a worthwhile proportion of the gold. Pickford had first to establish whether such a speculative project was technically feasible and economically tenable. This research project therefore began in 1954 in considerable secrecy, to prevent other salvors or the public getting to hear about it.

Because of the thirty-year-rule which keeps many official documents confidential until this period has elapsed, Pickford had a twofold secrecy problem. 'We couldn't find out as much in 1954 as we could many years later,' says Pickford, who now has his own firm researching wrecks around the world. 'There were the naval logs, for example, which were then covered by the thirty-year-rule. Our picture of the *Edinburgh* didn't become more complete until the late 1970s.'

Risdon Beazley approached the *Edinburgh* with definite caution. The cruiser was known to lie at a depth of between 700 and 900 feet, and no salvor at that time had worked in such deep and dangerous waters inside the Arctic circle. In fact, until the late 1950s, commercial interest in deep-sea diving was restricted to the occasional salvage operation and divers very rarely worked below 200 feet. Moreover, in the mid-1950s the Southampton firm, like many salvors in the immediate post-war era, were seldom short of wrecks lying in more approachable and shallower waters.

Risdon Beazley had built their reputation on the 'blast and grab' method of salvage recovery, a technique that relied on careful use of explosives. Pickford came to the conclusion that this method could be used on the *Edinburgh* once the wreck had been located. 'Our divers at the time worked in chambers instead of being in the water and getting into a ship under their own power,' explains Pickford. 'We never got into a ship; we opened up a wreck with explosives and then grabbed into it with a mechanical grab under the direction of a diver working in a chamber nearby.'

Pickford had had experience of bullion recovery before. Risdon Beazley, for example, had raised gold from the wreck of the *Niagara*, which had sunk during the war off the Australian coast. The researcher became convinced that the *Edinburgh* would present similar problems. 'You see, the gold often falls down between the ship's plates after it has hit the sea-bed,' says Pickford. 'The gold goes right to the bottom. So from our recovery method at the time we could not grab it very easily because we could not get our grab into the places where the gold would have lodged.'

In any event Risdon Beazley were uneasy about the challenge. Nevertheless, negotiations with the Admiralty continued. 'We had discussions, and even the Russians came over to see us,' says Pickford. In time the firm's proposals were submitted to the, then, Board of Trade. 'But Risdon Beazley decided not to go ahead. It was too speculative, especially at that time.'

Along with the prospect of five (maybe ten) tons of gold being raised by Risdon Beazley, there came an odd and contradictory twist to the story. In 1957, the War Graves Commission, a department of the Admiralty, designated the *Edinburgh* wreck an official war grave. Such a decision was curious, some might think hypocritical, in view of the fact that another Admiralty department had raised no objections three years before to Risdon Beazley placing explosives on the wreck and grabbing whatever gold was left behind after the blastings. Inter-departmental correspondence at the Admiralty in 1956 makes clear that the British government were still hoping to find a salvor prepared to take on the *Edinburgh* contract. So it would appear that one hand of government wanted the gold salvaged, while another apparently considered the wreck so sacrosanct a maritime cemetery that it should not be touched at all. Such conflicting official attitudes would years later have repercussions for the war grave and the bodies it contained.

But in spite of *Edinburgh*'s new status as an official war grave in

1957, a move partly designed to dissuade any 'pirate' attempts to seize the gold, there was little the British government could do in a practical sense to prevent an unauthorised entry into the wreck. There was certainly nothing to stop the Russians from making an attempt, assuming they had the technology to bring it off. For international law allowed anybody and any nation to work on wrecks lying in international waters, even in such a contentious East–West 'grey area' as the Barents Sea.

For the time being the British government's major ally was the simple, daunting fact that the cruiser was some 800 feet down on the sea-bed. In 1957 that was far deeper than any man had so far dived on any salvage mission. There was an additional obstacle to work beginning on the *Edinburgh*: salvors like Risdon Beazley were well aware that it would need a sizeable fortune to lift the bullion off the sunken cruiser. Interest in the gold was therefore shelved, though by no means forgotten.

Then, in August 1969, a sheriff's court in Scotland heard the remarkable story of a Yorkshire salvage diver who had helped himself unlawfully to bits and pieces he had found on a sunken German U-boat, lying within British waters and therefore the property of the British government. Keith Jessop, a bluff though genial small-time entrepreneur, admitted to the court that he had taken four torpedo tubes from the submarine and later sold them.

U-boat 570 was originally commissioned into Hitler's navy, but in 1943 her German commander had surrendered to a British aircraft off the French coast. The Royal Navy turned U-570 into HMS *Graph*, and the submarine remained in service until March 1944 when she sank in a towing mishap off the west coast of Ireland.

People listening to the court case that day heard a suitably contrite man in his mid-thirties explain why he had 'retrieved' brass from a submarine that had belonged to Her Majesty's navy. His explanation was given with the odd shrug and becoming smile of a man unused to tight and sometimes uncomfortable corners. Jessop received a sympathetic hearing in court, and his relaxed manner exactly matched the gravity with which he and the sheriff apparently viewed the charge. After all, the submarine was lying on the sea-bed and Jessop had no plans to return to the scene of his crime.

Jessop had been charged with another man from Keighley in Yorkshire, a diver who also described himself in court as a coal merchant. Next to them in the dock was a scrap-metal merchant who, the court decided, was the real villain of the maritime tale. For once Keith Jessop was out of luck. At the Keighley social centre, Jessop had shown photographs of the torpedo tubes to friends and talked about his good fortune with the German submarine which had been turned into HMS *Graph*. But unfortunately a detective had overheard the conversation and the salvor was later arrested and charged with theft.

The sheriff told Jessop and his colleague: 'You are both very experienced, and as far as can be judged, very fine men.' After such rather unexpected admiration came a guarded admonition and a ticking-off by the sheriff, who fined them £50 each and said they 'should have known better'.

Although the sheriff had not been entirely seduced by the charm with which he explained his behaviour Jessop had been lucky again. Considering that the four torpedo tubes were worth anything up to £1,000, a £50 fine and a mild rebuke were hardly a severe punishment.

In fact, in finding himself in court at all Jessop had broken, albeit unwittingly, the secrecy behind which most salvors traditionally prefer to operate. 'The salvage industry doesn't like discussing its plans or its operations with outsiders,' he told others often enough. 'And what salvors do under water is usually kept very secret.' Salvage could bring good profit out of the sea, but it could also easily end in abject failure, injury or death. Salvors, like bookmakers and builders, often went bankrupt. And salvors who disclosed too much about their activities on land or under water could be adding an unnecessary risk to their work.

Jessop's court appearance had attracted publicity and the unspoken disapproval of other salvors. For years afterwards, though, Jessop would disarm people he met by stretching out his hand and saying: 'I'm Keith Jessop. I expect you've heard about my criminal record. I'm a *terrible* lad.' Keith Jessop was eventually to become one of the world's most successful salvors, yet over the years he had certainly notched up a few notable failures. Apart from U-boat 570 and his appearance in the dock he had sometimes failed to find wrecks and at other times a promising specimen did not match up to his expectations.

But he did have the occasional, lesser discovery that paid well enough. In 1968, helped by a local lobster fisherman, he found the wreck of an armed merchant cruiser off the Hebrides. HMS *Otranco*, a former Orient liner, had been carrying several hundred American troops to Europe when it sank towards the end of the First World War. Less than twenty soldiers reached the shore safely. The cruiser was found some twelve feet below the surface and Jessop was able to salvage the boiler, propeller and other non-ferrous scraps. The ex-marine commando got back his investment, and made a good profit, but it was still a long way from a project like HMS *Edinburgh*.

Jessop relied at this time for much of his income from clearing underwater obstruction for the Northern Lighthouse Commission and a number of commercial concerns working off the Scottish coast. While doing so he always kept his eyes open for scrap and accessible wrecks. 'And ears open,' he says, 'because in the salvage game it's what you hear that can be important, like the odd remark from a fisherman who may have pulled up something in his nets that suggests a wreck in a position nobody previously knew about. Salvors, big and small, necessarily come to rely on their intelligence network.'

In the late 1960s, and throughout much of the next decade, Jessop had to mix his salvage work with jobs as a diver in the North Sea oilfields. He had a family and three children to support, and the occasional scrapping operation was risky and notoriously unreliable for a steady living. 'There was always the feeling inside me that I had to go for a really big job, a wreck nobody would begin to believe I might tackle,' he says. 'There were plenty of people around who laughed at my schemes, thought I was mad.'

Dreamers are common enough in the salvage world, as they are in any activity that combines an element of treasure-hunting, luck and reckless speculation. Jessop's detractors saw him as a small-town diver who was unlikely to progress from inconsequential scrapping to the more assured industry of salvage. Some even thought his schemes were ill-conceived. 'I know, half-baked, hare-brained, that's what people would say and not always behind my back,' he says.

For a man who lived in a modest semi-detached council house in Yorkshire (he bought it later), Jessop often cut a dash, and spun a boast, which brought him critics. For most of the 1970s he was almost fully committed to the North Sea oil industry for a living. In fact, although he had been involved in marine salvage since 1964, he had spent more years and had more jobs working for large diving concerns operating around the world. But it was Jessop's flamboyant approach to schemes, many of them obviously tenuous, others undeniably dangerous, that was to prove one of his key assets. His grand underwater projects, often extravagant in their scope, would in time be taken seriously by people with the capital which he needed but which he seemed to have no chance of raising himself.

Jessop was primarily a diver who in the burgeoning North Sea oilfields of the late 1960s and early 1970s began to appreciate the extent that new underwater techniques could affect future salvage projects. The Yorkshireman could see that 'blast and grab' techniques might in time be replaced by more sophisticated methods that relied to a greater extent on the diver moving outside the conventional deep-sea chamber. 'I began to see that there was no real reason why I shouldn't convert North Sea technology to the salvage game,' says Jessop. 'And for a number of projects around the world, the *Edinburgh* included.'

North Sea work had taught Jessop that divers wearing water-heated swimsuits and breathing a mixture of helium and oxygen could tackle salvage projects that many had hitherto dismissed as fanciful. But he was still tied to diving for an income and he was impatient with merely picking up a living from what amounted to scrap-salvage on the sea-bed. Equally he was irritated by the cautious dismissal of his ideas by some of the divers working alongside him. If he believed that millions could be raised from wrecks around the world, then surely others should share his unbridled confidence and optimism? But very few gave his notions even polite attention at the time.

With hindsight Jessop can be seen to have pointed out the obvious in the mid-1970s, and Risdon Beazley would eventually pay the price of bankruptcy for ignoring such tell-tale signs of change in their industry. This change centred around the increasing depth

and movement which divers wearing special swimsuits and breathing helium-oxygen mixtures were attempting. And the underwater
revolution was turning out to be as profound as the advances being
made in space travel and space technology.

Divers have worked underwater for thousands of years, but not
until the 1950s had they been technically equipped to work at
depths of 100 feet and more. Men like Arne Zetterstrom, a twenty-
eight-year-old Swedish engineer, had reached a depth of 363 feet in
the Baltic as early as 1945, breathing a mixture of oxygen and
hydrogen. But this mixture was dangerous, and he later died in an
accident while attempting a dive which reached 528 feet.

In any case a mixture of oxygen and helium, of which the United
States possessed the only readily accessible supplies, was known by
the mid-1920s to be a safer combination of gases for divers at great
depth. Using helium a Royal Navy petty officer, Wilfred Bollard,
broke the world record in 1948 by going down 540 feet; six years
later a Royal Navy lieutenant, George Wookey, broke the record
again by descending to 600 feet.

In 1962 Hannes Keller, a Swiss mathematician, descended to a
depth of 1,000 feet and planted his country's flag on the sea-bed.
But Keller was only able to remain at the bottom a few minutes.
Oilfield divers like Keith Jessop were needed for four hours of routine work, construction, inspection and servicing at depth, and not
just to break world records.

'The North Sea was an entirely new industry with many new
demands for the divers,' says Keith Jessop, who was in his early
thirties when the industry began to develop. 'You needed to know
about explosives and the use of different cutters and thermic lances
underwater. At depths of 300 feet and more some of these skills
were almost sciences in themselves.' Divers like Jessop were also
expected to use sophisticated underwater cameras which would
show supervisors on the surface what conditions were like below.
'Often the cameras see far better than the diver operating them,'
says Jessop. 'Later a diver can study what he has been filming on a
video system and thereby understand better the situation at the
bottom.'

Jessop was an enthusiastic diver in the 1970s and worked for
several specialised deep-diving contractors like Ocean Systems,

Oceaneering, Comex and Wharton-Williams. Diving gave the Yorkshireman a well-above-average income. He encouraged his two sons, Graham and Ian, who were still at school, to 'learn the diving trade'. But his thoughts were invariably centred on salvage and the possibilities which advanced diving methods now offered the salvor. Jessop was well aware that he needed the right projects and the capital to back them.

So while the North Sea oil industry went through a certain recession in the late 1970s, Jessop, with little money, envisaged mammoth salvage schemes at his modest house on a corporation estate in Keighley. Some of his projects would undeniably cost millions, but if they succeeded their profit margins were attractively wide, bountiful even by North Sea standards. 'The recession had led to a slump in the oil business,' says James Ringrose, a former Royal Navy officer who would later join forces with Jessop. 'Between 1977 and 1979 some oil business people were looking for a possible alternative use for their heavy plant equipment. It was a form of insurance they were seeking and very sensible in the circumstances. Keith Jessop was thinking about the *Edinburgh* at exactly the right time.'

The problem of raising money was a constant source of anxiety for Jessop. While he 'knew the diving game backwards' he had no real experience raising cash to get his projects off the ground. Although he was not without a chorus of detractors who thought him capricious, foolish or obsessive with regard to his salvage projects, he was not without a few supporters who took him seriously. He found an ally in John Jackson, the senior manager of the Salvage Association in London. This private but non-profit-making association represented owners with an interest in a wreck. Jackson, who headed his department, had the task of introducing wreck owners to salvors. The senior manager took a liking to the Yorkshireman who had no office other than the front room of his house. 'But I had known and observed Keith Jessop for several years,' says Jackson, who became something of a mentor, 'and he seemed to have both tenacity and enthusiasm. There was something about him which suggested grit and promise.'

Edinburgh was one of several ideas which Jessop toyed with. 'I became dedicated to the *Edinburgh* and eventually spent several

years researching her,' says Jessop. 'Diving is my game and once I
had an interest in the *Edinburgh* I never dropped it. I could go out
in the North Sea and earn £120, £130 a day, that was easy, but I
decided to forfeit all that to salvage what *Edinburgh* was supposed to
contain.'

Two diving contractors, Ric Wharton and Malcolm Williams,
with a firm called 2Ws had already contemplated moving into the
salvage business. In 1978, with the oil business contracting
throughout the world, they considered working on HMS *Hampshire*,
the British cruiser which had gone down with gold bullion in 1917.
That same year they approached John Jackson at the Salvage
Association, and eventually asked for permission to begin preliminary recovery work on the wreck of the *Hampshire*. In the end
Wharton and Williams turned to the *Edinburgh* project, perhaps
shelving *Hampshire* for another day. But much was to happen before
they became involved with Jessop and what was to be their first
major operation in the salvage field.

'Keith had to suffer a number of disasters before he finally got his
Edinburgh project underway,' says James Ringrose. 'Just how he did
it is one of those remarkable anomalies which could make some
people believe in pre-determined good fortune. Looking back, Keith
seems to have had that luck in fair measure.'

Jessop's immediate aim, by the autumn of 1978, was to discover
as much as he could about the sinking of HMS *Edinburgh*. It was
just possible, he told a few people including John Jackson, that he
would find a backer with enough capital to underwrite the operation of both finding the cruiser and recovering the gold.

Secrecy was necessary for a project of this kind, yet some people
were soon to learn what was afoot. On 1 December 1978, Jessop
wrote to the Ministry of Defence asking for specific facts about the
cruiser. There was no longer any confidentiality about *Edinburgh*
and its gold, and the Ministry pointed out that anybody could read
about the warship in files kept at the Public Records Office in
Kew, London.

Jessop was quickly to learn that another potentially damaging
problem would arise over any proposal to lift the gold. On 8
December, the salvor received a letter from the head of the naval
historical branch at the Ministry of Defence which included the

definite hint – some would read it as a clear-cut warning – that there would be opposition to any salvage operation:

Dear Sir,

With reference to your letter of 1 December 1978 to Mr Coppock, the full details of the loss of the HMS *Edinburgh* are available in the files held in the Public Record Office. The bullion was stowed in the aircraft Bomb Room, under and behind armour; this space was flooded with fuel oil as the result of a torpedo hit and the four hatches to the compartment above were shored down to check further flooding. These aspects alone would make salvage extremely difficult even without the depth of water and the final considera- tion, that of the acceptability of the idea of disturbing a war grave.

Repugnance at the idea of disturbing the wreck of a warship which con- tains the remains of those lost with her is based on principle, not politics, and it is improbable that this will become sufficiently eroded to result in any change of opinion for some time to come.

Yours faithfully,
David Brown.

Jessop viewed the letter with a mixture of encouragement and apprehension. 'I was not altogether surprised that the war grave issue would raise its head,' he said. 'But I didn't expect it quite so early.' Like most salvors Jessop had a matter-of-fact attitude to- wards wrecks and the bodies they might contain. He had certainly found human remains in the past and saw them as an inevitable part of the job. 'If they're there, what can you do but ignore them, go round them?' he asks in answer to such questions.

In the end Jessop knew that ignoring such a fundamental and controversial subject might prove worse than facing it head on. Jessop's instinct was right in this instance, for to the *Edinburgh* Survivors' Association any idea of salvaging the gold always seemed like grave robbery, 'sheer desecration'. 'Few in our Association were startled when we heard on the grapevine that several people were keen to go down for the bullion,' says Bill Daly, the Association's secretary. 'We somehow expected it. But that didn't mean we approved of it in the least. A grave is a grave, even on the sea- bottom, and should be left alone.'

Not every *Edinburgh* survivor agreed with Daly or the view that David Brown had expressed at the Ministry of Defence. Warships had been salvaged in the past and few had complained. And nobody had ever made any merchant ship an official war grave, although many had been sunk with an appalling loss of life in the Arctic convoys.

Inside the Ministry of Defence others joined in the controversy. The *Edinburgh* had been made an official war grave in 1957, a move partly prompted by the possibility of the bullion being salvaged one day. Twenty years later a certain element of hypocrisy had now entered into discussions within government departments; yet the fact remained that the cruiser was still a war grave. (In 1954, of course, the Admiralty had raised no objection to Risdon Beazley entering the wreck or recovering the gold, although in the event the firm had not attempted the operation.) Some officials hoped that the problem would disappear; perhaps video film of the warship would show a salvage attempt to be out of the question.

But lawyers inside the Ministry in the late 1970s found themselves tied to what had been agreed two decades before. Internal memoranda spoke of 'commitments to honour', agreements which, as one lawyer put it succinctly, 'one might wish did not exist'.

In effect, the British government was being pressed internally by the logic of its own correspondence files to accept the proposal to salvage the *Edinburgh*. The letter which the Admiralty had sent Risdon Beazley in 1954 had never been cancelled, and now it seemed far too late for it to change its position in the matter.

There was another critical and potentially embarrassing matter which had not escaped the MOD lawyers' growing concern. Salvage companies, of course, did not need permission to dive in international waters. One lawyer therefore suggested to his superiors that a possible compromise might be to negotiate with a salvor on the basis that 'no human remains would be disturbed etc.' Such an eminently respectable standpoint, it was argued, would show the MOD exercising 'control' over any salvage operation. The main consideration, therefore, would be the government's primary wish that 'no human remains should be disturbed'.

Exactly how a salvor proposed to approach the delicate war grave issue would, in effect, largely determine who would eventually get the official go-ahead to salvage the wreck. Government ministers responsible for the MOD readily accepted the advice of their officials. For one thing it appeared to escape the worst consequences of any disquiet there might be when the salvage operation plans became public knowledge.

For the moment nobody was certain how the public, or the survivors of the *Edinburgh* tragedy, would react to the news about the gold-raising proposals. But now there could be no hanging back; a decision had to be reached quickly. Soon the Department of Trade, another body which shared responsibility for any *Edinburgh* venture, agreed with the MOD's viewpoint.

The British government's emerging policy appeared to be correct on both moral and political grounds. In time such a policy would also prove to make extraordinarily sound economic sense. For one fortuitous by-product of the government's outlook on the war grave problem would be a hefty and highly acceptable slice of the bullion lying on the sea-bed. At the time, however, the government's lawyers had apparently decided that they had no real claim to the gold or to the wreck of their own warship.

Early in 1979 Jessop was anxious for permission at least to search for the wreck. By now he was taking advantage of a stroke of good fortune. An official at the Salvage Association had stumbled over a tin box during a visit to a government office in Southampton. The box was found to contain research notes compiled for Risdon Beazley in 1954. The Salvage Association took the view that it should not show favour to any party wishing to look for the *Edinburgh*. Risdon Beazley learned about renewed interest in the *Edinburgh* and joined what soon took on the appearance of a race.

To Risdon Beazley, and the salvage industry as a whole, the competition looked one-sided. Here was a well-established outfit with countless wrecks to its credit and of international standing. Backed by a well-heeled Dutch company and for years the official Admiralty salvors, Risdon Beazley apparently had all the experience, respectability and finance which the gold project demanded. But the company had been going through a bad patch, and the capital-intensive nature of its business, coupled with its insistence that 'blast and grab' methods could be used on almost any job, combined to hold back its chances in the race.

Jessop, meanwhile, had been introduced to a Norwegian company named Stolt-Nielsen of Oslo. Stolt-Nielsen were fundamentally oilmen who were keen to spread their interests into salvage

if the job looked feasible and profitable enough. 'Stolt-Nielsen approached the Salvage Association and said they were anxious to
become involved in large-scale projects,' says John Jackson, who
introduced them to Jessop. 'Jessop had a number of projects, one,
of course, being the *Edinburgh*. Not surprisingly a ship containing
some £45 million and lying so close to Norway appealed to them
enormously.'

Jessop had a domino effect on Stolt-Nielsen. Soon the small-time
British salvor was being asked to handle, not just the *Edinburgh*, but
other salvage jobs close to Norwegian waters. 'At first the Norwegians were brimming with enthusiasm and took up my ideas,'
says Jessop. The Yorkshireman told them that there were two wartime wrecks in their area which would help pay for the *Edinburgh*
operation. One ship was the *Chulmleigh* off Spitzbergen, which was
carrying a consignment of tin. The other was the *Waziristen*, a cargo
vessel which had sunk off Bear Island. The *Waziristen* had been
transporting a valuable cargo of copper ingots.

With the recession in the worldwide oil business, Stolt-Nielsen,
like other contractors, were happy to devote a ship and other resources to search for two wrecks which they hoped to salvage before
going on to find the *Edinburgh*. The Norwegians understood that
the *Chulmleigh* would take about twenty-four hours to find, the
Waziristen about a week. Jessop was confident he could locate the
wrecks quickly and then recover their cargoes. He was to be proved
wrong, and in time Stolt-Nielsen would claim, after they had
mounted a joint expedition to find the *Edinburgh*, that their connec-
tion with Jessop had cost them £500,000. But by the end of the
summer in 1979 they had not begun looking for the warship. 'The
Norwegians were a bit miserable about not finding the *Chulmleigh*
and the *Waziristen* almost overnight,' says Jessop. In turn Stolt-
Nielsen wanted reassurance from other quarters that they really
could still find the *Edinburgh* and that Jessop was the man to pull it
off.

In London, one official was hardly being discreet about his support
for the Yorkshire salvor. Chris Jenkins, a North Sea diving
superintendent, was startled when, on one occasion, this official began showing confidential material to Jessop at his City office. 'Keith
was shown private documents,' said Jenkins. 'There were letters from

rival companies. At one time we were looking at Risdon Beazley's mail. It was altogether odd.'

James Ringrose, the ex-Royal Navy officer who had served under Lieutenant HRH the Prince of Wales in HMS *Bronington*, was at something of a loose end when he heard about the *Edinburgh* project. At that time he knew little about the hard-nosed world of salvage. 'I was at a party with a Stolt-Nielsen employee and he was saying they were having a disastrous time searching for wrecks,' says Ringrose. Stolt-Nielsen were looking for people with specialist knowledge of wreck location. Ringrose had served in Royal Navy vessels designed for this purpose and knew his subject well. The Norwegians invited him to Oslo to discuss the *Edinburgh*.

'When I arrived, I met Keith Jessop for the first time,' says Ringrose. 'The Norwegians clearly saw the failure to find the *Chulmleigh* and the *Waziristen* as two major flops and there was a certain coolness between Stolt-Nielsen and Keith.' But by now Jessop and his Norwegian partners had permission from the Ministry of Defence to search for the sunken cruiser. So too had their great rivals Risdon Beazley, who were also mounting an expedition to visit the Barents Sea.

'I was positive we could find the *Edinburgh* at the end of the 1979 season, and we almost did,' says Jessop. 'Sure, they were putting a lot of money into the venture but once you've started there's no point in holding back.'

Stolt-Nielsen had eventually agreed that the *Sea Hawk* could look for the *Edinburgh*, and their search vessel left Norway for the Barents Sea in October. 'We had every reason to be confident of finding the warship,' says Ringrose, who agreed to join the expedition. On board the *Sea Hawk* were miniature submarines which hopefully would descend to the wreck once they had located its position. Then the *Edinburgh* could be surveyed on film and the results analysed in London and Oslo.

'Whoever found the wreck first and filmed it on the sea-bed would almost certainly be awarded the contract to recover the gold,' says Ringrose. 'That was the assumption at the time anyway.'

From the outset Jessop accepted that the Russians would have to become involved. After formal approaches to their embassies in Oslo and London, the Russians indicated that, like the Ministry of De-

fence in Britain, they had no formal objection to a film survey of
the *Edinburgh* taking place.

Again, luck appeared to be on Jessop's side. In 1978 the Russians
had started an underwater search in the Barents Sea, using echo-
sounders and camera equipment which could film at depth. Western
military observers at first suspected that the Russians might be
looking for a missing nuclear submarine. In fact, it later emerged
that they had been seeking the *Edinburgh* but, not for the first time,
had failed to find it.

'The Russians had to be brought into any scheme, even in
international waters,' says Jessop firmly. 'I knew that from
the beginning. However hard it might be I had to accept
that.'

In spite of the preparation which went into the speculative venture, the Stolt-Nielsen–Jessop expedition failed to find the wreck
which held the gold. 'During the first seven days we searched two
square miles of sea-bed and we found nothing, not a solitary thing,'
says Ringrose. 'The submarines were costing anything up to 2,000
dollars a day, but they weren't even used.'

Jessop and the Norwegians began to squabble again, occasionally
over trivial details, sometimes over where the wreck might be. The
British salvor had earlier interviewed a trawler skipper whose nets
had been caught in a wreck in the area for eighteen hours. 'Eventually the skipper freed his nets and when he brought them to the
surface found what was obviously a bit of the wreck itself,' claims
Jessop. The piece brought on board the trawler was thought to
come from a British warship. 'It had to be the *Edinburgh* because
there are no records of any other sunken British warships in the
area.'

Jessop eventually managed to examine the log-book references to
trawler sightings of such finds. On 9 November 1967 one British
trawler captain had written in his log: (we) 'picked up something
very heavy ... quite a bit of iron-work that was the bulkhead etc.
of a navy ship – I suppose this was the HMS *Edinburgh* – after this
there were two explosions underwater that could only be bombs or
depth-charges.'

But the Norwegians, and Ringrose, were not convinced. 'When
we rang the fisherman we discussed the basis of his position,' says

Ringrose. 'He'd caught his nets on a wreck in 1960 and he seemed uncertain exactly where the incident had happened.'

Altogether the expedition spent forty-two days searching for the *Edinburgh*, half of the time being used to analyse what information they had on board the *Sea Hawk*. It turned out to be inadequate. The expedition was searching in an area the size of London, over 1500 square nautical miles, the equivalent of an area bounded on the north and south by Luton and Crawley and on the east and west by Brentwood and Windsor.

'We started to move towards the north but the weather grew worse,' says Ringrose. 'The Norwegians ran out of patience and called off the search. We were told to return to Norway; they were extremely unhappy. Somehow they felt they had been misled. Anyway, there was a general air of unhappiness.'

Whose fault it was would be debated for years, but the fact remained that Keith Jessop had promised to find three wrecks and their cargoes, and he had so far failed to find one. By Christmas 1979 Jessop, the salvor who was now without an office or a job, was back in Yorkshire making excuses. After all, he argued, the first rule of treasure-hunting is that one sometimes fails to find what one is looking for. In any event Jessop was out in the cold, alone again and without anybody in sight to back his dreams.

For Keith Jessop, who was never to falter in his fervent belief in finding *Edinburgh* and her gold, 1979 had produced a somewhat beguiling mixture of encouragement and despair. While he had succeeded in persuading the British government to let him search for the sunken warship he had not fulfilled his own initial hopes or any of the rich ambitions of his Norwegian backers. Moreover, *Edinburgh* was still hidden somewhere in silt and débris 800 feet deep in the Barents Sea.

4

Jessop Lands the Contract

Early in 1980, after the disastrous *Sea Hawk* fiasco the year before, Keith Jessop found himself in an uncomfortable legal squabble with Stolt-Nielsen. By now the Norwegians had, perhaps not surprisingly, lost much of their confidence in the ebullient Yorkshire salvor. They preferred to hire a fresh British consultant and continue the *Edinburgh* project independently. 'Finding the warship and recovering the cargo now looked less difficult than getting the contract,' said Stolt-Nielsen.

Back in Keighley Jessop pondered his next move and his least expensive way out of yet another tight corner. Money was short and to return to diving in the North Sea would be an open admission of failure. Fortunately his wife Mildred and their three working children brought some money into the house, though not enough to take on a large international oil company in the courts; or, for that matter, to underwrite the family's continuing passion for treasure-hunting inside the Arctic circle. Jessop fell back on raising some additional money on his already mortgaged house.

James Ringrose remembers Jessop's resilience and apparent insulation from the fuller implications of the Norwegian débâcle. 'Once in Norway Keith and I were waiting at Stolt-Nielsen's office in Oslo,' says Ringrose. 'The Norwegians were preparing a document which set out the terms of their breaking away from the partnership with Keith. The proposal came through on the telex and I'll never forget Keith giving it a cursory glance and saying: "Ah, that looks fine." And then he just signed it on the spot. The Norwegians were staggered.'

Back in Britain Jessop told Ringrose, and anybody else who would listen, that 'hundreds of people' would be only too happy to

put money into the *Edinburgh* operation. Few were prepared to
throw money at such a deep-sea gamble or at any rate had the
amount of capital to fund a new expedition. When Jessop did help
bring a consortium together later that year the different parties
between them would be asked to find £2 million. And in time there
would be other expenses to pay for.

Jessop had a remarkable habit of making people trust his no-
nonsense confidence. He would tell people with the ardour of a
John Wesley: 'You *must* believe me. I'll do it. That gold has my
name on it.'

This was, at least for some people who observed the man, a rather
disquieting experience. 'He was like a prophet,' said one financier
who met him in 1980. 'Here was a man with a speculative gamble
written all over his personality like the tablets of Moses. But he had a
message about a shipwreck which never tired him and which he never
for a second even considered might turn out to be Yorkshire's answer
to the South Sea Bubble.' Like some other money-men at a critical
moment the financier told him he was wasting his time and his energy.

But there were those who did not turn their back on Jessop and
his abiding preoccupation with the *Edinburgh* story. Ringrose was
one man who somehow could not get away from the salvor and his
pursuit of the gold. 'Why? I frankly don't know the answer to that
question,' says Ringrose. 'I'd like to say there was a single academic
answer, but the truth was more complicated in this case. I'd seen
Keith in Norway and felt, whatever the circumstances were, that
he had tried his best to find the wreck. And I'd watched him behave
in multifarious situations where he sometimes came off second best.
But the *Edinburgh* operation was more than a dream in my view.
Anyway, I somehow never drifted away.' Ringrose was convinced
that Jessop could not mount another Arctic expedition on his own.
The salvor needed sound legal advice and, above all, he had to
have capital. The problem was that Jessop had very little collateral
and yet was talking about continuing negotiations with the British
and Russian governments. But as the poet Horace had pointed out
in an ode: 'Gold can a path through hosts of warders clear, And
walls of stone more swiftly can displace Than ever lightning could.'
And gradually Jessop found a small and varied group of advisers
and other enthusiasts collecting around him.

One of the most important figures at this time was a young Manchester commercial lawyer named David Bona. Jessop's barnstorming approach to business Bona found perplexing but at the same time not without its own candid charm. 'Keith was either right or completely wrong about the *Edinburgh* project,' says Bona. 'His burning faith that he could pull it off was either misplaced, quirkish or magnificently correct.' The quiet, rather shy lawyer thought hard about Jessop's gamble and decided that he, and his firm, would join in the risk. Bona would help provide the legal backing for a new expedition to the Barents Sea.

But first Bona had a fair amount of clearing-up to do. In Norway Jessop had placed himself in a difficult position with his former partners, Stolt-Nielsen. Bona set out to extricate Jessop from the telex proposal he had hastily signed in Oslo. Jessop had agreed to take 10% of the net proceeds, after expenses, of any profit the Norwegian firm might make from a successful *Edinburgh* operation of their own. The Yorkshireman had thereby effectively written himself out of most of the proceeds from the bars of gold he had been pursuing for so long.

In any event Bona and Jessop eventually agreed with Stolt-Nielsen that they would release each other 'from their respective rights, interests and obligations of whatsoever nature as existing between them up to and including the 26th February this year [1980] in respect of the first survey, and any future proposed survey and salvage of the cargo of the wreck of HMS *Edinburgh*'.

Bona had won back Jessop's independence, and Stolt-Nielsen were free to join in the race to find *Edinburgh*'s gold, a freedom which the Norwegians were intent on pursuing. Meanwhile, of course, Risdon Beazley in Southampton were quietly planning their own operation. By spring 1980 three salvage companies had formal permission from the British and Russian governments to search and film the wreck of the British cruiser.

The Norwegians had a large workforce, huge cash reserves, ships and equipment, and a hard-nosed international reputation for being successful. Risdon Beazley in Southampton employed almost 200 people and for years had enjoyed the confidence of the MOD's salvage division and governments around the world. By early 1980 both companies had proclaimed their enthusiasm for the *Edinburgh* project and stressed to the Salvage Association their determination to find the wreck and win the joint Anglo-Russian contract to recover the gold.

In marked contrast Keith Jessop was an inveterate one-man band with a distrust of offices, overheads and business routines which might impede his activities. His new lawyer had encouraged him to set up a private limited company called Jessop Marine Recoveries. The salvor would be the chairman and major shareholder and the mailing address Bona's office in Manchester. Jessop Marine, with a registered capital of £100 and no reputation one way or the other, would deal with its *Edinburgh* plans and any other salvage operation which might look feasible in the future.

'My philosophy has always been that everybody has to earn their keep and make their own way,' says Jessop. 'No cure, no pay.' Such a simple homespun outlook would in time serve the salvor well. Instinctively Jessop wanted the people gathering around his *Edinburgh* project to share the risk. He wanted little, if anything, to do with salaries, offices, employees and all the usual encumbrances of a business. And he certainly would not have Jessop Marine Recoveries listed in the Yellow Pages or even in the local telephone directory. Jessop slowly turned his outlook into a demonstrable virtue: he needed nobody; others needed him if they were to get their hands on Stalin's gold.

For Jessop, such an unflinching strategy was simply his way of telling the truth as he saw it. In his own mind he was the only person *entitled* to the *Edinburgh*. 'If it weren't for me nobody would even be thinking about the ship and the gold,' he would tell people at the time. There was, of course, a rather spurious logic to what amounted to a boast, but legally it was meaningless.

Such flamboyant assertions often served to irritate some of those who had taken up his cause. 'We supported that man, borrowed money to pay his living expenses and gave him moral support,' explained Ringrose. 'But I don't think we imagined for one moment that Keith would ever remember or thank us for it. He somehow saw anybody who became involved with the *Edinburgh*, even on his own side, as a potentially malevolent interloper.'

For in his own eyes Jessop, the near-penniless salvor in 1980, *was*

the *Edinburgh* operation; the two were indivisible. The trouble was
that image-making costs money, and Jessop, unlike his rivals, had
no reliable income other than what his family were bringing home
in wage packets. When he left Keighley on business jaunts he tended
to stay in guest-houses or with friends. From his early days in the
mid-1960s there had been grumbles about finance, how to scrape it
together and how to make it last underwater on relatively trifling
projects.

Compared with the *Edinburgh* operation, any salvage venture
Jessop had ever worked upon now looked a mere trifle. Jessop
Marine, the fledgling outfit which early in 1980 few in the salvage
business even knew existed, were looking for more than spare cash
to raise the *Edinburgh* gold. Gone were the days when a handful of
pounds would fund lifting brass from a rusting hulk off the Scottish
coast.

'We faced a very formidable task in 1980 because, not only did
we need speculative capital, we also had to convince the British
and Russian governments that we were serious contenders for the
Edinburgh contract,' says James Ringrose. 'For many in the salvage
world there was a three-horse race except that many also saw us as
a non-starting donkey.' Jessop was familiar with people scoffing at
his schemes. 'I know people have laughed at me and to tell the
truth I've found that a spur on occasion to keep going,' he says.

But the problem of raising money was a constant source of anxiety
for Jessop and his newly-found partners who made up Jessop
Marine. His lawyer, David Bona, had no specialised knowledge of
the salvage business or the sea; Ringrose was a professional seaman
and survey specialist but had no real experience of raising investment capital on the risk money market. Long hours were spent
contemplating countless schemes, different approaches to bus-
inessmen, bankers, anybody in fact who had money to dole out
lavishly on a dream. Many people who were later to kick themselves
heartily rejected Jessop Marine's offer of a slice of the gold.

In the end it was contacts of Jessop's lawyer who would come
up with the money and the backing he so desperately needed. But
before they came into the picture and agreed to join him he heard
what at first were rumours. The salvor had learnt that Risdon
Beazley had sent a survey vessel within the Arctic region to examine

a wreck. Once the *Droxford* had completed the first survey he understood they would begin searching for the *Edinburgh*. He also knew
that Stolt-Nielsens were endeavouring to mount a second expedition
to the Barents Sea. With his competitors beginning to breathe down
his neck, time for Jessop appeared to be uncomfortably short.

Jessop had discussed the *Edinburgh* with David Morrice, a salvor
in his own right and a man who might have substantial capital to
invest in the right project. But he turned the opportunity down:
'Naturally I regret that decision now. Who wouldn't? I didn't end
up with a damn penny.'

Jessop turned next to a company called Star Off-Shore, tested,
well-financed and carrying the weight which would undoubtedly
impress the British government if they agreed to become involved.
Jessop Marine presented Star Off-Shore's board with its proposal to
salvage the British warship. After a fairly short deliberation the
company flatly rejected the scheme. In their view it was speculative
to the point where shareholders might ask why the company's
money was being thrown down the drain.

Bona cautioned Jessop repeatedly about talking to too many
people about the *Edinburgh*. If news leaked out that he was being
turned down by would-be backers, others might decide there must
be good reasons. 'Frankly I didn't blame people for their apparent
lack of interest,' says Ringrose. 'The presentation was poor and
people were getting to hear about the failure to raise money for the
Edinburgh project.'

Jessop's only remaining trump card, apart from his boundless
enthusiasm, was the original permission to survey and film the warship once it was found. In August 1979 his Norwegian partners,
through their London office, had received a letter from the Salvage
Association setting out the terms of that permission. Jessop and his
son Graham were mentioned in the letter and were clearly beneficiaries of a British government bounty upon which luckily there
was no stipulated time-limit.

John Jackson's letter laid down the British government's conditions which allowed Jessop to survey the *Edinburgh* wreck:

(A) Only the external features of the wreck to be sighted or filmed.
(B) No attempt to be made to land on, or gain access to the inside of the

vessel or to disturb, touch or in any way interfere with the wreck.
(C) You comply fully with the requirements of the Norwegian authorities
     to whom full details of your proposed venture must be given and copied
     to this Association.
(D) All results of your survey are to be made available to this Association.

Jackson added at the end of his letter: 'Lastly, we are requested
to remind you that the wreck of HMS *Edinburgh* is still classed as a
War Grave and must therefore be given due respect.'

Jessop naturally made the best possible use of the letter. The
Yorkshireman believed that he was the catalyst to make the
Edinburgh project succeed, and the letter was part of his back-up
campaign to raise the capital on which his aims finally relied.
Within a few weeks of breaking away from the Norwegians Jessop
asked two diving contractors in Scotland, Ric Wharton and
Malcolm Williams, if they might be interested in ten tons of
Russian gold. Jessop could claim he had some sort of contact with
the two entrepreneurs who had already made a fortune out of the
North Sea. On occasion he had worked for their company, 2Ws
(Wharton-Williams Ltd), just as he had worked for several oil outfits
employing deep-sea divers.

Ric Wharton was a well-qualified civil engineer who had left
university and worked on diving contracts in Britain, the Middle
East and the Gulf of Mexico. In 1971 he had joined the French
diving company Comex as the general manager of their British
subsidiary. At Comex Wharton prospered and in time began plans
to branch out in the North Sea on his own.

Wharton met Malcolm Williams, an ex-British Army officer, at
Comex. Williams followed in Wharton's footsteps as general
manager of Comex (UK) until the two men decided to strike out
independently with their own company Wharton-Williams. Both
men brought individual talents to their new enterprise; Wharton
was decidedly flamboyant, Williams was a more retiring and cautious administrator, but together they flourished. In Aberdeen,
where the partners based their deep-sea company, financiers and
competitors watched their success with a mixture of envy and per-
plexity. Although the oil business seemed to be heading for a slump
from 1976 onwards, 2Ws apparently thrived on fears of an industry recession. When they linked up with the established American firm,

Taylor Diving, 2Ws entered the world league of deep-sea diving contractors.

Jessop, the one-time employee, decided to tempt 2Ws with his
Edinburgh operation. Wharton and Williams had the men and the
equipment to dive on a wreck 800 feet down inside the Arctic circle,
and they importantly had the means of raising the capital to back
their expertise.

Jessop went with Bona to see Ric Wharton at his Aberdeen office.
In front of Wharton both men displayed an almost missionary zeal
for their plan to raise the gold. Jessop talked about just over ten
tons of gold worth some £90 million lying on the sea-bed. Many of
the convoy shipments from Russia had been ten-ton consignments,
and Jessop was happy enough to accept the figure which, as we
have seen, had the provenance of Admiral Golovko, who had been
in command of Murmansk when the gold had been loaded aboard
the *Edinburgh*.

Jessop had been open about the failure of the Norwegian expedition to find the warship and about the role he himself had played.
But Wharton, and later Williams, gained the distinct impression
from the salvor that the *Edinburgh* would not be difficult to pinpoint.
'Keith positively burbled about there being ten tons and not five-
and-a-half tons,' said Williams. 'He said ten tons over and over
again. That was one of the negative factors that came up when we
started checking. While a lot of research had been done a tremend-
ous amount hadn't been.'

The Aberdeen diving contractors had never got involved with
such a high-risk gamble before. But Wharton was particularly taken
with the idea of the *Edinburgh*; Williams, however, was apprehensive
about being seen to participate in out-and-out treasure-hunting.
They could fail and lose a fortune; there could be accidents and
divers might die.

Ric Wharton, who began diving at university, has been collecting
artefacts from the sea-bed for many years. His castle, which he insists
on calling a house, is littered with souvenirs he has picked up from
the ocean floor.

'When someone comes and talks to me about a wreck, I'm interested,' says Wharton. 'I've known Keith for a while, he's worked
for us in the past, and I knew him as a man of integrity. We have

the most advanced diving technology in the world and we can dive as deep as anybody. And Keith had this project of a wreck from living memory. He could actually talk to people who saw the gold loaded on that ship.'

Although the venture was speculative, Wharton says he is not a gambler. 'I've never put a pound on a horse. But I'm a bad loser. Anyway it is a bit different putting a pound out of your own pocket on a horse rather than a pound of your own company's on a horse.'

Wharton believed Jessop's scheme had about a ten per cent chance of succeeding. 'I thought about ten per cent because, firstly, there had been attempts to look for the wreck already and they were unsuccessful.' The diving contractor estimated that the cost of looking for the *Edinburgh* would be about £300,000.

But the rewards were obviously great. 'The total amount of money depends on the gold price,' he explains. 'The value of gold changes from day to day and recently it's come down from its thousand-dollar peak. It's between £40 and £45 million. So we're looking at a potential pay-out of £20 million for the salvors for a potential expenditure of £4 million, so it's a 5:1 bet.' In the event the costs would turn out to be almost half the original estimate.

Malcolm Williams explained that 2Ws had spread its risks. 'We had to supply a certain amount of equipment for the original survey to find the wreck, but the cost was only about £50–100,000.' He added: 'If we found the wreck and decided that we could go ahead then the risk would jump dramatically.'

'But such an enterprise could damage our public image,' said Williams. He had other reservations. 'I went back with whole strings of questions to Jessop Marine. Were we looking for ten tons of gold or half that amount? The answer was important for our calculations. And how difficult would it prove to find the *Edinburgh*?'

In spite of his doubts Williams agreed with Wharton that 2Ws should join in the venture. What amounted to a verbal contract was worked out between the two companies: a formal detailed contract could follow later. 'We signed the contract without having any other participants on a 90%: 10% basis [90% to the 2Ws, 10% to Jessop Marine],' said Williams. 'We thought it all right.'

Jessop had put in the idea and 2Ws would put up the men and the equipment to back it. From the outside it might appear that

Jessop was giving away a massive percentage in return for a tiny slice of the gold. 'But I had to be realistic at the time,' says Jessop. 'I didn't have £2 million although my idea had raised the money.'

Williams formed a positive impression of Jessop but felt the diver had placed rather too much faith in the salvage operation. 'I liked Keith,' says Williams. 'He was a diving man, a practical man, a man who knew the sharp end of the business. It was Keith's concept, his idea and nobody's else's.' But Williams feared there were dangers in such absolute commitment to one gamble, win or lose. 'I felt Keith was hanging too much on the *Edinburgh*,' says Williams. 'I thought at the time: "If this fails and failure is possible, distinctly possible, it will be very damaging to Keith." I felt it could almost destroy him.'

Jessop seemed to rise above criticism of his passion for *Edinburgh*. He would simply disarm those who attacked him, however well-meant their concern might be, by producing some obscure new fact about the wreck. He was never, for example, to lose his belief in there being ten tons of gold on the sea-bed, or that its recovery would be 'straightforward, no real problem'.

In his financial standing Jessop was a minnow compared with the freshly-minted fortune which 2Ws had made from four furious years working the North Sea. In fact, in investment terms he no longer had any money to put into *Edinburgh*. But he impressed Malcolm Williams by getting his idea off the ground at all. 'How the hell he ever got as far as he did is beyond my comprehension,' says Williams. 'But he had established, it appeared, a good working relationship with the Salvage Association and we formed the impression we were in with a chance as far as the Anglo-Russian contract went. Keith had got himself in a position where he could beat his rivals.'

Keith Jessop would retain a bitter memory of the deal Wharton and Williams struck with him. Giving away 90 per cent of 'his' gold to outsiders – for that is how he tended to see the split later – was tantamount in his eyes to a man squandering his birthright. 'I don't know exactly what Keith felt afterwards, but at the time he was relieved that Wharton-Williams had agreed to join in,' remembers his lawyer David Bona. 'Keith brought the concept and some research material, but the others who were to join the consortium we were putting together had to put in much more. Keith's ten per cent may seem small, but everybody had to evaluate what they were putting into the operation.'

The 90:10 split would later bring out all the salvor's combative instincts. One day there would be in his mind a question as to whether perhaps he deserved more from the split, a more 'morally' justifiable chunk of the gold which he had years before laid claim to owning. 'Look, I'd never doubted the gold was just waiting for me and I *knew*, I really *knew*, my operation would one day bring it to the surface,' he would say months later. 'Wharton-Williams, or any diving contractor I chose, would no doubt do a good job but there seemed something wrong to me that I was forced to sell my idea so hard. In my mind it was always foolproof once it had been worked out: an invitation to one of the biggest underwater fortunes in the world.'

For the moment, however, romantic illusions had to take second place to the urgent financial demands which were crowding upon him in early 1980. By the last day of May that year Jessop's company was ready to present its formal proposal to Wharton-Williams in Aberdeen. By now two other parties who would in time form part of the consortium had been approached. One of them was the West German shipping line OSA, which had agreed in principle to provide the vessels needed for the operation. The other was Racal Decca, a large company based at Leatherhead in Surrey, which had agreed to provide the sophisticated navigation equipment for pinpointing the wreck.

Keith Jessop had found in Wharton-Williams the diving specialists his consortium needed, and in turn 2Ws had introduced their one-time employee to the OSA, Offshore Supply Association. OSA had some ninety vessels, but the pride of their fleet was the 1400-ton *Stephaniturm*. Uli Reinecke of OSA thought his company's costs would be about £1 million. 'We had to put in a lot of research before we could approach our board and convince them to make the decision to go ahead with the project,' said Reinecke.

'We had convinced ourselves that 2Ws would find the divers and the expertise to recover the gold, but that was only part of the problem,' says James Ringrose. 'I'd suggested Racal Decca and we then discovered that 2Ws knew OSA, who owned the *Stephaniturm*.'

At their original meeting on Wednesday 7 May 1980, Ric Wharton had spared ninety minutes to hear David Bona and Keith Jessop outline the basic concept of recovering the gold. The businessman had warmed to the sheer audacity of the scheme and, in effect, had virtually committed his company on the spot. Events began to move remarkably quickly after what amounted to a verbal contract between 2Ws and Jessop Marine.

In London Wharton introduced Jessop Marine to OSA's British representative John Clarke, a retired Royal Navy marine surveyor.

Clarke knew the *Stephaniturm*'s capabilities well. Part of his work was to find commissions for the ship anywhere in the world.

'The vessel was ideal for the task,' he said. 'Basically, it has got two thrusters for'ard, rotating thrusters for'ard and one aft.' The dynamic positioning system, linked to the ship's computer on the bridge, would hover over the wreck like a helicopter.

Ringrose went off to Leatherhead to outline the overall plan to Racal Decca. 'We wanted to form a consortium quickly, get the contract and get to the Barents Sea as soon as we could,' says Jessop. The salvor had good reason to hurry. When he had finally broken with Stolt-Nielsens in February that year, says David Bona, it was 'in the spirit of may the best man win'. Bona had formed the clear impression from the Norwegians that they did not expect Jessop even to get to the starting-post of mounting his own expedition.

Jessop Marine's joint venture proposal, which Jessop presented to 2Ws in early June, was the length of a short novel, and some remarked afterwards that, in part at least, it tended to read as such. In spite of the British government's records showing that five tons of bullion had been stowed on the cruiser, Jessop still preferred the Russian version of the story. 'On board at the time of the sinking was approximately 10/10½ tons of slab gold bullion, representing payment for war material sent to Russia,' the proposal, which ran to almost a hundred pages, had started confidently. 'We always stressed that 10/10½ tons were uncorroborated,' says Bona, who had been largely responsible for bringing the written proposal together.

Jessop Marine detailed its two major objectives: 'Stage 1 – The carrying-out of a photographic survey of HMS *Edinburgh*. Stage 2 –

The carrying-out of a salvage operation to remove the gold bullion
from HMS *Edinburgh*.'

Although 10½ tons of gold was a great deal of money, almost
£100 million at the then current gold prices, there were a few
snags, and the proposal made clear from the outset that the British
and Russian governments would also expect a share of the bullion:

Normally, permission to search for a wreck is not required. However, for
a wreck and cargo of this nature, permission is most certainly required, for
the following reason:

1. HMS *Edinburgh* is a designated 'War Grave'.
2. The ownership of the gold – two-thirds belongs to the Russian government and one-third belongs to the British government.
3. The geographical position of the wreck.

Keith Jessop had always reluctantly agreed to himself that the
Russians would have to be brought into any deal, just as the British
government were claiming financial interest. And Jessop was not
the only person who thought it possible, even in international
waters, that the Russians would stop or seize any gold brought up
so near to their own waters. Such fears were probably misplaced.
NATO and the Warsaw Pact countries regularly patrol the Barents
Sea and it was therefore unlikely that the Russians would risk an
international incident over a salvage vessel quietly treasure hunting.

But no salvor could take the chance of the Red Navy turning up
and demanding the gold at gun-point. Or so some officials believed
at the Ministry of Defence in London. In any event, it was a fear
which in turn would give the British government a healthy financial
bonus it otherwise could not have hoped to receive. And, of course,
it gave the MoD a guiding hand around the sensitive war grave
and human remains issue.

Jessop Marine's 30 May document showed they had at the very
least done some homework at the Public Record Office in London.
And the MoD's naval historical branch, despite their chief's strong
disapproval of the project, had also provided helpful charts and
other *Edinburgh* memorabilia. There were photographs, too, of the
crippled cruiser and HMS *Harrier* taking off survivors, and there
were also pictures of the wreck's sister ship HMS *Belfast*.

Captain Hugh Faulkner (left) and Rear-Admiral Stuart Bonham-Carter, on board the cruiser HMS *Edinburgh (below)*.

Launching a Walrus aircraft by catapult from HMS *Edinburgh*.

On board the HMS *Edinburgh* inside the Arctic Circle.

Above left Seaman Hermann Galewsky in 1942: his torpedo crippled the *Edinburgh*. *Above right* A photograph, taken on the day the cruiser sank (2 May 1942), annotated by a survivor. *Below* A dramatic view of the damage to the cruiser's stern.

The quarter-deck, 'curled up like a sardine-tin' after the first torpedo attack.

Above Survivors being transferred from the crippled cruiser to the minesweeper HMS *Harrier*. *Below* A souvenir of HMS *Edinburgh* produced in Britain by survivors later in the war.

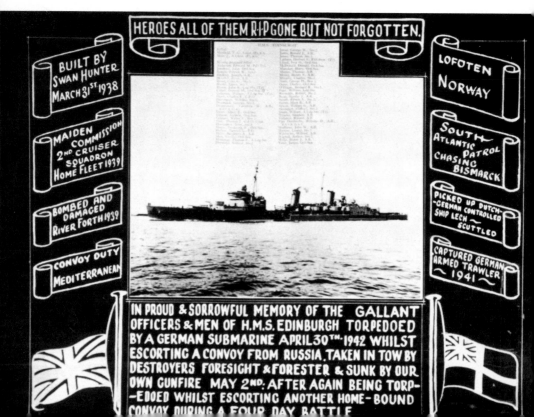

HEROES ALL OF THEM R·I·P GONE BUT NOT FORGOTTEN.

BUILT BY SWAN HUNTER MARCH 31ST 1938

MAIDEN COMMISSION 2ND CRUISER SQUADRON HOME FLEET 1939

BOMBED AND DAMAGED River Forth 1939

CONVOY DUTY MEDITERRANEAN

LOFOTEN NORWAY

SOUTH ATLANTIC PATROL CHASING BISMARCK

PICKED UP DUTCH-GERMAN CONTROLLED SHIP LECH SCUTTLED

CAPTURED GERMAN ARMED TRAWLER 1941

IN PROUD & SORROWFUL MEMORY OF THE GALLANT OFFICERS & MEN OF H.M.S. EDINBURGH TORPEDOED BY A GERMAN SUBMARINE APRIL 30TH 1942 WHILST ESCORTING A CONVOY FROM RUSSIA. TAKEN IN TOW BY DESTROYERS FORESIGHT & FORESTER & SUNK BY OUR OWN GUNFIRE MAY 2ND. AFTER AGAIN BEING TORP-EDOED WHILST ESCORTING ANOTHER HOME-BOUND CONVOY DURING A FOUR DAY BATTLE

Above From the bottom of the Barents Sea – a video-picture of one of *Edinburgh*'s 6-inch gun turrets, taken by a robot camera from the survey ship *Dammtor*. *Right* How divers, working from the *Stephaniturm*'s diving bell, later cut their way into HMS *Edinburgh*.

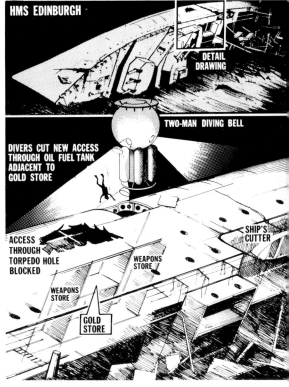

HMS EDINBURGH

DETAIL DRAWING

TWO-MAN DIVING BELL

DIVERS CUT NEW ACCESS THROUGH OIL FUEL TANK ADJACENT TO GOLD STORE

ACCESS THROUGH TORPEDO HOLE BLOCKED

SHIP'S CUTTER

WEAPONS STORE

WEAPONS STORE

GOLD STORE

David Bona, the Manchester lawyer who became chief executive of Jessop Marine.

Above left James Ringrose (right) with the Prince of Wales on board HMS *Bronington*. *Below* Keith Jessop (right) on board the *Stephaniturm*, with David Keogh, a salvage officer from the Ministry of Defence.

Above Ric Wharton (with beard) and Malcolm Williams, the diving contractors from Aberdeen. *Below* Igor Ilin (left) and Leonid Melodinsky, the Russian observers on board *Stephaniturm*.

Above left Débris – including trolleys – being brought up by crane from HMS *Edinburgh*.
Above centre One of the metal cages used to bring up the gold bars. *Above right* The
American Don Rodocker fitting Legs Diamond with his diving helmet.
Below The *Stephaniturm* in position in the Barents Sea: viewed from close-by the Russian
'protection' vessel.

The diver Dougald Mathison helps to haul in the diving bell's 'umbilical' deep-sea cables.

Above The control shack log-book records the discovery of the first gold bar, by John Rossier from Zimbabwe (right).
Below The gold comes up; seen here (from left) are Ron Morris (life-support team), Dave Keene (supervisor), Harry Neave (LST), Jim Tucker, Pete Croft, Keith Cooper, Brian Cutler, 'Banjo' West, Geoff Reudavey – all divers.

Celebrating the gold – Rolf Nommensen, a German crew member (left); Leonid Melodinsky, in the bullion room (above right); and the man with the mystery role – Dr Sidney Alford (seated), with Paul Blewett (life-support team) and Ted Setchell (supervisor, deck).

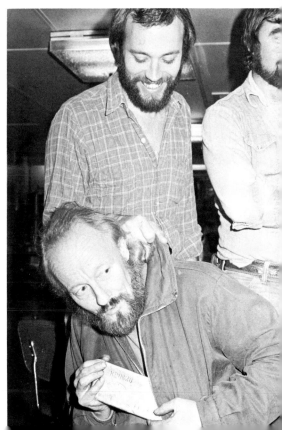

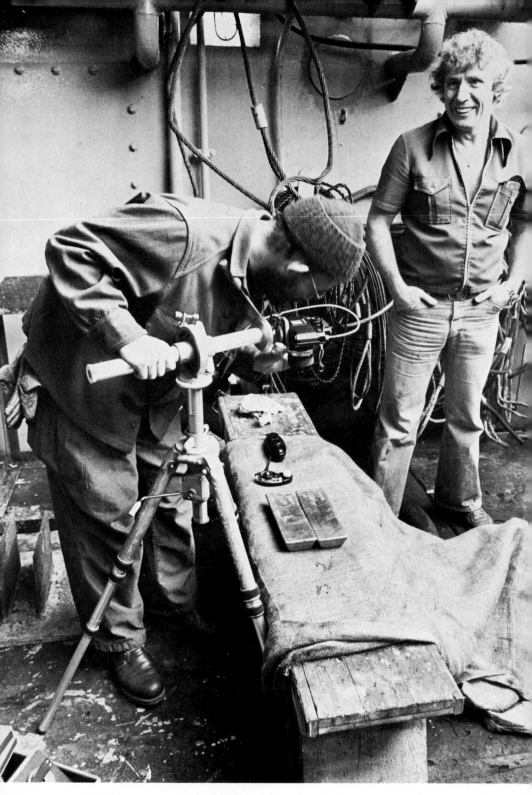

Keith Jessop watches *Sunday Times* photographer Ian Yeomans at work, photographing each gold bar.

Gold bars at Murmansk, with *Stephaniturm* in the background, October 1981.

Above The Kola Inlet of north-west Russia seen from the *Stephaniturm*; it was from here that HMS *Edinburgh* sailed on its last voyage in 1942. *Left* The remaining gold leaves Peterhead in a Brinks security truck.

There was much more besides included in the proposal. Jessop Marine, which had never undertaken a salvage operation before, had even worked out the code they would use on the two proposed expeditions. Called the 'random number code' it would be used in the normal daily telex messages between the salvage ship on location in the Barents Sea and the land-based operations back in Britain. James Ringrose, who helped devise the code, appeared to have covered most eventualities and dangers the salvors might experience, including possible problems from a Russian presence on board the salvage ship.

For the outsider or the cynic, it tended to read like a plain person's guide to undercover work and spying. The instructions began:

All coded messages will be transmitted by telex to the base office.

The coded signal will for most of the time be sent along with the normal daily telex report. All the coded part of the message will be prefixed with the identification word 'operation'. For example: 'Operation 5.7.4.' means – 'We have found a large wreck. The wreck is on its port side. We are having no problems with the Russians.'

Then followed a fuller list of code phrases, a useful warning to other parties in the planned consortium of the dangers that could lie ahead:

5. We have found a large wreck.
19. The wreck is in one piece.
39. The wreck in in two pieces.
6. The wreck has collapsed.
29. We have found the stern section.
37. We have found the bow section.
20. This is the wreck we are looking for.
7. The wreck is on its Port side.
36. The wreck is on its Starboard side.
3. The wreck is upright.
30. The wreck is upside down.
18. We have found the *Hermann Schoemann*.
1. The Russians are becoming a problem.
4. We are having no problems with the Russians.
21. We are returning to port because the Russians are becoming a problem.

 2. The situation in the bomb area is . . .
17. The bomb room is intact inside the wreck.
31. The bomb room is broken open.
 8. We can see the gold bullion.
 9. We are unable to determine the situation regarding the bomb room.
10. The wreck has collapsed in the area of the bomb room.
15. This part of the wreck is underneath and cannot be seen.
25. Everything looks OK – stand by to mobilise for next stage of operation.
12. The situation looks impossible.
34. I will return and report.
24. Please call us.
28. Location marked with a transponder.
11. Do you wish us to mark the wreck with a transponder.
23. Conditions inside the wreck are . . .
35. There are lots of nets on the wreck.
16. There are no nets in the area.
42. Visibility in the area is good.
41. Visibility in the area is bad.
27. The tide is a problem.
40. The tide is no problem.
13. Bottom conditions are good.
32. Bottom conditions are bad.
26. We are returning to port.
33. The video is working well.
22. The video is broken down.
14. We anticipate completion (number of days).
43. We have started the video programme.

Secrecy and salvage are words often synonymous in the competitive cargo recovery business, and *Edinburgh* was to be handled in keeping with this highly-prized tradition. Jessop often repeated the salvor's dictum: 'The salvage industry doesn't like discussing its plans or its operations with outsiders; and what salvors do under water is usually kept very secret.'

Under 'Security' Jessop Marine had declared in its proposal:

The maintenance of a high degree of security is of paramount importance, thus: all charts and information concerning the cargo and wreck will be kept in the hands of the Surveyor and Keith Jessop or Graham D. Jessop as the onboard representatives of the 'Joint Venture'.

The ship's crew will be told only what is deemed necessary and this will be done by the Ship's Master.

A cabin should be made available for the Surveyor and Keith Jessop or Graham D. Jessop to enable them to maintain a high level of security when using charts and photographs etc., and also for the use of meetings of the Survey Team. No other persons on board will have access to the information referred to above.

Out of thirty-six major tasks which the consortium would face during the *Edinburgh* operation, assuming it won the contract, only seven would be the responsibility of Jessop Marine. Wharton-Williams, if they needed reminding, were learning in detail in the proposal why Jessop had agreed they could take ninety per cent of the gold, *if* the recovery plan worked in the Barents Sea. Such tasks included anything from locating the wreck of the *Edinburgh* to providing remote-control video cameras, a satellite receiver, scan sonar and the cost of providing a highly-sophisticated salvage ship.

In keeping with his maxim to whittle costs and personnel to a bare minimum, Jessop would only become chairman and managing director of his company when the proposed joint venture agreement was signed with 2Ws. Jessop Marine's would-be directors, including Bona, Ringrose and Graham Jessop, found themselves in the same position.

'No cure, no pay,' Jessop had always propagated, and now he seemed to be putting his basic tenet into play. Wharton-Williams and in turn their new partners, OSA and Racal Decca, agreed to join in the hunt for the gold along lines outlined by Jessop Marine. The Yorkshire salvor got 2Ws' signature on his proposal and went on to become the chairman and managing director of his own company.

But from the outside Jessop's chance of snatching the *Edinburgh* contract from beneath the noses of Risdon Beazley and his Norwegian rivals still seemed remote. In spite of his new-found backing his company was untested and the methods he proposed revolutionary. Surely the British government would plump for a salvage outfit with whom they had pulled off many lucrative jobs and whom logic suggested would appeal to the Russians?

Jessop had been introduced to David Bona in 1980, and the Manchester lawyer was quickly to prove himself invaluable. Now he was as keen as Jessop for the *Edinburgh* operation to take place that year. On 10 June 1980, David Bona wrote to John Jackson at the Salvage Association informing him that Jessop had set up his own company. The salvor, with the £100 company, stressed that he would be looking for the *Edinburgh*, but his ambitions by no means stopped at the gold. 'The ultimate object of JMRL . . . is . . . to be exclusively engaged throughout the whole of the world in the field of marine salvage, wreck removal and ancillary activities.'

Jessop's company decided in June to strike a diversionary blow against their rivals. Instead of merely looking for the wreck as they were already allowed to do, why not make an immediate bid for the contract? On 18 June, Jessop Marine, now the £100-funded company heading a consortium worth millions, began to make the running by applying to the government for the *Edinburgh* contract. 'We wanted to discover whether the British government was really serious about recovering the gold,' explained David Bona. 'Perhaps they might want to salvage it themselves. Although the Royal Navy doesn't have its own salvage department, the MoD has.'

Until then the salvors anxious to win the contract had assumed that the first outfit to find the wreck would automatically get the Anglo-Soviet go-ahead.

David Bona's master-stroke – for such it turned out to be – threw the opposition into confusion. In the mid-summer of 1980 Risdon Beazley and Stolt-Nielsens suddenly found themselves hastily having to prepare their own formal proposals to secure the British contract. Just over a month later the three rival salvage firms were summoned for interviews by a panel of experts at the Department of Trade. Jessop Marine, the outsiders in the race, had brought their competitors to the starting stalls before they were really ready to run.

The ploy could end in nobody getting a contract, but it was a gamble worth risking. Government officials had already decided the *Edinburgh* contract had to be settled without delay. Warning voices between the ministries hinted that unauthorised parties might go ahead and rob the warship of its gold without any permission being sought. After all, the technology existed to dive on a wreck at 800 feet and the bullion was undeniably a rich and beckoning prize, especially if a 'pirate' salvor were to keep all the money for himself.

In making the running unexpectedly Jessop had effectively forestalled his formidable opposition. The Yorkshireman could not be certain, but it was unlikely that his rivals would have enough time to compile such smoothly polished proposal documents.

There were other factors behind the scenes which began to benefit Jessop's bid. Information continued to reach the salvor about his competitors' activities. Photocopied documents from the Department of Trade and the Salvage Association, some marked on a 'for your eyes only basis', began to turn up in Jessop Marine's post-bag.

Salvors must necessarily succour themselves on information about wrecks and the progress of their rivals. And the more confidential and classified the inside information, the better. Jessop therefore found himself in the embarrassingly happy position of being covertly kept in the picture through the equivalent of an undercover agent with an interest in the *Edinburgh*. Such a 'mole' kept Jessop cheerfully aware of almost every stage of the race in which he was now anxiously engaged. In mid-June, for example, he learnt that asking for 45 per cent of the cargo would guarantee he won the contract.

'Over the years you build up contacts and get to hear bits and pieces,' he would answer disarmingly when quizzed about the information that was reaching him regularly over the months. 'I've said before: every salvor has to have his intelligence network or he'll starve for wrecks.'

When Jessop and his team presented themselves for interview in front of a panel of experts at the Department of Trade he had every reason to feel he was now in with a reasonable chance. In fact, there was no question in his mind about which company would win; it was only a question of when, with the contract, he could leave for the Barents Sea. Inexplicably for some, Jessop's confident cantering that summer was fast turning into a gallop. And such confidence was beginning happily to affect the consortium which, on paper at least, he was now heading.

The directors of Jessop Marine at this point agreed between themselves to establish a charity which in time would benefit a variety of good causes. Assuming the consortium won the Anglo-Soviet contract and brought back the gold, more than £100,000 would be placed in a special 'charity' account. Later, more money would be added to a charity designed to benefit the relatives of men who had died on board the *Edinburgh*. Others were told that they would also get donations, including a London hospice, a Royal Navy charity and the trust which is currently recovering the wreck of the Tudor warship *Mary Rose*. Prince Charles, who is an enthusiastic patron of the *Mary Rose* Trust, sent James Ringrose a letter thanking him for his interest and the promised donation.

To some outsiders the charity idea might seem a mere ploy to impress the British government. But officials in Whitehall, faced with the delicate war grave issue, could hardly be criticised for welcoming a charity that might help balance any public controversy the *Edinburgh* project might arouse. In fact, the offer of a charity was a superb gesture in the overall strategy of winning the salvage contract.

'Cynics will interpret the charity differently perhaps,' said James Ringrose, 'but we were genuine about setting it up and I was privately delighted that several causes would benefit.'

On the morning of 22 July the salvor gathered with his close advisers at OSA's offices in London. Like actors in a play each man went over the lines he would read the government panel of experts later that afternoon. Reading from an up-dated proposal document, Jessop and his team were soon word-perfect. Not surprisingly, when the full circumstances became apparent, the meeting at the Department of Trade went like a well-padded dream. Soon afterwards Jessop Marine heard that their two rivals had 'not given such good performances'.

By introducing an urgent note into the interview Jessop and his team had won over their audience. In the preface of their black-bound proposal file, Bona had written: 'It is now within the interests of all the parties concerned, not only the beneficiaries of the cargo, but the other interested salvors of which there are at least two of other nationalities or with associations abroad, if the question of a salvage contract could now be resolved.'

Jessop had introduced an element of chauvinism which was less than fair and scarcely accurate. In his proposal document Jessop argued that 'if JMRL [Jessop Marine Recoveries Ltd] were to be awarded a salvage contract, the operation would be an all-British venture, and could include British Royal Navy personnel should they wish to participate in the actual salvage operation.'

OSA, of course, were agents for VTG (Vereinigte Tanklager und Transportmittel), who were proudly German and the owners of the 1,400-ton salvage ship *Stephaniturm*, which was earmarked for the *Edinburgh* project, had been built in Bremen and was crewed by Germans. Ironically, too, the revolutionary helmets which the divers would use on the *Edinburgh* were invented by Americans and, as it turned out, would be operated by an American on the *Stephaniturm*.

Jessop also knew where to hurt his opponents at the interview, and much stress was laid on the fact that his company was adamantly against using explosives on the sunken warship. 'The use of a conventional salvage technique, such as "blast and grab operation", would be abhorrent in relation to a "war grave" . . . saturation diving . . . would enable the company, without disturbing the "war grave", to enter the wreck and remove the cargo by hand.' And so the proposal document went on, adeptly darting rings around the competitors.

John Jackson, from the Salvage Association, was present during the interview which took place in July and heard each salvage company present their case. 'Jessop Marine satisfied the panel on the points raised, especially over the war grave issue,' says Jackson. 'That was a telling feature in my view.'

Jackson was quite unequivocal about his personally disinterested but professional support for Jessop Marine's application. In a report marked 'confidential' he told the MoD and Department of Trade that Jessop Marine – known as 'Group 3' – were 'a group of men each an expert in his own field and each independently financially sound so far as is known. The combined experience of Jessop & Son, Captain Morrice and Captain Hodson as Salvors is almost unbeatable in the Diving/Salvage field.' In fact, although Jessop warmly welcomes such an accolade to his talents as a salvor, Morrice and Hodson never did play a significant role of any kind in the *Edinburgh* operation.

But for the two other rivals Jackson had some harsh judgements to make. About Stolt-Nielsen – 'Group 2' – he said they were 'under considerable pressure' to get the contract and had 'expensive equipment lying idle and personnel laid off'. About Risdon Beazley – 'Group 1' – Jackson commented: 'Has no equipment or personnel or any of its vessels to enable anything but a "Blast and Grab exercise guided by a Diving Bell" '; and 'I have personal reason and experience to doubt them as a Company' and 'Reasonably reliable but distinctly unforthcoming in provision of details of their operations'.

For Jessop Marine Jackson had nothing but confidence. Under 'Reliability' he wrote: 'No experience of this group as such as yet but have every reason to believe in the personal reliability of those forming the Group.' When he turned to 'Trustworthiness' he stated: 'I would trust them as a Group and as individuals on this job.' When it came to the cost of the operation Jackson had no doubts that Jessop would prove the cheapest salvor, although he had yet to submit his likely costings. He added: 'As this would be Group 3's first operation I have no doubt that they would be the cheapest. Jessop has found the wreck once and can find it again and this would obviously cut down the expense of the operation.' But Jackson was particularly critical of how Risdon Beazley might handle the sensitive matter of the war grave and the human remains it might contain. According to the Salvage Association, Risdon Beazley 'has never to my knowledge taken any heed of the human remains which might have been in any of their targets, would not welcome Naval personnel involvement and in any event would "Blast" the wreck.' Such a document again made sweet reading to the Yorkshire salvor into whose hands the 'confidential' document suddenly fell.

Jessop was highly delighted when he heard that his company had won the contract, but he could not say that he was entirely surprised or spellbound by the welcome news. After all, he was a missionary with a message that only he could find the *Edinburgh* and win the gold back from the sea. Any fair-minded panel of experts would see that, and they had.

At the beginning of August 1980, a few days after Keith Jessop and his team had been questioned by the British government officials at Parliament Square House in London, the Yorkshireman received a photocopy of a highly-confidential report of the three formal interviews of the month before. Marked 'Commercial-in-Confidence', it told Jessop what his rivals had told the government board at their interviews. Such information was priceless at the time.

But suspicions that Jessop was too well-informed had already been noticed by Risdon Beazley. When they went to Parliament Square House on 22 July 1980, Graham Harvey and Fergus Hinds of Risdon Beazley raised the question of leaks. Ironically, Jessop could now read in the leaked document what the Southampton firm had alleged was happening.

'Although not within the terms of reference of the meeting Messrs

Harvey and Hinds immediately launched into an attack on what they claim were (a) complete changes in Government Policy on the issue of salvage contracts and (b) breaches of confidence by HMG [Her Majesty's Government] in allowing information to be passed to competitors.' The report went on: 'RB [Risdon Beazley] were assured that there had been no change of policy and certainly no breaches of confidence.'

'You rarely discuss your cargo recovery method because it's confidential and you risk losing the job,' said Graham Harvey, then Risdon Beazley's managing director. 'Fergus Hinds and I were very conscious that here was a government body asking me how we would do the job. I was fearful that my method might leak out; I had a hunch and you must read what you like into that.' But the report had leaked out and made clear that Risdon Beazley proposed using 'blast and grab' methods on the official war grave, a technique the board thought was 'not acceptable'. At Stolt-Nielsens' formal interview on 23 July the board, consisting of officials from the Ministry of Defence, Foreign Office, Department of Trade and the Salvage Association, noted that 'their records seem somewhat less complete than the other interested parties'.

At the end of the report was a summary of what the three salvors had told the board. About Risdon Beazley Jessop read: 'We were left with the impression that RB's location and underwater equipment has not kept pace with modern technology.' Stolt-Nielsens were 'obviously extremely competent and well equipped for operation within their normal sphere of activity [North Sea Oil] but are not experienced in salvage work of the type required in this particular case.'

Jessop, of course, was able to read what the government board had thought about his application for the *Edinburgh* contract.

'The presentation of this company was extremely professional,' Jessop read with a warm glow. 'They have obviously researched every angle in great detail and have got together a strong team with every man an expert in his own field.'

Rather rashly perhaps, Jessop did not always cover the tracks of his mole. The privileged paperchase which his man had dropped in Jessop Marine's postbag had alerted the salvor's fellow directors. 'I was amazed about the information and later the documents which Keith kept getting in the post,' says James Ringrose. 'Most were anonymous, but once there was a note on official headed notepaper. By comparing the handwriting it became quite clear where the material was coming from.' Ringrose and Jessop Marine's lawyer warned Jessop strongly about the risks he was taking and the embarrassing implications it had for the company. But surely the salvor could not be blamed if an official chose to leak documents to him? And the information was extremely valuable.

'For example there was one letter where Keith was told how to apply for two wrecks which might interest him,' said Ringrose. The two vessels had sunk in 1889 and had cargoes of tin on board. Such inside information was invaluable to any salvor, especially one as ambitious as Keith Jessop.

Jessop's intelligence network was so good that at 2 p.m. on Wednesday afternoon, 23 July, his company knew much of what had been said at the Stolt-Nielsens meeting that morning. The ever-helpful mole had telephoned to say that the British government's panel had had a preliminary discussion and Jessop Marine 'had definitely come out on top'.

The Yorkshire company also learned that Jessop's 45 per cent take of the gold bullion 'would undercut the Norwegians and be looked at in a very favourable light'. In fact, the mole had also telephoned to reveal that Stolt-Nielsen would bid for 50 per cent, while Risdon Beazley wanted 55 per cent of the gold cargo. It was vital information. Apologising for not having more time to speak that afternoon, the official had urged Jessop to hurry with his application. The Russians, he said, already knew that the Norwegians wished to retain the first ton of recovered gold; Jessop's counter-bid, based partly on his tip-off, might turn out to be the trump card that would scoop the pool.

In late August the British government informed their Soviet counterpart that in their view Jessop Marine should be awarded the *Edinburgh* contract. The Russians were inclined to accept such a high-level recommendation, but not before hiring a City of London specialist in company affairs to take a close look at Jessop Marine.

Captain John Banister, a marine surveyor, had been asked to investigate the company by Mirislav Krumin, who was the resident legal adviser to the Anglo-Soviet Agency in London. Banister had been able to find out that Wharton-Williams were substantial, but he had failed to discover much about Jessop's new, and still un-registered, company.

Adroitly, Bona thought it better to take a suite at the Tower Hotel in London and meet there. Jessop had no offices, and a cor-poration estate in Keighley might not prove the most salubrious backdrop for a question-and-answer session with Banister. When Jessop, Bona and Ringrose met one Thursday afternoon in October 1980, it was therefore in the impersonal surroundings of a luxury hotel in London.

David Bona advised his chairman to let him answer Captain Banister's questions when the City expert cross-examined them about Jessop Marine and the *Edinburgh* operation. 'I'd set up the company and I felt it better that I should answer any points which might crop up,' says Bona. 'And I obviously knew more about the legal background to the project.'

For the sake of such meetings Jessop agreed to abandon his wide-checked jacket, which seemed to some more suited to the golf course. After visiting the high street outfitters, Hepworths, the salvor turned up at the Tower Hotel wearing a smart grey suit. He had also put on a collar and tie to complete the new-sprung image of affluence and City respectability.

The British marine officer, temporarily investigating for the Soviet government in London, seemed apprehensive about the new and untested Yorkshire-based company. 'I told them, here you are, a £100 company, with no office or even a telephone, heading a multi-million pound consortium searching for a fortune in gold,' said Captain Banister. 'Something doesn't seem right somehow.' But Jessop Marine got through their rigorous interview at the Tower Hotel. Banister told the Russians they could go ahead, although he outlined any reservations he had in a report which ended up in Moscow.

Jessop Marine may not have had an office or a listing in the telephone directory but they had brought together an impressive array of technological talent. The Yorkshire salvor had quietly cleared another obstacle on his run to the gold lying about 170 miles north of Murmansk. But there was no hurrying the Russians into agreeing formally that Jessop had won the contract. 'We had thought that through diplomatic channels the Russians might reply almost at once,' said Bona. 'We were waiting hopefully on a speedy answer and in the conviction that as we were dealing with the British government the Russians might just endorse the official view in London.'

Jessop's hopes of getting an expedition underway before the end of the 1980 season were to crumble slowly with the passing weeks and worsening weather inside the Arctic circle. Although the *Stephaniturm* was ready to sail at one point, and divers were briefed to join the salvage ship, Wharton-Williams and OSA eventually had to demobilise the vessel berthed at Peterhead in Scotland. 'Not only was it costly to prepare the expedition, it was somehow nerve-racking not knowing one way or the other if we were leaving or not,' said Malcolm Williams, who was overseeing the preparations in Aberdeen.

With the 1980 diving season over Jessop was now running into a personal financial crisis. Jessop Marine had won the British end of the contract but the Russians were being irritatingly slow in their negotiations from Moscow. Jessop's company found at one stage that it had just £100 in its solitary bank account. In desperation its chairman and managing director turned to Wharton-Williams for a loan to keep the company afloat. 'Keith went to India as a diving supervisor for Wharton-Williams,' said James Ringrose at the time. 'I'm afraid it didn't do our credibility much good. We were seen to be a company with no money and yet we had convinced them we could make them millionaires many times over.'

Suddenly the Russians showed a flicker of interest again. Over David Bona's telex machine they announced that a delegation would be leaving Moscow for London in January. 'Hopes soared again, of course, but nobody knew what their attitude would be,' said Bona. There were seven officials in the party which visited Britain in January 1981.

For ten days the Soviet delegation delved into some of the finer intricacies of lifting the gold from the sea-bed. In Scotland they inspected the *Stephaniturm* and visited Ric Wharton's restored 17th-century castle outside Aberdeen. Back in London a memorandum was signed at the Soviet embassy and, amid vodka toasts, the *Edinburgh* project seemed to be pushing ahead again.

In January 1981 in London Soviet officials negotiating the contract had some reservations about the Yorkshire salvor. In a document which came into Jessop's hands the Russians had commented: 'It was discussed that Jessop in their own identity did not own or possess any of the relevant equipment seen at Aberdeen.' But the company with just £100 in its account – and undertaking an operation which Ric Wharton thought could cost £4 million – were ultimately unaffected by these early 'reservations'. Yet again Jessop had got to know what other people, and governments, thought about him and his company's drawbacks.

But the Russians appeared baffled over press reports in the West that claimed unequivocally that the *Edinburgh* had already been found by a British salvor. In Moscow the Russians were sent newspaper articles which said that Risdon Beazley had surveyed the wreck before Christmas. One newspaper story began: 'Found – the £50 million golden cruiser . . . one of the world's great sunken treasures has been found by a British salvage company . . . After frequent unsuccessful searches by British, Russian and Norwegian salvage experts for twenty-five years, the wreck was found this summer by a Southampton-based company, Risdon Beazley. "It will be one of the most difficult salvage operations ever," says the company's cargo recovery manager, Fergus Hinds. "But the wreck is there, the gold is there and the job can be done."'

Not unexpectedly Russian officials in Moscow were perplexed by such claims. The Soviet embassy in London were told to find out what was happening. The Jessop Marine consortium was also gravely concerned. Had another salvor simply ignored the two governments involved and found the wreck already? If a salvor had located the *Edinburgh*, might he not also have helped himself to the gold?

'Those newspaper reports gave some of us apoplexy,' explained James Ringrose. 'At a sensitive moment in negotiations, especially with the Russians, it could all have ended in muddle and confusion.'

In the event Risdon Beazley's claims were not to be substantiated. If the Southampton salvors ever did find the wreck they failed to photograph it or at least to produce such film as evidence of their discovery. Several months later Risdon Beazley closed for good and almost 200 people were made redundant. Exactly why Risdon Beazley told newspaper reporters they had found the *Edinburgh* remains a mystery to this day. But if they had sought to startle Jessop Marine during their negotiations with the Russians they had certainly succeeded. 'If we'd won the contract the operation would have kept the firm going,' said Tom Pickford, who sixteen years before had researched into *Edinburgh* and her gold. 'And the jobs would have been saved.'

Meanwhile, with the Russians apparently now satisfied that the cruiser was still intact with its cargo, Jessop and the British government representatives were invited for further talks in Moscow. While Stanley Holness and a lawyer from the Department of Trade arrived in Moscow with John Jackson from the Salvage Association, Keith Jessop decided to travel separately. On 28 March the chairman of Jessop Marine arrived in the Soviet capital with Thomson Holidays on a package holiday costing £150. And it was to be Jessop's adventures in Moscow which would mark the beginning of his first real chance of becoming more than a mere millionaire.

At the Intourist hotel close to Red Square, Jessop's team planned the negotiating strategy for the imminent top-level talks with the Russians. Jessop and his team would be battling with hardened Soviet negotiators from the mighty Ingosstrakh organisation, Russia's equivalent to Lloyds of London. When he was not deciding on the odd stratagem he would use or when he was bored with the meetings, Jessop the keen amateur photographer would slip away from his hotel to take photographs of the Kremlin from Red Square, preferring prints rather than transparencies.

The Yorkshireman and his fledgling firm had already made the tortuous but successful journey from Keighley to London and impressed the British government. From his initial triumph in one of the toughest capitalist heartlands it now remained to be seen if he would have another overnight success at the business centre of the Communist world.

With £45 million at stake, some 125 million in roubles, the Soviet Union had much to gain if an authorised salvor retrieved the bullion which Stalin had been sending to the West thirty-nine years before. But there were potential snags and underlying suspicions which had to be ironed out in Moscow if the Soviet government was going to give its official blessing to the treasure-hunt.

At the Ingosstrakh offices in Moscow, officials had listed some of their misgivings and possible objections to the expedition. One problem concerned the amount of gold which might be packed inside HMS *Edinburgh*. The fact was that the British government said there were five tons on board; Jessop Marine had reason to think the true figure could be more than double. 'The Russians told us they were missing some $3\frac{1}{2}$ tons of gold from their wartime stocks and that this might be on the *Edinburgh*,' said Jessop. 'That was in addition, of course, to the five tons which Captain Faulkner had signed for in Murmansk and which all the parties agreed should be in the wreck.'

In Moscow the British government was represented by Stanley Holness, an experienced official in the shipping division at the Department of Trade. By his side at the negotiating table was Colin Ingrams, who was well versed in marine law. In addition to Jessop, David Bona and James Ringrose, John Jackson, the Salvage Association's senior manager, also attended the negotiations. Jackson had an independent and tricky function to follow because his Association, a long-established and respected body around the world, had been formally asked to represent both the British and Soviet governments in the talks. In time the Association would play a major role as arbitrators in disputes, which might, and did, crop up during the actual salvage operation and its controversial aftermath.

At the Moscow talks Jackson played an important, though backroom, part in the assembled cast. The most vocal negotiator was A. L. Zlobin, a bespectacled official and the vice-chairman of the main Soviet insurance house. Zlobin wanted to know how security could be maintained over the gold, not only when the bars were lifted on board but on the sea-bed itself. 'Oh, they were very suspicious,' explained Jessop, 'in case the divers helped themselves to the odd bar. I told them: "I'm just as interested as you are in that! They'll be my gold bars as well, you know."'

Jessop agreed to film the whole operation in the Barents Sea, filming both in the wreck and on the salvage ship *Stephaniturm*. Video film would guard against gold bars being misappropriated and would ensure that the terms of the contract, particularly over the delicate war grave issue, would be strictly followed.

While the Soviet government knew that Jessop Marine was by no means a rich established British company – in Moscow in March the firm still had no telephone or telex of its own – it was felt that the salvor's consortium had the technology to pull off the operation. The Russians were not being asked to invest a penny or kopek in the speculative venture; that was entirely the responsibility of the consortium. Although they might know that Jessop had turned up for the Moscow talks on a cheap package tour, they apparently did not think it significant. If they had discovered that Jessop Marine had only a few pounds in their account they would probably have shown some concern.

After all, they no doubt argued, surely the British government would not enter into multi-million pound contracts with a man of straw? And Jessop had said plainly enough that the *Edinburgh* would only be one of many big future contracts, some of them well inside Soviet waters. His proposal document which he had brought with him to Moscow underlined the point and his ambitions after the *Edinburgh*. 'In the short period of time since its formation, the Company has already established its presence within the marine salvage field,' JMRL's manifesto cheerfully claimed. And it went on to promise: 'The successful recovery of the cargo from HMS *Edinburgh* would enable the Company to fulfil its declared objective more readily and establish itself as a major UK Salvage Company.'

Never slow to miss a basement bargain, a policy which Lenin had begun by selling caviare to the West shortly after the Revolution, the Russians saw the spectre of other lucrative deals in the future. What had Moscow to lose but negotiations, the occasional lavish function, and a couple of official trips to London? The rewards on the *Edinburgh* alone were tempting: some £16 million for permission to dive in international waters which did not belong to them.

Even 'defence' considerations, always a sticking point for the Russians, did not seem to concern them unduly. The wreck was about 170 miles north of Murmansk and in waters frequently used by their nuclear submarines and the pride of the Red Navy fleet. If they suspected the West might take advantage of the *Stephaniturm* being in a Soviet-claimed area they kept such concern out of the negotiating chamber. In any event it had been agreed that two Soviet officials would be on board the salvage vessel throughout the operation. As an added precaution the Soviet fleet would send a ship to protect the *Stephaniturm* from anybody showing an uncalled-for interest in the gold.

The Ministry of Defence in London were painfully aware that the Barents Sea is a highly sensitive military area and within the Soviet sphere of influence, despite the fact that NATO planes still fly regularly over it. Indeed it was the simple fact that the *Edinburgh* was close to the Russian coast that had persuaded the British government to involve Moscow in the first place. 'There's no argument when one's looking down the barrel of a gun,' the MoD official with responsibility for the *Edinburgh* project stressed. 'The wreck is in their backyard even if our planes do fly overhead.'

Jessop knew that East–West politics were almost certain to intrude in any *Edinburgh* project. Already he was beginning to experience the hostility of the *Edinburgh* Survivors' Association, although not every member individually opposed his salvage plan. In Moscow the Russians had not been particularly concerned about the war grave issue, but they concurred with the British government's strongly-held view. Jessop now accepted again that several hundred gold bars would be divided on the basis of two for Moscow and one for London; that would account for some £25 million; his company would collect the remaining £20 million, and in turn JMRL would pay the other members of the consortium.

'In Russia we were in a clear-cut situation where we had to recognise that the wreck was a designated war grave and in Russian-claimed waters. And I had to accept,' he added, 'that the two governments were collecting the lion's share of the cargo's value.' But Jessop and his consortium were prepared to settle for £20 million. With the expedition costs estimated at £2 million the gold left behind for the vaults of the Bank of England represented a handsome enough profit by almost any standards.

Negotiations in Moscow in March 1981 continued for a week. Usually eighteen people, mostly Russians and their interpreters, clustered around a large rosewood table to finalise the complicated contract. On occasion Jessop grew tired of the seemingly endless rounds of talks and long hours of enforced idleness in his Moscow hotel room. After three days he decided he would miss one session at the table and take snaps of the Russian capital. 'I managed to see some of their underwater diving equipment while I was there,' he said. 'Very primitive and cumbersome. I'm sure they go down

deep but I couldn't see them using it in the *Edinburgh*. They're
years behind.'

Russian backwardness in deep-sea diving technology was
believed, by some British officials at least, to explain the Soviet
government's willingness to participate in such a unique international venture. By involving themselves in the operation and
securing the right to observe the gold being recovered stage-by-
stage, the Russians would learn much about the West's latest diving
techniques. But the lure of the gold on the sea-bed had swept aside
any considerations of secrecy being breached. For the British
government, as much as for the salvors, the bullion equalled business
and for Whitehall, sound, practically unearned income.

By the first week of April Jessop had a draft, but initialled, Anglo-
Russian contract in his pocket. As far as he was concerned the gold
was also as good as there as well. Before leaving Moscow Jessop
pondered on the irony of the Soviet Union's role in the *Edinburgh*
operation. As he looked around the austere Russian capital it did
seem odd, not to say bizarre, that the heart of the Communist
world would possibly turn him into a multi-millionaire before the
year was out. The irony was especially apposite when he remembered
that his company's bank account had only the statutory minimum left
in it. Even his package tour to Moscow to negotiate his multi-million
pound contract was being paid for with borrowed money.

Jessop's astute legal adviser had guarded the company's interests
by insisting that all contracts and negotiations in pursuit of the gold
had to be undertaken and vested in Jessop Marine, a company
which had yet to leave the chrysalis stage. Although Jessop's company had contracted 2Ws in Aberdeen to pay for most of the actual
operation costs, it had nonetheless undertaken to finance several of
its own. Keith Jessop was Jessop Marine, and the salvor and his
company only had the *Edinburgh* project upon which it could generate any money. And when Jessop came to sign the Anglo-Russian
contract on 5 May 1981 he had still only £100 in his company's
bank account and no immediate prospect of raising much more.

Before the Anglo-Soviet contract would be formally signed in
London on 5 May, Jessop was still wrestling with his encroaching
money problem. He was concerned not only to honour his company's obligations to the Arctic expedition; he was also anxious

about his day-to-day living expenses. Living on borrowed time and money, he was sustained as always by great expectations of the gold. He had felt rather uncomfortable having to take a stop-gap job with a Wharton-Williams project in India in early 1981, but frankly, he admitted to a few close friends, he desperately needed the money. His lawyer had made some arrangements for loans to tide him over, but such money would not last for ever.

Even when he had money Jessop was instinctively cautious about the way he spent it. True, he took a certain private delight in saving money by staying at cheap guest-houses when he moved around the country, but his pride as the guiding force behind the *Edinburgh* project was dented by his enforced parsimony. While Ric Wharton was in his castle and Malcolm Williams on his farm, the consortium's chairman could sometimes afford bed-and-breakfast houses during his trips to Scotland. Jessop had a house on the edge of a council estate and was no commonplace snob, but he could not hope to compete with the magnificence of his partners. When the Soviet delegation had visited Britain in January they had been lavishly entertained at Wharton's castle on the outskirts of Aberdeen. The representatives from the world's first avowedly proletarian state did not have Keighley on their itinerary around Britain.

'Keith had taken the diving supervisor job from 2Ws and some saw him slipping into a more backroom role,' says Ringrose, who had become Jessop Marine's operations director. 'The planning for two expeditions, to find the wreck and then attempt to recover the gold, was nudging Keith out of the picture, and he naturally resented it.'

Meanwhile, Stolt-Nielsens were remarkably philosophical about not winning the salvage contract. 'We suspected an official was helping Keith Jessop,' said Stolt-Nielsen from a hotel in St Moritz. 'We were playing a game but the outcome was already decided.' Risdon Beazley were understandably more bitter about Keith Jessop getting the contract; losing the *Edinburgh* contract had helped force them out of business for good. But did Harvey and his fellow directors at Risdon Beazley suspect that there had been leaks and questionable business behavior in the race for the *Edinburgh* job? 'Oh my God, no,' Harvey replied. 'That wouldn't be cricket; we live in England.'

5

The Wreck is Found

With the scheduled April expedition to the Barents Sea to look for the *Edinburgh* almost upon them, Wharton-Williams were slipping their organisation into top gear. Their project manager, Mike Stewart, another ex-Royal Navy officer, was already scouting for freelance divers who would be willing to work on a 'no cure, no pay' basis. The Scottish contractors had taken the lead from their Yorkshire partner in promising gold or nothing: not even expenses.

Prepared for visiting the Arctic circle the previous year, 2Ws felt frustrated, even flustered, on occasion about equipment not arriving and deadlines not being met on time. But OSA had their survey ship *Dammtor* standing by and Racal Decca had supplied the vessel with an array of the latest deep-sea gadgetry.

Much of the equipment and extra cabins were installed in welded-down blue-and-orange containers on *Dammtor*'s boat deck. Compared with *Stephaniturm*, which OSA intended using for the gold-lifting operation later in the year, *Dammtor* had the appearance of a large rust-coloured barge. While *Stephaniturm* looked convincingly as if it belonged to the space age, *Dammtor*, with its containers on deck, looked more like a well-ordered building site.

In Peterhead, Scotland, the consortium made hurried last-minute preparations. Significantly for a man who had always clutched his project tightly around himself, like a child with a toy it fears may be snatched by a rival, Jessop was not going on the first expedition. James Ringrose believed that his chairman was not quite as confident as he outwardly appeared.

For somebody who had always declared so vociferously that *he* would find the *Edinburgh*, Jessop seemed to be acting out of character. After his failure with the Stolt-Nielsen expedition in 1979, some people felt he would demand to be on board *Dammtor* in April. Jessop dismissed puzzled inquiries with a shrug or the retort that all his research data had been passed to the consortium. Finding the wreck would be a technical accomplishment based on his all-important information.

In fact, with an area the size of Greater London to survey, the task was formidable. Moreover, if Risdon Beazley really had tried to find the wreck when their survey vessel had been in the Arctic region they had singularly failed to find anything.

Jessop Marine's operation director, James Ringrose, who had Royal Navy experience in the location of wrecks, some of it highly classified work connected with nuclear submarines, would sail on *Dammtor* in place of Jessop. 'Keith could have come but his presence was not central or essential,' says Ringrose. 'Though some thought he might like to be in at the kill, assuming of course we found the wreck.'

Months before the April expedition got underway, Jessop, still acutely short of money, had had his first encounter with what would turn in time into an avalanche of publicity. In the previous summer Jessop walked into the offices of Yorkshire Television in Leeds. For a company chairman heading a rich consortium with a secret mission it was a move that the salvor would later admit had been rash.

In his second-hand Cortina Jessop turned up at YTV and offered to sell his life story, a life that now centred almost exclusively on *Edinburgh* and the gold bars. Two astute journalists, Clive Entwhistle and Barry Cockcroft, sensed a dramatic story and told the salvor they could build a documentary film around him and the sunken warship. 'They told me I would become the Red Adair of the salvage world,' said Jessop later.

In the autumn of 1980 he talked to the two journalists about the *Edinburgh* project. In restaurants and at a party, attended by a few local television personalities, Jessop launched into his story with considerable gusto. The journalists enthusiastically agreed to make a film which could then be offered to YTV for transmission after the gold had been raised.

Although Jessop Marine's lawyer had skilfully retained the 'intel-

lectual rights' to the *Edinburgh* project, its chairman had not told
his board about his meetings with journalists. In any case he had
not raised any money from his discussions, only promises, and in
any event he had decided, just before Christmas, to fly to India and
take up the diving supervisor's job which 2Ws had offered him. For
the time being work in India solved the salvor's immediate crisis
over money. His son Graham, now a Jessop Marine director, was
despatched to Brazil to earn money as a diver, and that also lessened
some of the responsibility he felt for his family.

Back in Britain in the winter of 1980–1 Jessop began talking
again to Entwhistle and Cockcroft. In February Jessop told a
startled Ringrose and Bona about his links with YTV. His fellow
directors were horrified; Jessop had let a valuable cat out of the bag
and breached the very secrecy upon which the Yorkshireman had
always insisted the salvage world rested.

On 25 February, Bona and Ringrose, in the company of their
errant yet defiant chairman, arrived at Yorkshire TV's studios in
Leeds. Jessop, apparently cheerful and as loquacious as ever, tried
to talk his fellow directors into allowing a documentary film to be
made. The televised programme would centre on his life and on the
Edinburgh operation and would give him some much-needed ready
cash.

With only a month before their vital Moscow negotiations, and
another month again before the *Dammtor* would leave for the Barents
Sea, Bona was anxious that no further news about the operation
should leak out. Well aware that information about their rivals'
activities was vital to their own success he had no wish for others to
learn of Jessop Marine's confidential business plans. Yet news of
these had already reached journalists and Bona's task was to shore
up any damage before the situation deteriorated further. The lawyer
decided to stall and attempted to bring Jessop quickly to heel once
more.

In any event talks between Jessop Marine and the Yorkshire
journalists did not go well. Ringrose openly laughed when he heard
the offer to 'turn Jessop into a Red Adair figure around the world'.
Behind the scoffing that day was real concern. Premature publicity
could alarm the two governments involved and the consortium itself
and could alert Jessop Marine's competitors. 'But we were also

concerned about the war grave issue being ventilated to our disadvantage,' says Ringrose. 'The Ministry of Defence and the Salvage Association had repeatedly warned us that this was a highly contentious subject and one that potentially could scuttle the project before the contract had been awarded.'

Ringrose also knew that John Clarke, OSA's representative had been talking to *Edinburgh* survivors and at least one of them, Bill Daly, was adamantly against the war grave being touched. Daly, of course, was the *Edinburgh* Survivors' Association secretary and therefore well placed to create dangerously bad publicity for the operation.

Clarke had talked to Daly at his home in Warrington in July 1981. At first the former Royal Navy surveyor believed that Daly and his wife, who helped with Association work, would assist the additional research he had undertaken to do for the consortium. In fact, Daly turned out to be an unyielding and hostile critic of the gold recovery scheme. Oddly, though, it was to be many months before he took his Association's case to the press and sent a protest telegram to Buckingham Palace. Simmering rumours about the *Edinburgh* had quietened until Jessop made his own remarkable overtures to the press by trying to sell his life story.

The approach to Yorkshire TV had been slowly stifled by Bona's open distaste for such early, and potentially disastrous, publicity. But Jessop had still not accepted the danger fully and, with a Yorkshire journalist's help, turned to Express Newspapers with his story. The newspaper's colour magazine section was willing to pay up to £20,000 to the salvor for the exclusive right to cover the whole *Edinburgh* operation. In turn the *Express* could syndicate the story all over the world.

Jessop wanted to effect a sale before the *Dammtor* left Peterhead on 30 April. £20,000 was a tidy sum for a man living virtually from hand to mouth. Ringrose and Bona would know nothing about his newspaper negotiations until the survey vessel returned in triumph from the Barents Sea.

Meanwhile, Ringrose had much greater problems to occupy himself than unwanted press publicity. His major concern on the *Dammtor* was to make certain that he and the Racal Decca survey team now found the wreck. The young marine surveyor and friend of Prince Charles had already taken part with Jessop in one search which had failed abysmally and cost Stolt-Nielsens half-a-million pounds. On that occasion the survey had taken a gruelling and fruitless forty-two days.

Ringrose wanted no misunderstandings on his second venture inside the Arctic circle. Before leaving Peterhead he told Bona in writing where he believed the *Edinburgh* had sunk. He suggested that Keith Jessop should also write down his favoured position on the chart, but the salvor chose to give his view verbally. 'Remember we'd been once already and when we failed we went through hell,' says Ringrose. 'We'd suffered in my view partly because Keith in October 1979 had boasted so definitely that he would find the wreck. So I wanted my position left with the company's lawyer before the *Dammtor* left Scotland.'

While Ringrose had agreed to put his estimate of the wreck's location in writing, Keith Jessop decided against such a move. In the event Ringrose's estimate was within six miles of the *Edinburgh*; Jessop's position turned out to be some twenty-six miles wide of the mark. But by then it hardly mattered; the cruiser had been found.

Positioning reports were largely based on official records made by British and German vessels taking part in the naval engagement in 1942 which had led to *Edinburgh* sinking. Ringrose and Kip Punch of Racal Decca had also taken into account reports of 'fasteners' (obstacles which snag trawling gear on the sea-bed) from British and Norwegian fishing vessels. The survey team on board *Dammtor* recognised that there was a cogent explanation for the perplexing range of positions left behind in historical records. Survivors' accounts, too, had stressed that poor visibility and the cruiser's zig-zagging manoeuvres had made navigation and establishing a position extremely hazardous.

'We had about twenty positions to eliminate in an area the size of Greater London,' says Ringrose. 'That's an area of 1,500 square nautical miles. Eventually we narrowed the relevant fixes down to those from the *Edinburgh*, three destroyers and two U-boats.'

Oddly the Russians, who had so much to gain from locating the wreck, had not provided reports from their official records. Apparently accounts made in 1942 on board their destroyers *Sokrushitelni* and *Gremyaschi* had been lost. And naval and marine authorities in

Moscow had proved singularly unhelpful in finding documentation or eye-witnesses.

But in early May a Soviet observer, Igor Ilin, had joined *Dammtor* on its way to the Barents Sea. Soon the reserved Russian, whose wife was a Moscow judge, began poring over charts piled high on the *Dammtor*'s bridge. In faltering English, and with the aid of a pocket English dictionary, Ilin familiarised himself as best he could with the survey positions already known. Ringrose and Kip Punch's team outlined to the Soviet government's representative their major problems.

While the surface ships of both sides were assumed to have faced identical navigation problems during the battle in 1942, German submarines in the area were believed to have been acting independently of the surface vessels and had different ideas of their positions. 'Matters were further complicated by the German use of the "Quadrat" code,' explains Kip Punch. 'This "Quadrat" divides the earth's surface into rectangular areas, the smallest of which in the Barents Sea area covers about five minutes of latitude and twenty minutes of longitude.'

Correlation complications linked to differing Anglo-German navigation methods were studied along with the possibility that mistakes in the German 'Quadrat' coding might have taken place in 1942. 'You must remember, too, that few of the vessels involved in the action were fitted with automatic plotting tables,' says Punch. 'These might have helped in obtaining more accurate positions, but in any case would not have been able to follow entirely the erratic ship movements with frequent changes of course and speed.'

Before leaving Peterhead the Racal Decca survey team had largely discounted fishing vessel 'fastener' reports. Like Ringrose in 1979 on the first *Edinburgh* survey expedition they also dismissed the claim that pieces of a British warship had been trawled up as 'potentially high value' but probably untrue.

Interest on *Dammtor* centred on the naval reports of the mine-sweeper HMS *Harrier* which had helped evacuate survivors from the crippled *Edinburgh*. Racal Decca had established one error in *Harrier*'s accurate navigational reports and yet this had opened up another search area with a five-nautical-mile radius. The two areas turned out to be fifteen nautical miles apart from the prime area to the north-west of the secondary area.

'I'd been very interested in *Harrier*'s reported positions, and I'd read accounts by Eric Hinton,' says Ringrose. Hinton had commanded *Harrier* during the battle. His reports would prove to be crucial.

Tension on board *Dammtor* grew as the survey vessel steered closer to the search area. While the Russian observer studied the intricacies of computer chess in the ship's recreation room, OSA's John Clarke pondered on the chances of pinpointing the wreck. Clarke had recently been made redundant when OSA closed their London office; the ex-navy surveyor had decided to put all his available cash, and future, into the gold being recovered. Failure could ruin him.

Ringrose, too, had staked his future on the wreck in spite of the salutary lesson he had been taught with Stolt-Nielsens in 1979. Everything he owned was committed to the *Edinburgh*, including his time; he would end up spending three years on the project.

Now that the *Dammtor* expedition was well underway it began to take on a scientific air; absent was the note of burlesque and instinctive guesswork which Jessop had sometimes brought to the project. Men in clean bright overalls were turning areas of the prosaic-looking, russet-brown vessel into cramped makeshift laboratories. Orange Aquafix transponders, commonly called 'pingers' because of the sound they emit on the sea-bed, added another dash of space-age colour to the scene.

Jessop's dream was gradually turning into a reality which relied almost exclusively on exactitude and equipment which smacked of Cape Canaveral. Position-fixing and wreck-detection equipment, along with data logging and processing units, were necessarily replacing ambitious, yet blind, hopes about the gold.

A 2MHz Hi-Fix ranging system was chosen for primary position-fixing with 'slave' stations at Vardo and Gamvik in Northern Norway. To make quite certain that signal levels would be adequate, 20-metre masts with 100-watt transmitters were necessary; such sophisticated technology would help plot the wreck and then, with satellite aid as well, ensure that the survey ship remained above it while *Edinburgh* could be filmed.

The main underwater search tool was a Klein 50kHz side-scan sonar with Klein 531 triple-channel recorder. Such computerised circuitry, baffling to many and unromantic to others, was checked and re-tested as the *Dammtor* reached the Barents Sea on 4 May.

On board Ringrose thought again about the position for the wreck which he had left in writing with David Bona in Manchester. He wondered, too, if Jessop's position would prove to be accurate. Others, like Kip Punch, had done their calculations and made marks on their charts. Would anybody be right and therefore able to claim that they had found the *Edinburgh*?

Not everything on the expedition had gone smoothly, although to the casual observer the machinery appeared to be functioning well enough. Racal Decca's real problems had been on shore. Vardo and Gamvik were still under snow and conditions were far from ideal. 'The shore equipment, including masts, had been air-freighted to Norway, but snow ploughs had been needed to reach the sites where the slave installations were to be built,' explains Kip Punch. 'It was a race against time.'

In fact, the first slave installation at Vardo was finished by 5 May and was on the air five days later. Two days later the second slave mast at Gamvik was fully operational. Meanwhile, on *Dammtor*, technicians tried out their impressive array of sonar equipment. By now the seas were light but the temperature had fallen to minus 5° C and a thin coating of ice covered the deck.

From the survey ship the sonar could detect any large object within a 400-metre slant range and once spotted it would become a squiggle on a graph and exactly pinpointed. But the *Sea Hawk* had carried gadgetry and yet had not found anything during its forty-two-day search.

The *Dammtor* left Peterhead on 30 April, thirty-nine years to the day after the cruiser had been torpedoed. Fifteen days later, a large 'contact' was made on the port trace of the sonar record. People on board gathered together with mounting excitement as *Dammtor* turned for another run. Could this be the 10,000-ton wreck of the *Edinburgh*? One voice suggested it was probably the *Hermann Schoemann*, which had been sunk by the cruiser and was known to be close to her one-time adversary.

'We picked up the same contact,' says Ringrose, recalling the sudden tension of the moment, 'and then other checks showed conclusively it was a large wreck.' *Dammtor*'s sonar searches had first pinpointed a wreck at 2.21 p.m. on the afternoon of 14 May. By the following morning the expedition was still unsure whether they had found a British or a German warship. There was also the outside possibility that the sonar beam had struck a large and wholly unknown wreck.

At exactly the wrong moment the weather began to worsen. Already the Scorpio remote-controlled vehicle, looking like a complicated bedstead with two yellow cylinders 'sleeping' in the middle, had been sent down to inspect the wreck. But *Dammtor* was not moored close enough and Scorpio was brought back on deck. Disappointment, mixed with a certain understandable impatience, began to spread through the survey vessel.

Igor Ilin, the quiet Russian, returned to another game of computerised chess. Ringrose, meanwhile, sent back coded messages of their progress to Jessop and Bona. Characteristically, the salvor said he felt sure they had finally found the British warship. He could not face the prospect that it was the German destroyer.

For several hours *Dammtor* circled around searching for the *Hermann Schoemann*, waiting for sea to calm before returning to the original wreck their sonar had pinpointed. If a second large wreck could be found it was almost certain that the expedition had found the two warships which had sunk in May 1942. 'Certainly it was nail-biting but it was also rather frightening,' explains Ringrose. 'I suddenly remembered that finding the wreck would be one thing; but that was only the beginning. Assuming we had found the *Edinburgh* we still had to come back to try for the gold.'

But on 16 May, just before 4 a.m., *Dammtor* was able to hover above the wreck she had found. Scorpio was slipped into the water and descended slowly. Soon video pictures were being studied in the control room on board. Some people were despondent at first. Perhaps they had found the *Schoemann*; the camera ran slowly back and forwards along the size of a vast expanse of grey metal. 'Gradually we became convinced it was the *Edinburgh*,' says Ringrose. 'There was incredible tension on board. I clearly remember suddenly seeing the *Edinburgh*'s massive gun turrets on the underwater video, it's a moment I won't forget.'

Igor Ilin produced some genuine Soviet vodka and others produced bottles from their belongings. And time and again men stood staring at the video pictures which brought them remarkably clear images from 800 feet down in the Barents Sea.

The unique video film ran for almost four hours and showed the *Edinburgh* lying on her port side. Clearly seen were her 6-inch gun turrets, her triple torpedo tubes, and, oddly, a modern plastic shopping bag which had drifted down and attached itself to a guard-rail on the cruiser's upper deck.

Weirdly, there were few fish swimming about her, but the film showed clearly where the ship was hit by the first German torpedo, near to the bomb-room compartment where the gold had been stored at Murmansk. Several men watching the picture of silent desolation on the sea-bed wondered aloud if the gold had been scattered and destroyed by the torpedo explosion. It was a very real fear.

But the *Edinburgh*, despite its ruptured and twisted hull and broken bridge, appeared to be in an astonishingly good condition. After all, in his secret report to the Admiralty in 1942 Rear-Admiral Stuart Bonham-Carter had said that the *Edinburgh* had broken her back. From what could be seen on the television screen on *Dammtor* the British warship looked game enough for another fight.

Ringrose said: 'The ship looks extremely well when you remember that German submarines hit her three times before the Royal Navy destroyer hit her with a fourth torpedo. But when she was hit her internal structure was bound to have been badly distorted and the gold bars may well have shifted downwards in the wreck, like bricks falling off a tipper lorry.'

News that the *Edinburgh* had been found reached Keith Jessop in Keighley the same day. He celebrated modestly enough with a drink and lapsed for a time into an uncharacteristic, yet controlled silence. With the video pictures from the wreck would now come at least an attempt to raise the £45 million in gold which she contained.

Dammtor and the men who had found the hitherto elusive *Edinburgh* wreck berthed quietly at Peterhead on 22 May. Luckily for the expedition their singular success had not leaked to the press, and few took much interest when the survey vessel was demobilised at the small and remote Scottish port. On the quayside were the bearded figure of Ric Wharton and his taller partner Malcolm

Williams, waiting anxiously but approvingly by a custom-built Range-Rover. Hours later the two English entrepreneurs would be seeing their first eerie glimpse of *Edinburgh* at their company's office in Aberdeen.

Until the wreck, shrouded in a soft grey light, appeared on their television screen, Wharton-Williams had not taken the seemingly preposterous plan to raise the gold as seriously as they had taken their bread-and-butter oil diving contracts. Although Jessop's scheme was no South Sea Bubble adventure, it had some of the hallmarks of a very speculative gamble. For that reason 2Ws had laid off some of the risks by bringing in other treasure-hunters ready to place long-outsider odds on a coup. Just how eager 2Ws were in the race for gold was a question that worried Jessop Marine. The contractors had been willing enough to invest in the idea from the moment they learned about it in 1980, but did they actually *believe* their chance bet might come off spectacularly and win them a fortune?

Doubts about their rich partners' stamina for the bullion project were even raised formally at a Jessop Marine board meeting. A newspaper article had brought several simmering elements to the surface and on 3 June 1981 Jessop found his company facing a crisis. Bona and Ringrose had called a special meeting in Manchester to discuss with Jessop an article which had appeared prominently in the *Daily Express* two days before. The mood was sombre. Jessop, it transpired, had continued talking to journalists after the *Edinburgh* had been found. Express Newspapers were now keen to pay at least £20,000 for the salvor's exclusive story and discussions had taken place in Fleet Street. But the tempting offer had been thwarted by Bona as chief executive; he and Ringrose contended that unwelcome publicity could lose Jessop Marine the confidence of their powerful partners and possibly the Anglo-Soviet contract itself.

On 1 June, the *Daily Express* had boldly headlined an article about the *Edinburgh* being located: '£45 million in sunken treasure hunt by Charles's old shipmate.' Below, the *Express* reporter had claimed: 'A British company has won the contract to make a sea-bed hunt for £45 million in gold, thanks to royal backing . . . Prince Philip, who as the Duke of Edinburgh shares the British warship's name, and Prince Charles both expressed an interest in the venture. One of the company's operations directors is Mr James Ringrose, an ex-naval officer friend of Prince Charles. They served together during their naval careers aboard the minesweeper *Bronington* while Charles was in command of the ship.'

The clear inference that Buckingham Palace had helped swing the salvage contract in Jessop Marine's direction, said Bona, was very damaging and personally embarrassing to Ringrose. And some of the information which the *Express* had published had come, without payment, from Keith Jessop, who had happily talked to their reporters. At the extraordinary board meeting in June, Bona had claimed that 'the article might by now have caused irreparable damage to the project as a whole'. The board minutes of 3 June then raised the troubling question of 2Ws' commitment to the whole project.

Bona suggested controversially that: 'Until the Operations Director [Ringrose] on the *Dammtor* had actually located the wreck of the *Edinburgh*, it was . . . true to say that Wharton-Williams Limited had basically treated the Joint Venture as a joke . . . they . . . had seen the Company as just a façade, and had lost all faith in the Company's credibility. But,' added Bona pointedly, 'once the wreck had been located, the operation had had, for the want of a better expression, "a massive injection of penicillin" which no one could then ignore.'

Dejected at the need for such an uncomfortable and urgent meeting, Jessop had listened to a catalogue of sobering facts and complaints about his performance as the company's chairman. But the time had clearly come, as the board minutes recorded, 'for a frank and open expression of views'.

Bona calmly reminded the salvor that he was living on borrowed money; his company had no real assets, no office accommodation, telephone, telex or photocopying facilities. Jessop's dream about *Edinburgh* was finely balanced on his company's appearance to the 'outside world' and had now been endangered at a most critical moment.

'We weren't just worried about the media,' says Ringrose, who agreed with the need for such open boardroom castigation. 'We feared that the British and Russian principals, and the consortium we had formed, not to mention the Salvage Association, could pull the carpet from under us. Our standing was at grave risk.'

Bona had soon established that Jessop had been the unwitting source for some of the information in the *Express* article. The slim dark-haired lawyer, twelve years younger than Jessop, gradually changed his role into that of disapproving schoolmaster. The bluff Yorkshireman took much of the chiding, adopting a suitably contrite manner. 'Well, I apologised to Ringrose for any embarrassment the *Express* piece had caused him,' says Jessop. 'Well, it had happened. I felt we should forget it and concentrate on the *Edinburgh*.'

But Bona had not finished with his fellow director. He told him he was 'in the real sense of the word "a salvage man"; he did not by his own admission possess the appropriate expertise or credibility to survive in the world of corporate entity, in which he now found himself.'

With hindsight Jessop could see that he had been unwise to approach 2Ws for a job that winter. Working for them in India had shaken confidence in his company and had 'created the ludicrous situation . . . where the managing director of the principal salvage company in a £45 million salvage operation was employed . . . as a diving supervisor.'

The chairman, Bona went on, had no right to sell his life story for £20,000; the *Edinburgh* story belonged to the salvor's company and not to him personally. Jessop saw such lawyer's parlance as no doubt correct, but somehow ironic and too fine a shade of pale legal detail for his taste.

Some of the minutes that day read like the strictures of a magistrate or a Methodist preacher with a liking for strict temperance. Jessop was reminded of his drinking bouts around the world. 'When the Soviet Delegation visited Aberdeen at the end of January of this year [1981], Mr Jessop was seen to be the worse for drink on one particular occasion and had compromised the Company,' the 3 June board meeting's record.

Bona had learned that the Soviet delegation had intimated that they might fly home to Moscow and abandon the talks. The lawyer had given various assurances to the British government about the Aberdeen incident but there had been a further scene at a cocktail party given at the Soviet embassy in London. According to the minutes: 'Despite being discreetly advised to leave, Mr Jessop had declined this advice and had found himself standing on his own in a room full of Russians some forty minutes later.'

In Moscow the salvor had extravagantly demonstrated his liking for vodka, although there was absolutely no suggestion that he was an inveterate tippler or an alcoholic. Jessop saw himself as a sociable *bon viveur* in a business world where entertaining was the norm. 'I like a drink and I hold it well,' said Jessop months later, 'and most of the lads in diving are the same.'

Jessop made little comment at the lengthy board meeting, but he appeared to be taking such criticism to heart. At one stage he admitted he had become 'bored and frustrated over the winter period' when he returned from the job he had taken with 2Ws in India. He agreed he had drunk too much at the 'incidents mentioned' and added with disarming honesty that he had 'found it difficult to adapt to the commercial environment which he was now in'. Jessop's candour apparently knew no bounds that day. He 'acknowledged that he had behaved rather foolishly and gave his assurance that he would endeavour to play his part to the full, in the future, to ensure that the operation was a success.' And, for good measure, he told his board: 'He didn't really feel comfortable in a suit and tie.'

Some of the observations made by the Manchester lawyer, however, and recorded chillingly in the minutes that Wednesday, were of a far more serious kind. Bona told the meeting that he had gained the impression from Mr Jessop that he regarded it 'as a fact of life . . . that backhanders were paid in the salvage world to get people to either give you information or do things.' Bona sternly told his fellow director that this was 'totally unacceptable' and had 'reiterated to Mr Jessop that no such promises or payments were to be made, whilst [he] was in any way connected with the Company. They were not only illegal, but it would be downright foolish to be involved in any such dealings.'

Jessop would later explain that the subject had been rather misunderstood. But the board minutes record a different interpretation of what the salvor had told his colleagues on different occasions. 'Mr Jessop had also indicated that he was considering the possibility of giving some sort of payment/benefit to an official . . . in recognition of his individual involvement,' one paragraph began. But the account went on: 'Again, Mr Bona reiterated that this was completely out of the question for obvious reasons and should be put to rest.' It is clear that this matter was discussed in more direct and detailed terms, but the company minute contains merely a discreet summary.

By chance Ringrose had overheard Jessop talking with an official, now identified as the mole, and he made clear his dislike of such 'insider' information reaching the company. Bona, bound by the strict demands of the lawyer-client relationship, had his own insider view of what was happening, and how his client's actions might be misconstrued if the facts ever became public.

Jessop had apparently been told by the official, who claimed he might be able to influence the awarding of the Anglo-Soviet contract, that the equivalent of a bar of gold would not go amiss in his pocket. This discussion was overheard. The Yorkshireman had listened to the official's offer with the chuckling cynicism of a salvor who had heard that such things occurred in the scrap world. Jessop would not pay up and in any event by June 1981, with the contract in his pocket, he had no need whatsoever to become involved in any underhand dealings. The official, who had wanted a suitcase stuffed with banknotes to be left on his desk, was to be disappointed, although he kept his hopes alive for months afterwards.

Jessop had not quite heard the last of the complaints about his behaviour as chairman and managing director of a multi-million pound consortium. In fact, the salvor had made gaffs in Moscow in March that year which had, according to a British government official, almost lost him the contract. Bona told the board that the *Edinburgh* project was 'one of the biggest coups of the century' if it could be brought off. But Jessop had to behave in a manner 'that befitted his status'.

Jessop again was not spared some of the details of his alleged laxity in Russia. For a salvor who believed in secrecy he had been too open about his *Edinburgh* plans. In Moscow, the board minutes record, 'some of this information had apparently been given quite freely to one young lady, then a croupier at Ladbroke's in London, who was giving quite an adequate résumé of the *Edinburgh* operation, one morning at breakfast, when Mr Bona and Mr Ringrose arrived to eat.'

In fact, Stanley Holness, the senior British government representative at the Moscow talks, had called a meeting to warn Jessop about 'loose talk'. Holness had asked for an assurance in words of one syllable. He feared his delegation would leave the Russian capital without getting the contract.

But Jessop was not yet out of the dangerous woods in which he found himself at that crucial June board meeting. If the *Daily Express* did not publish a retraction of their article of 1 June, and they might well refuse, Jessop might have to resign from his own company. Saddened by the tortuous train of events after the *Dammtor*'s success in finding *Edinburgh*, Jessop ruefully agreed that he would resign if the *Express* stood by its story's claims. But before the week was out the newspaper published an apology and retraction, and stated that it was wrong to say that the Royal Family had helped Jessop Marine win the *Edinburgh* salvage contract.

Jessop had survived another tricky obstacle in his path to the gold bullion. Now the ever-burgeoning pressures swept into new areas of controversy surrounding the wreck. Newspaper articles dwelled on the war grave issue and the risk that human remains might be disturbed. The *Sunday Times*, which had agreed to observe the salvage operation from start to finish with fifty per cent of any syndication fees going to charity, tackled the matter in their first article on 31 May.

Bill Daly had told the newspaper: 'There would be no way of getting the gold without moving bodies. I have had dozens of calls from survivors and next of kin saying how upset they feel.' The Survivors' Association secretary had labelled the operation as sheer 'desecration'. But Jessop Marine pointed out that they would not be using explosives to reach the bullion; they were using revolutionary methods which made that unnecessary, and bodies would not be disturbed. Moreover, clause two of Jessop's contract with the British and Soviet governments stated: 'The wreck is classed as a British war grave . . . and every effort must be made by the contractors to cause as little disturbance as possible.'

In Moscow the Anglo-Soviet talks had worked out a procedure to follow should human remains be found on *Edinburgh*. The contract stated that the British government representative had to be told and that the 'Secretary of State for Trade of the United King-

dom is to be informed immediately.' There would be 'a solemn
burial of any remains found at sea', and 'identity discs or other
means of identification found on the remains are to be handed over
to the Secretary of Trade of the United Kingdom'. Contractually
London and Moscow, and the consortium, were agreeing to take
clear note of their legal obligation and solemnly to respect the war
grave where so many had given their lives in 1942.

There was a distinct fear in the government departments involved
that ballyhoo about bullion on a warship could backfire and raise
public disquiet. For some, treasure-hunting in an officially designated grave would be in the poorest taste and, for others, distinctly irreligious. Officials at the Ministry of Defence feared questions in the House of Commons and angry protests from serving
and retired Royal Navy personnel.

But James Ringrose, the ex-Navy officer, did not expect to find
any remains on the wreck. 'In our experience with other wrecks,
bones decalcify,' he said in a *Sunday Times* article. 'There are no
longer bodies or human remains down there, especially after almost
forty years.' Certainly the video film, which had been taken in
April, had shown no signs of bones or bodies. But what would the
divers find when they laboriously made their way inside the twisted
labyrinth of the warship?

PART III
Recovery

6

Preparation

By midsummer 1981 Jessop, with the Anglo-Soviet contract in his pocket, was anxious to begin diving for *Edinburgh*'s gold. With the high-jinks of Moscow behind him and the boardroom barracking a blurred nightmare, he was ready to make for the centre-stage in an operation the *Sunday Times* dubbed 'the salvage mission of the century'.

Though Jessop had been taken aback by the biting remarks of his co-directors, he had bounced back in July with relish, believing that little now stood in his way. The simmering controversy about human remains he tended to dismiss as a passing irritant. Even the £20,000 he had been told by his company to leave behind in Fleet Street was dismissed as a lost bagatelle.

When Jessop Marine learned from Moscow that the Soviet government would pay him in gold bars, rather than sterling as originally agreed, he was not really perturbed. And when the salvor heard he might have to pay VAT on his bullion he felt confident that his new London financial advisers would clear such a hurdle with ease.

But Moscow's decision to pay the salvor in gold rather than pound notes was more than a silly hiccup, and his advisers were forced to take the threat to his would-be fortune on the sea-bed seriously. Common Market regulations placed no VAT on cash coming into Britain, but owners of gold were liable to pay swingeing taxes.

Jessop's advisers had top-level discussions in July with Bank of England and Department of Trade officials to resolve the cruel

143

dilemma. For some weeks the company feared it could end up with only £2 million, barely covering the costs of bringing up the gold. When the salvage company held their secret negotiations in Moscow the Russians had agreed in the draft contract to pay the sterling equivalent of 1.6 tons of bullion. British currency would be handed over at Murmansk in return for the Russians getting back their share of the gold. But later Soviet officials began insisting that the salvor be paid in gold bars, and so began Jessop's first hint of tax problems.

'We were put in the position where we were being told by the Russians: "Take it or leave it,"' says James Ringrose. 'We were told in July that we could face paying 15 per cent VAT on our gold once we landed it in Britain. That was laughable. With 52 per cent corporation tax, 60 per cent personal tax and the company's outlay, we might wind up with paying back almost everything to the government that contracted us to bring up the gold in the first place.'

British government officials who took part in the negotiations with Moscow and Jessop Marine were unhappy that the Russians decided to do an 'about-face' on the original deal. 'They clearly prefer to keep our pounds in their pockets rather than their gold in the State Bank of Moscow,' said one civil servant involved. 'And it looks as if our Exchequer might gain an unexpected wind-fall.'

Meanwhile, customs officials in London confirmed that they would demand 15 per cent VAT on Jessop's bullion when it was landed in Britain. They added that the company would need to pay VAT 'in cash' or 'certified bank cheque', like anybody bringing gold into the country.

But Jessop, now making final preparations for his voyage to the Barents Sea, learned that there could be a legal detour around the regulations. Jessop Marine might be able to sell any gold to the Bank of England or a bullion dealer. Unlike salvors or anyone who wishes to import bullion, the Bank of England does not pay VAT on imported gold. 'If we were to sell the Bank of England our gold *outside* British waters we could then avoid paying VAT,' Ringrose had told Jessop. 'We may have to say to the bank: "Would you care to buy a portion of the gold at sea later this summer?"'

While Jessop's new financial advisers wrestled to ensure that their client's firm earned £20 million and not £2 million from the salvage project, Jessop was turning his mind to how he might spend some of his money. For some, such unbridled confidence seemed premature. Nonetheless the salvor and his co-director son Graham decided they would each buy a Porsche, and Mildred could also have a new car out of the gold. By August he conceded that the millions he might soon be bringing to the surface could force him to become a tax exile. 'The money will come in very handy,' Jessop told acquaintances, 'but I want to use most of it for new salvage schemes after I've finished with *Edinburgh*.'

The Yorkshireman had told himself often enough that the Arctic region, rather than the British Isles, was the place where rich untouched wrecks could still be found. He wanted to spread his salvage net farther and, of course, deeper than anybody else in the industry. 'There are thousands of wrecks around the British Isles but you can pretty well say that most have been looked at,' he said. 'The Arctic Ocean, the Barents Sea, they're the areas, but the salvage industry doesn't like discussing its secrets.'

While Wharton-Williams and the rest of the consortium methodically went on recruiting men and ordering equipment and materials for the Arctic voyage that summer, their chairman and managing director found he had a more backroom role to play. For the time being anyway he would keep a low profile; his flirtation with the press was temporarily over.

Eager to prove his Arctic operation was no gimmicky jaunt on the cheap, the salvor could show pictures of *Stephaniturm*, the impressive salvage ship that cost at least $10,000 a day to run. Commissioned in 1978, *Stephaniturm* was a familiar sight in the North Sea. Although she had sometimes been idle, and berthed for days on end at ports in Britain and France, there was no doubting she was the best vessel in the world for work on a wreck like *Edinburgh*.

Such a project now needed a code-name, a designation which each party to the consortium would recognise in telephone and telex traffic to and from the *Stephaniturm*. Jessop had a dog named Sam; Keogh a dog named Henry; and so Operation Greyhound was born, although nobody in the consortium actually owned a racing dog.

In Keighley Jessop waited for a definite sailing date. Originally he had wanted to leave in midsummer but by early August *Stephaniturm* was still on hire to the French diving contractors Comex. Inside the consortium in Scotland some feared the delay might well endanger the expedition, particularly if bad weather in the Barents Sea further held back the diving operation. By the end of October conditions within the Arctic circle would probably make deep-sea saturation diving impossible. *Stephaniturm* was technically able to hover over an exact spot, give or take a few inches, in a Force-six swell, but not if weather conditions worsened into gales. 'My main worry in August was that the weather would turn and the exercise might then be half-completed and abandoned,' explained a genuinely concerned Jessop. 'Naturally I was pressing to leave as soon as *Stephaniturm* was loaded.'

For the moment *Stephaniturm* was still being demobilised in Cherbourg while the gold-seekers anxiously wanted her in Peterhead. Such a delay was not wasted by the parties making up the consortium; divers were interviewed, extra research was done on *Edinburgh*, and in London Jessop's financial advisers and the Bank of England sorted out the VAT conundrum.

In Aberdeen Mike Stewart, 2Ws' project manager, was putting the final touches to his months of preparation. Stewart's responsibility in the end was to decide how many divers to use on the operation. *Stephaniturm*'s compression chambers could take thirteen divers, but the ship itself could carry more in reserve. He had to face the prospect of divers going sick or being injured while working on the wreck 800 feet down. Or indeed worse: fatalities in deep-sea diving were common.

Stephaniturm was fully air-conditioned for work in the Arctic – or in the tropics for that matter. In addition to the ship's impressive array of gadgetry – including radar, two gyro compasses, autopilot, echograph, telex and weatherfax – the deep-diving system itself was built to reach 1,316 feet. Ten divers could be in saturation at any one time, 'blown down' to 'atmosphere 23'.

On board, Mike Stewart explained what 'saturation' diving really meant. 'It's a descriptive term which is given to the actual physiological process that takes place when a diver descends under pressure. As the diver goes down it is necessary for him to breathe oxygen, and that oxygen must have with it a further volume of inert gas, which in deep diving is normally helium.

'The helium is there to make up the extra volume that is required to fill up all the lung space. As a diver inhales he will be using on this job 3 per cent of oxygen in a total 100 per cent mixture; the remainder will be helium.

'The helium is dissolved in the bloodstream, through the lungs, as the energy is taken in from the oxygen and helium. It has quite a specific gravity which allows it to dissipate into the system very quickly and the term actually is that it *saturates*. Your body is like a sponge and it takes up the helium very quickly.'

On *Stephaniturm* the divers would live in the two deck decompression chambers; DDC III was the larger single lock chamber and could take six men with toilet and washing facilities; DDC IV had facilities for four divers.

Compressing or 'blowing down' the divers takes some twelve hours; but bringing them back from an atmospheric depth of 800 feet can take almost a week. Why the difference and why so long?

'If you consider all this gas which has been saturated into the body tissues,' said Mike Stewart, 'it needs to get out from the body. It's gone into every nook and cranny in the diver's system and the only way it can get out is the way it came in: through the lungs, mouth and nose. If you look at a bottle of soda it appears calm – that represents the diver at depth. But should you pop the cork all the bubbles start coming out very quickly; well, all the energy in those bubbles is similar to the gas that is trapped in the body tissues of the diver. If a diver were brought up too quickly he would be dead within a very short period.'

In fact, his body would explode, a fate which a decade ago overtook one unfortunate diver. But now sophisticated technology makes that awesome prospect remote, even in the unlikely event of *Stephaniturm* breaking up in an accident or storm. The deck decompression chamber DDC IV can, in an emergency, take ten divers and be launched over the side and connected to an attendant life-boat.

The diving bell was designed to accommodate three divers, but in the event Stewart decided that two, with all their equipment, were enough. One extra man made movement inside the bell almost impossible.

Once the divers were inside and ready to dive, the bell would descend from *Stephaniturm*'s 'moonpool' like a slowly-moving cage in a coal mine. 'The diving system utilises a cursor system on rails,' explained John Clarke. 'This hydraulically connects the bell beneath the "moonpool" to the cursor and then lifts the bell within the ship. The transfer of the bell to the double-lock transfer chamber is done hydraulically. And the bell is positively under control throughout the launch and recovery once it's "latched" onto the cursor. Within the "moonpool" the weight of the cursor eliminates movement of the bell.'

As far as the *Stephaniturm* was concerned, Stewart felt he had no major headaches. The recovery vessel had repeatedly proved its prowess and reliability for other contractors in the North Sea. But the situation in which they would find themselves working was substantially different. Though the thirty Germans who formed *Stephaniturm*'s regular crew were used to contrasting conditions, they had mainly worked in areas where ships and oil platforms were regular sights. In the North Sea diving vessels can find themselves working alongside each other. Oil installations contain medical and transport facilities; in some areas of the marine oilfields the brightly-lit jacket platforms have the beckoning welcome of small modern towns, even when surrounded by raging waters.

At a spot inside the Arctic circle where the *Edinburgh* was now known to rest, *Stephaniturm* would be without any other support ship. The nearest port where emergency rescue facilities would be available was the small Norwegian port of Vardo, twelve hours sailing time from where *Stephaniturm* would remain hovering over the wreck. The 1,400-ton *Stephaniturm*, 224 feet long, $44\frac{1}{2}$ feet wide, was nevertheless well equipped in the event of accidents. But would the emergency facilities on board prove sufficient, Stewart pondered in Aberdeen, for a major diving accident 200 miles from anywhere?

On board *Stephaniturm* there would be a purpose-built medical room, but 2Ws decided they would not carry a doctor on the expedition. Although the recovery vessel was insured to berth sixty men, places were short. In fact, in August there was a last-minute scramble for a place on the unique voyage.

The decision not to employ a doctor would later prove controversial. Stewart, however, banked on his divers, most of whom were paramedics, escaping injury or sickness. If the worst did come about a doctor could be brought out to the survey vessel. Stewart was not by any means without back-up emergency systems on *Stephaniturm*. Built around a decompression chamber and a diving bell, the ship had an emergency second chamber which could be launched and attached by an umbilical cord to a life-boat.

Stephaniturm's main compression chambers, cigar-shaped and each of them the size of a tiny living room, had a complete life-support system: medical supplies, communications, telephones and even entertainment facilities. Whether they would prove sufficient in the intricate manoeuvres to find the gold would only be established on site in the Barents Sea.

Exactly where *Stephaniturm* was destined to hover Keith Jessop would not disclose before the expedition was ready to depart. Although he had been censored by his company's board in June he still, on occasion, displayed the recalcitrance that he believed had won him the *Edinburgh* contract. *Edinburgh*'s precise position, inside the Arctic circle at 72° north, 35° east, and some distance away from the official log made by Captain Faulkner in 1942, was a secret he firmly kept to himself. Like others lured by Stalin's gold he could not altogether rule out that 'pirate' salvors might just get to the wreck before they did. 'Even worse,' he admitted several times to close colleagues, 'is the nightmare that others have already worked on *Edinburgh* and taken off her cargo.'

By the final week in August *Stephaniturm* had slipped quietly into Peterhead in readiness for loading supplies and the gas and gadgetry upon which, along with the divers, the success of the expedition would ultimately depend. Already the nucleus of the consortium's high command was beginning to assemble. 2Ws in Aberdeen urged their American suppliers to hurry with their deliveries of helium and oxygen. Divers were chivvied into action and some told about the ordeal before them. Life-support teams, backroom boys who supervised divers in saturation conditions on board, wondered how their work would differ from an oil job in the North Sea.

Stewart had drawn up a sketchy list of some of the oil industry's better known divers the year before, when Jessop's consortium first began planning. 'I heard a definite whisper about the *Edinburgh*

idea a year before we actually sailed for the wreck,' said Derrick
Hesketh, one of the most colourful diving supervisors in the North
Sea. '2Ws took us into the know about a secret, really hush-hush,
operation and we were not to breathe a word about it to anybody.
But it soon became known. People came up to me in Aberdeen and
said: "Oh, you're going after the *Edinburgh* gold!" '

An Australian diver, Geoff Reudavey, had learned from Jessop
about the project many months before the *Stephaniturm* was being
mobilised in late August 1981. Reudavey had the Yorkshireman's
word that he would be included in the diving team. In spite of the
'no cure, no pay' deal, the challenge to dive on the world's deepest-
ever salvage had its own prestige and a man stood to make a small
fortune from recovering the gold.

There were a considerable number of men to sound out about
the Arctic dive. Within weeks of finding *Edinburgh* in April, Stewart
was approaching potential recruits with the knowledge that work
would begin on the wreck before the year was out. The ex-naval
lieutenant, who was also a trained diver, had a rather different
background from the men he had in mind. An ex-public schoolboy,
with a becoming gift for esoteric twists and turns in his conversation,
Stewart had a certain shyness which some saw as the aloofness of an
officer trained in the discipline of Dartmouth Naval College. But
few doubted his ability to bring together a colourful and experienced team to raise the gold. He viewed each recruit with the eye
of a racehorse trainer, convincing himself that every candidate had
the right stamina, skill and proven cold courage to work at dangerous and icy-deep depths.

In Malta with the Royal Navy Stewart had tackled explosives
underwater. *Edinburgh* was a warship packed with shells, bombs
and ordnance, especially in that part of the wreck where the gold
had been stored. It was hard to imagine a more difficult job and he
needed specialists who would not baulk at handling devices that
would put their lives at constant risk. Choose a suspect diver and
men could die; an expedition could be aborted through human
frailties operating at perilous saturation depths.

Today large groups of divers gather anywhere in the world where
they can find well-paid jobs on sea-bed oilfields. Many favour an
instantly recognisable image rigidly cultivated from frayed jeans,

personalised T-shirts and pricey jackets. Along with cowboy boots and the regulation Rolex timepiece they are often as identifiable as a City businessman carrying a tight umbrella and wearing bowler and pin-stripe grey.

Picking the tough reliable deep-sea diver from such a dressy bunch of extroverts, nonconformists, mild extremists, the odd social misfit and the genuinely brave is not easy. Because their work all over the world leads them to a mildly bohemian life-style, divers rarely work for one boss all the time. Though some men earn their reputations as strong talented divers, project managers like Stewart have to know how to weed out the careful performers from the capricious cowboys of such a high-wage industry.

Stewart was quietly confident about the contrasting team he had helped pick for the *Edinburgh* operation. Barry 'Banjo' West was a bright extrovert from the North, with theatrical gifts which could have led him to a colourful career on the boards. But West's effervescent high spirits never outweighed the cool professional skills he brought to his work.

Like 'Banjo' West, Keith 'Scouse' Cooper brought a warm zany humour to his job as a deep-sea diver. But both West and Cooper were skilled hands with explosives and Royal Navy trained. Stewart envisaged them diving on *Edinburgh* first and eventually clearing a path to the bomb-room where the gold was believed to be.

Altogether twelve divers were chosen for the operation along with a diving superintendent (who also knew about explosives), two supervisors and a group of men who would make up the life-support teams. Racal Decca, who had provided the sonar equipment which had pinpointed the wreck in April, were bringing along just two men to relocate the warship.

Meanwhile *Stephaniturm*'s owners, OSA, were taking on huge multifarious supplies at Peterhead that August. The expedition could last anything up to three months, and vast quantities of food and other materials would be needed to sustain the sixty men who were going to sea.

Wharton-Williams had opted for a recycled gas for the divers to breathe on the sea-bed. Stewart had invited an American specialist called Don Rodocker to supply the diving helmets, again on a 'no cure, no pay' basis. Rodocker's system used an improved helmet which instead of expelling the helium and oxygen mixture actually allowed each diver to recycle the gas. 'There's a saving of over 90 per cent on some dives,' Rodocker claimed before leaving Peterhead. 'In some cases the saving can be more.' Rodocker's system meant that *Stephaniturm* could last longer in the Barents Sea before a supply vessel would need to bring more giant gas cylinders to replenish the helium-oxygen which would be lost.

Stewart had convinced 2Ws that they should take the risks which might arise with Rodocker's helmets and recycled gas. Some divers were known to favour a more conventional gas system; the reservations they expressed were partly conservative and partly because, in the past, men had died before Rodocker and others arrived on the scene with a helmet they claimed was now safe. 'There's obviously a huge potential saving,' said Mike Stewart, before leaving Peterhead. 'When you consider we're loading about 1,500,000 cubic feet of gas, costing about £75,000, it represents a large investment.'

Although the grandiose salvage project had been the perspicacious hunch of Keith Jessop, the salvor took little part in the preparations now taking place on board *Stephaniturm*. For some weeks Jessop had been in the background. He continued to rely heavily on Ringrose and Bona in the daily affairs of his company, and he appeared to see them in the role of lieutenants, putting the final touches to his inspiration. Now all was ready, and *Stephaniturm*'s journey was the one voyage he would not miss for the world.

7

Departure

Keith Jessop's niche in salvage history is secured by his success in turning a Cinderella-wish into a real-life, £2 million-pound Arctic expedition paid by oilfield princes he barely knew. Inside his consortium there would be much dispute about who made the major contribution on board *Stephaniturm* and who should be blamed for major mistakes. Nobody, however, disputed that it was Jessop, the down-to-earth jack-in-the-box, who had popped up in the middle of a world recession with a notion that could turn men into millionaires and even raise a rich golden glow for governments on both sides of the Iron Curtain.

When *Stephaniturm* finally sailed from Peterhead in the early hours of 30 August 1981 she carried with her the embers of rows only temporarily cooled. If gold bars were found Jessop Marine would leave little to chance. A 'security procedure' had already been agreed by the British and Soviet principals and within the consortium itself. Each bar would be photographed three times and on the bullion room door on the stern would be fitted 'a rimlock, and . . . two separate padlocks, all of which will have two keys . . . the door to the strongroom compartment will be kept locked at all times.' Altogether there would be six keys, all of them spread between the parties on board *Stephaniturm*.

Jessop Marine's lawyer had wanted any gold they salvaged to remain in their interest-earning hands until the bullion was back in Moscow's State Bank or the Bank of England. Wharton-Williams had threatened to call off the operation and invited two British government representatives and the man from the Salvage Association to listen to heated exchanges within the fragile consortium.

While Bona and Ringrose stayed away on the day *Stephaniturm* sailed, choosing to record their costly arguments by telex and telephone, Jessop tended to agree with his adversaries during a critical meeting in Aberdeen. 'Bloody hell, 2Ws were going to abort before we'd even left port,' an anxious Jessop explained later. 'I wanted to get going, for God's sake, so I agreed with the other side.'

Faced with capitulation by their chairman on the spot, Bona and Ringrose knuckled down to new 2Ws' conditions which permitted the survey ship to leave. But separate disputes were allowed to smoulder at critical moments later in the expedition.

Doubts were expressed at the wisdom of having a *Sunday Times* reporter and photographer on board. David Keogh, a salvage officer from the Ministry of Defence, claimed he had not been told that the press, and a documentary cameraman, would be observing the operation. John Jackson from the Salvage Association demanded to know who would be 'vetting' despatches for publication in the Sunday newspaper. 2Ws, smarting somewhat from the fact that Jessop claimed 'intellectual rights' in the gold and might dominate the news in the event of success, shared similar fears about publicity. 'What happens if things go wrong on the voyage?' asked Malcolm Williams. 'The project could prove a fiasco. We might not find the gold; divers could be badly injured, even perish.'

Tucked away in the background were secrets which were known only to certain parties within the consortium: confidences destined to slip out embarrassingly during the course of the operation. One secret revolved around a short, casually dressed man with a wispy beard, who had furtively slipped on board *Stephaniturm* at night. Earlier he had arrived at 2Ws' Aberdeen offices hidden under a coat on the back seat of a car. Before *Stephaniturm* steered in the direction of the Barents Sea, this Puck-like figure had brought on board a well-padlocked container and had had some of the divers sworn to secrecy about his mission.

Jessop claimed he knew little about such mysteries, feeling increasingly that he was not always fully in the picture now about the finer details of the mission. In his comfortable high-deck cabin, always reserved for the charterer, he would tell visitors he was grateful that the expedition was at last under way and that he should be in charge.

But only days before *Stephaniturm* left Peterhead 2Ws threatened to pull out of the consortium. They had demanded that once any gold had been found and taken to Murmansk it would at that point come into their legal possession. David Bona argued strongly that the bullion would remain in Jessop Marine's charge until they returned to Britain; after all, they were the main contractors.

Wharton-Williams were adamant that they would not sail if Jessop's did not agree to this late condition. Indeed to demonstrate how strongly they felt they informed the British and Russian governments of their decision. While Bona argued from his office in Manchester, Keith Jessop decided to side with 2Ws.

'There was nothing I could do,' said Jessop. 'There was this terrible meeting in Scotland and they said they'd pull out. Without 2Ws we couldn't go. And I was desperate at that stage in time to get the expedition going.' Jessop, as charterer and chairman of the firm heading the consortium, was technically in overall control, and few could question his being the guiding light in the whole gold-raising idea. But now there were other interested, and powerful, voices which had to be heeded.

Stephaniturm's captain, Ronnie Götz, a pragmatic German who would later reveal an understandably querulous side to his nature, was certainly in command of his ship. But he had to take notice of the ex-Royal Navy surveyor, John Clarke, who represented the vessel's owners, OSA.

While the charterer and the captain had individual cabins on the top deck, Clarke and other officials on board shared neat cabins one deck down. David Keogh, who announced that he represented the Ministry of Defence and Department of Trade, was paired with the mysterious stowaway with the wispy beard.

Nearby the two Soviet officials, Igor Ilin and his bigger, tougher-looking companion, Leonid Melodinsky, shared a cabin. Igor Ilin was the division chief of the Salvage, Towing and Dredging Department of the Ministry of Merchant Marines in Moscow. Leonid Melodinsky, from Leningrad, was the head of department of the Emergency-Rescue Salvage Services Company in the Baltic Sea, again a division of the Ministry of Merchant Marine.

Stewart paired with Clarke, and the two diving supervisors and the superintendent were also found berths on the middle deck. Most of the divers, sonar technicians and life-support teams were fitted into steerage quarters another deck down. But steerage passengers, four to a cabin, had scarce reason to complain, because some divers had to sleep in the compression chambers. *Stephaniturm*, with its complement of sixty, was full: packed with men and machinery and the back-up supplies to keep them going for a very long time.

The British-led party had been quartered on the survey ship with the deference to social comfort which one of the officials clearly thought appropriate. Jessop, who sported a pair of shorts for much of the Arctic trip, may not have resembled a Captain Scott figure but he was rightly given pride of place on board. Before leaving Peterhead, Malcolm Williams, of 2Ws, who was not sailing, told the British party and the ship's captain: 'Without Keith Jessop we would not be here today.'

But Williams, ominously for Jessop Marine, had nudged the control conch closer into 2Ws' hands as the project progressed. He had admitted at the prior-to-sailing meeting on *Stephaniturm*: 'As you're all probably aware, Keith, to a certain extent, has put this all together for the past two years, starting with what he was going to do and how he was going to do it. Now he is handing over to Wharton-Williams and the other venture partners who will carry out the work.'

2Ws from the outset held in check their enthusiasm for the formidable challenge they faced and seldom disguised the genuine anxiety they felt about its outcome. Williams had warned people on board that the ship was crowded and there could be conflicting interests 'especially when the diving begins and the operation becomes exciting'.

The sun-tanned entrepreneur pointed out that the divers' control room, small and cramped by gadgetry panels, would be the nerve-centre of events taking place on the sea-bed. Video monitors would show some of the work being carried out on the wreck. But space was a problem. 'In the control room there is a shift supervisor who is on duty for twelve hours,' explained Williams. 'He directs the location of the diver from the surface. He has two assistants and then the diving superintendent will be up for some of the night. The work will go on with two shift teams, day and night.' Work must not be hindered by people 'badgering' the supervisor while he talked to the divers throughout his twelve-hour shift. 'It's in our own interests that everybody knows what's going on,' Williams added. 'There are no secrets, nothing you won't hear about. If anything does go wrong in a diving operation a supervisor may say: "Hey, everybody out." But you'll pick up the news half-an-hour later. I'm very keen we get a good rapport on this operation.'

On *Stephaniturm*, project manager Mike Stewart promised compelling pictures from the deep. 2Ws had made arrangements, he said, for a pan-and-tilt TV camera and a hand-held camera, and there was the chance of sound too from 800 feet below. 'You'll be fully up-to-date with what's going on because you'll hear it, and see it, on TV,' said Stewart confidently. The monitoring screen would be in a separate cabin.

But 2Ws stressed that some pictures they would not like to see shown on public television. 'This business venture can very easily in the eyes of publicity be converted into a treasure-hunt,' Williams had explained at the quayside in Peterhead. 'If I have an accident, I'm a long way from home, no rescue vessels nearby. If I have an accident and lose a diver on this it will be extremely damaging.' Williams wanted no pictures of divers injuring themselves or, worse, being seen by the outside world. Jessop Marine were contracted to keep a documentary filmed record of the expedition for the British and Soviet principals; the public might not be shown everything happening on the voyage.

At the first meeting on *Stephaniturm* the *Sunday Times* reporter heard, oddly enough, that no telex or telephone messages could leave the ship. Keith Jessop, whose company had invited the newspaper to syndicate the story of the gold, seemed disconcerted but said nothing. 'As far as I am concerned there'll only be one call made,' said John Clarke purposefully, 'and that will be a call in code saying we've done the job and that's the end of it.'

Behind Clarke's attitude was an apparent concern for security. If several tons of gold bullion were brought on board, the survey ship could become a prime terrorist or criminal target. Concern about the gold had already troubled Ministry of Defence officials and Brinks-Mat Ltd, the security company ultimately responsible for taking any recovered bullion to the Bank of England after the operation was over. David Keogh, the tall, slim MoD official, would be technically responsible for any gold landing on the salvage vessel.

Keogh had been dismayed at an article about Keith Jessop which had appeared in the *Sunday Times* a week before *Stephaniturm* left Scotland. Jessop had told the newspaper that once any gold was lifted, the ship would sail to Murmansk and £25 million would then be divided between the British and Soviet governments on a basis of 'one for London, two for Moscow'. The rest, some £20 million, would be brought back to Britain and 'unloaded at a spot near Tower Bridge . . . with most of it ending up in the vaults of the Bank of England.'

According to Keogh, public disclosure about exactly where the gold would be landed was tantamount to an invitation to thieves or terrorists. John Jackson of the Salvage Association had been equally disturbed at the news leaking out. Jessop, not for the first time, had seemingly jeopardised the venture, albeit innocently. Jackson, who demonstrated concern for the Yorkshireman's so far unrecovered gold, could not believe that such information had come from Jessop Marine for publication.

Press interest in the prospect of gold bars being hauled from the Arctic sea-bed was already increasing throughout the world. In the United States CBS News carried pictures of the *Stephaniturm*; in London ITN's reporter David Smith gave the first of several reports about the salvage mission. Smith, who was not on the voyage, interviewed an *Edinburgh* survivor who had helped store the gold in 1942. 'What sets this [salvage job] apart is not just the treasure,' Smith told several million viewers, 'but the fact that man rather than just machines will do it. Eight divers, veterans of the North Sea, will be locked into a decompression chamber, early next week, to acclimatise themselves to the prospect of going deeper for salvage than anyone has done before. The divers' confidence is absolute.'

For officials on *Stephaniturm* public interest in the 'salvage mission of the century' was a mixed blessing, and their reputations would hardly be helped if the job were a failure. But with Jessop's gargantuan appetite for promoting his company, and in the light of his contractual obligation to record events for London and Moscow, public interest, already aroused by the sheer audacity of the project, was rapidly growing.

As the divers played cards in their cabins, waiting for the moment when they would finally go into their saturation chambers, they expressed a buoyant enthusiasm for what lay ahead. At briefing meetings organised by Mike Stewart, anxiety rarely showed through and was firmly contained behind a constant stream of jokes and occasional horseplay.

'We're a hundred per cent confident,' said 'Banjo' West, an intelligent man who had already bought a comfortable home and adopted a suitable life-style from the money diving can bring. 'The worst things we are expecting are the weather and extreme cold. Not just for the divers themselves but also for the equipment; gauges, for example, freezing over.'

Stephaniturm steered northwards at a steady ten knots in a relatively calm sea. Within hours she was picking her course between the oilfields of the North Sea. Individual 'jackets' on massive stilts, some exuding powerful jets of flame into the night sky, were readily named like big hotels in a major capital. Thistle Fields, Murchison Fields, Brent Fields, Hutton Fields – divers and members of the life-support teams alike recognised them. After all, this was where many of them had gained much of the experience which would prove critical in the Barents Sea, still five days sailing time away.

During the day divers gathered for the daily briefing sessions in the recreation room. On the wall was a squawk box which linked them directly to the control room 100 feet astern on the same deck. In one corner of the recreation room was a large plastic model of the compartments and bulkheads which cocooned the bomb-room where the bullion had been stacked in rough deal boxes. 2Ws had even gone to the trouble of having a heavy wooden box made the same size that the Soviet-made originals were thought to be. The weight, too, was the equivalent of four gold bars, some 112 lbs.

Explosives on *Edinburgh* were a major consideration in the catalogue of dangers which the divers would experience. Mike O'Meara, the fair-headed and dark-bearded superintendent, brought with him a wealth of practical know-how about explosives and the kind of unexploded ordnance the divers might stumble across on the wreck. Divers were told that men with Royal Navy experience like himself would be 'locking out' of the bell first. 'Banjo' West learned that he would be one of three men going on the

first bell run. The well-built, hefty diver had the chance of establishing a world record in this method of salvage recovery and
might become the first man to walk inside *Edinburgh* for almost
forty years.

The classes in the recreation room bore the aspect of a sales
pitch to the divers. O'Meara instinctively knew that the men needed
to be encouraged like athletes and brought to their best by a mixture
of firmness and psychological prods peppered with good humour.
Nobody had to teach the men to dive at great depth or how to
handle underwater cutting gear. But this dive was to be different,
and in a remote part of the world, and O'Meara wanted his divers
to pay attention at the briefings.

At dawn one morning the divers had assembled for a secret
meeting where they were shown diagrams. Keith Jessop was not
invited and nor were Igor Ilin and Leo Melodinsky, the two Soviet
officials. And it would only emerge weeks later why the small man
with the wispy beard had also turned up for the meeting behind
closed doors.

Open briefings for the divers sometimes concentrated on the video
film of the wreck. 'Gun turrets are pointing over the starboard
bow,' an official explained as the cruiser's 6-inch guns came into
view on the monitor. 'In May we were unable to make a complete
excursion right through the bow because débris and the shattered
remnants of the ship endangered the umbilical cord attached to the
Scorpio remote-control vehicle.' Gradually the massive shadowy
hole torn out by the first German torpedo despatched by U-456
came into view. 'The hole appears to be the size of one sheet of
armour plating,' the voice continued, 'and we're now looking inside
the hole.'

A lone silver stick-fish, thinner than an infant's index finger, zig-
zagged into a shattered hole through which a bus could pass. 'I'm
glad to see there's not much moving down there,' joked 'Scouse'
Cooper. Gigantic eels and gourd-like monk-fish, though not necessarily dangerous, were familiar features of the North Sea underwater
installations. The waters around *Edinburgh* looked empty of life.

When the video film had been viewed by the divers they were
given a medical briefing. Although all of them had received some
paramedic training in the past, *Stephaniturm* had no doctor on board.

The North Sea has produced its own crop of specialist doctors who have studied the effect of saturation diving on men working at enormous depths. But 2Ws, of course, had not included one at the beginning of the voyage, a curious decision the contractors were later to regret.

Keith Roberts, who was part of the night-shift life-support team, had worked for several years in the North Sea oilfields. A quick-thinking wit whose barbed tongue was equally pointed at midnight as at midday, he had been brought along to talk to the divers about special problems which might arise at 800-feet diving.

'Scouse' Cooper lay flat on the fixed oval table in the recreation room and acted the diver injured in the bell. 'I'm going to show you a few techniques: setting up a drip, giving injections,' said Roberts. 'If we should need to use any of these we'll be talking you through it over the radio and monitoring it on the TV.' A colleague from the day life-support shift took over and demonstrated how to feed an injured and unconscious diver. Treating a man underwater, especially in a bell at depth, presents formidable obstacles. At 800 feet a diver would be wearing a thick hot-water suit, and access to his injuries would be tricky in the tightly-packed chamber hovering close to the sea-bed. *Edinburgh* was certain to contain swilling oil from fuel tanks close to the bomb-room in the wreck; the diver would no doubt be covered in oily muck.

The thin Scot, Sam Sutherland, from the life-support team explained how to give a diver cardiac massage, take a pulse from the neck and increase his circulation and breathing; it was a demonstration a paramedic finds tiring enough on land. Reviving a diver, injured and dragged back to the bell in icy-cold conditions, would by no means be the same operation at depth. The mood of the briefing was momentarily grim and silent.

'What about piles on the sea-bed?' asked David Keene, the day-shift diving supervisor, to ease the sudden tension in the room. Keene was popular and widely thought to be lucky at his job. With a gold Rolex and aeroplane to his name, he had a reputation, by no means common in the North Sea and Middle East oilfields, for hanging on to the money he earned from diving.

'What about a doctor if one were needed?' enquired one diver quietly. In the event of an emergency a helicopter would fly out to the ship. 'An English-speaking doctor?' said one diver. Nobody seemed quite sure. 'There's not a lot a doctor could do for you down there,' commented Derrick Hesketh, the night-shift supervisor known as 'Cyclops' after losing an eye in an accident. In saturation diving a doctor rarely gets a chance to examine his patient other than through a chamber window and over the radio link.

Diving superintendent Mike O'Meara then explained that it was vital for divers going into saturation to begin using their special ear-drops: an important precaution against sea-bed bacteria which can cause excruciating pain and wreck a diving operation.

O'Meara told the divers, soon to live in the compression chambers on board, how their days and nights would be patterned by their life-support teams. 'What we are going to do is to leave eighteen hours of each day, during which period of time you will be up and awake,' said the superintendent. 'And then there will be a six-hour window into each day and this will be your rest period when you will be required to sleep. You will all keep rigidly to that routine and cooperate with us in the control room. It's to make decompression easier on you.'

Roberts added that there was no point in having rest periods and divers not sleeping in them. If divers slept in the morning and not within the allocated time they would take longer later to come out of saturation once the job was completed or aborted.

Before the briefing was over divers were told they could not take cassette recorders into the chambers. Batteries at depth are a risk; taped music would be piped to them from the control room. *Stephaniturm* was supposedly a 'dry' ship; divers would not be able to take alcohol into the chamber. 'No drink will go into that chamber in any shape or form,' O'Meara insisted. Divers were also told about other chamber prohibitions; they must not wear 'woolie bears' (textured underwear) beneath their hot-water suits; they would wear regulation rubber underwear whatever their contention might be about 'woolie bears' being warmer and more flexible.

While divers and their back-up teams attended the daily briefings, Keith Jessop spent time in his cabin writing his diary. One day, he said, he would produce his life story and an account of how he tackled the *Edinburgh* gold. 'It's the most remarkable bloody story,' the Yorkshireman would tell visitors invited to his cabin for a beer. 'If people only knew a tenth of the way the contract was won; well they'd gasp. The truth is sheer bloody mind-boggling.'

Jessop was confident his autobiography would become a hot property in the publishing world: a veritable 'I reveal all' bestseller about what some human beings get up to on the sea-bed. His exuberance for any task he tackled was characteristic. But if he went through with his plan to tell the truth he might create numerous problems for himself, and at least one man linked to the *Edinburgh* enterprise could end up facing censure, if not worse.

Already chastened by his lawyer about the subject of 'backhanders', even though none had really been given, he was underestimating the implications of earlier events when such matters had been broached. Did he really believe that he could write openly about, say, 'backhanders' without drawing risky attention to himself from startled Whitehall officials?

Jessop had steadily collected a stream of documents based on his *Edinburgh* project: these, he believed, would prove invaluable for his memoirs. But some the salvor realised could not be mentioned. Just how had Jessop acquired top-level, highly confidential memoranda between the Norwegians and the Russians in 1980? Who was the mystery figure sending Foreign Office and Department of Trade papers to the Yorkshire-based salvage company, and what were his motives?

Jessop's swashbuckling approach to business morality meant that he could not interfere with a well-placed deep throat who brought priceless information. What another man might do, photocopying papers and sending them illegally to Jessop, was not his responsibility. After all, he had initiated nothing; if his postbag brought the odd windfall then he was simply lucky.

On board *Stephaniturm*, now cutting its way effortlessly through the calm beauty of the Norwegian fjords, the salvor had endless hours for contemplation. In his cabin he was happy to talk about how he had beaten his formidable opponents to the wreck. But what would the Norwegian firm Stolt-Nielsens do if they knew the full story of Jessop's eager mole? In March 1980 Stolt-Nielsens and Jessop had formally agreed to take their separate paths to the gold. Yet on 28 May, when the Norwegians signed an agreement to split, they had also successfully negotiated a draft contract with the Russians in Moscow. That contract had rested on the British government being informed and agreeing to Stolt-Nielsens getting London's approval; if they had succeeded Stolt-Nielsens would have beaten Jessop into the ground.

Shortly after the Norwegian-Russian draft agreement in May, signed in great secrecy, Stolt-Nielsens had passed a photocopy of the document to the British ambassador in Oslo, Sir Archie Lamb. The embassy had then passed this to the Foreign Office in London. The Soviet government, too, recognised that Britain had rights on their sunken warship and that they would also need London's approval of the Norwegian contract. Stolt-Nielsen's Chris Delmer in Oslo had passed over the document in the strictest confidence.

At the Foreign Office, Simon Butt, who then worked on the Russian desk, showed the contract to others before passing it to the Department of Trade. Within a short space of time the document, which contained a clause covering the fact that it was strictly confidential, had ended up in Jessop's postbag, without Butt's knowledge. Butt was certainly not the 'mole'; civil servants had no idea apparently that papers were leaking from government offices concerning the contract. Knowing that his former partners were already close to winning the contract with the Russians had spurred Jessop, in 1980, to hurry ahead with his application. Like Ali Baba, and helped by the mole, Jessop had outmatched Stolt-Nielsens and proved the value of insider information.

Now he began to play down some of the earthier facts of his own past. In the month he had won the £45 million *Edinburgh* contract Jessop had also paid £200 for a car, in hopes of profit, and had been forced to scrap the vehicle in Yorkshire when the deal went wrong. The car was worth only a few pounds, and on paper the salvor with an eye for metal had lost badly at a time when he could least afford it. More interesting, perhaps, for some, the car had belonged to one of the officials who had recommended that Jessop should get the salvage contract.

On *Stephaniturm* life was very different and Jessop eased into the contractor's role without difficulty. Instead of worrying about scrap metal deals he would talk to the two Russian observers on board, speak to the captain about the weather, and weave his way round chatting to people he had brought together for the operation.

At midnight on 1 September the salvage vessel had reached Tromsö in Norway. The next morning, at 10.43, eight of the divers scrambled into the orange-coloured compression chambers to be 'blown down'. While *Stephaniturm* would not reach the wreck until the following afternoon the divers had to be got ready. Within five hours the life-support team in the control shack had blown them down to 500 feet, although of course they remained in the ship. Some men would not emerge from the chamber for forty-two days.

Mike O'Meara had already told the divers what their schedule would be before they reached the wreck. 'When we get you to 500 feet we'll stabilise you there for six hours,' he had explained at a briefing. 'After that we'll take you to 750 feet; then we'll go down at half rate. The exercise will take between twelve and fourteen hours. By the time we come to dive you should be in good shape already.'

'Scouse' Cooper was no stranger to saturation diving, although he – like everybody else – had never been down to 800 feet within the Arctic circle. 'When we go into saturation we don't feel any physical difference at all,' he said. 'There is no illness or stiffness. You get tired more than anything else. You try and relax and read and you're a little bit on edge because you have to dive. It is quite weird, but surprisingly after a few minutes inside everybody acclimatises straight away and you can all understand each other's conversation quite clearly.'

Before they had climbed into the chambers the divers had checked and re-checked the equipment they would rely on to survive at 800 feet. Hot water is vital for the suits; without it, should there be an accident, a diver would die in minutes in the bitterly cold waters.

As the divers disappeared into the chambers on 2 September each shook hands with Keith Jessop and other officials wishing them well. The atmosphere was decidedly that of men going into the unknown and risking their lives in pursuit of profit and challenge.

'This is an historic moment,' commented Igor Ilin solemnly. His Soviet companion flicked through his pocket English dictionary to find the word 'historic'. When he found it he nodded vigorously.

Jessop, his daily routine filmed and photographed for posterity, talked about his feelings now that *Stephaniturm* was so close to the wreck itself. 'We're starting to get the feel of the operation now we're getting near,' he said. 'It's exciting when you see all the equipment that is being brought into readiness. The divers are getting into the feel of things.' But the operation might not go according to plan. 'Things could go wrong with the weather, for example, apart from anything else,' said Jessop, 'but the charts are showing off pretty good just now. There are lots of little problems but at this moment the main problem will be the weather.'

On the ship's bridge the weather forecast spluttered slowly, like a telex message, from one of the machines. The weather was fine and the sea calm, a welcome sentence which was entered into the contractor's log that Wednesday.

Jessop, in shorts and carrying his camera, enthused cheerfully about the divers who would be looking for the bullion within hours now. 'I'm delighted with them,' he said, an older diver commenting on a younger crop. 'Wharton and Williams have brought together a superb bunch of lads. Some of the divers I've dived with in the past and they really are some of the best from the North Sea and around the world.'

John Clarke, OSA's representative, was similarly confident about their chances of success. He had convinced his employers that it was worth deploying *Stephaniturm* on the gamble. At one stage the owners had become sceptical and had considered pulling out of the gold hunt. 'It was a hit-and-miss affair, but when we found the wreck it kept the momentum going,' said Clarke. 'The past three months have been centred on getting all the parties together on this ship. Now, as a marine surveyor, the task is to find *Edinburgh* again. But the risks are there; we don't know if the cargo is still on the ship and whether the technology will work. But we can't get away from the fact that others may have been there already. Moreover, it's possible that the cargo could have fallen out at the time of the action in 1942.'

Such potential nightmares had occupied the minds of officials for months. Now the problems were narrower and grouped around the challenges the divers would meet at 800 feet, whether or not the 'cargo' was there – for officials on board rarely mentioned the word gold at this stage, believing it smacked too coarsely of treasure-hunting.

Mike Stewart, who had overall charge of the divers, looked out at the Barents Sea and talked about his team. 'Half of the problems of a job like this is getting the right people,' he said. 'They've got to have a dual role; it's no use a man being just a life-support team member, he's got to be a nurse as well.' Most men were competent in more than one skill on board. 'We're not in the normal environment of the North Sea where you have the psychology of having a periphery of help,' he added. 'The logistics of keeping the guy on the sea-bed is one problem, but it's got to be the right person. I wouldn't say we have the best team, nobody can ever say that, but we have a strong band of people. They've got to cut into the wreck using their dual skills. Some have had a lot of time disposing of unexploded ordnance. They're all burners who know how to cut metal, but there's also a coded pipe welder, who has spent years cutting, and an underwater photographer who can also burn well.'

Stewart stressed that 'whatever the target' his main aim was to 'bring the complete team back in one piece'. Although Jessop Marine had told the British government that their consortium was 'all-British', the truth was rather different. *Stephaniturm*'s captain and crew were German, and the divers ranged from Australians, New Zealanders, South Africans and a man from Zimbabwe who had served in the Rhodesian SAS. But there were a good number of British divers, along with the life-support team. And the one American on board, Don Rodocker, who supplied the special diving helmets, would turn out to play a vital part in the operation.

For the outsiders some of the divers might appear incorrigibly lighthearted about what lay ahead. In spite of *Stephaniturm*'s captain declaring the ship 'dry', some divers had drunk heavily before going into the compression chambers. 'We're all taking it seriously,' explained Keith Cooper, 'but we've had to treat everything as if we were enjoying it. If you didn't enjoy it you couldn't put up with some of the hardships.'

Cooper explained that many divers were attracted by the excitement of the job. In the early days men could work on the sea-bed without having a supervisor watching them too closely. Now that was all changing, and with video cameras the diver was directed increasingly from the control shack on the surface. 'I've been caught up in the whole *Edinburgh* story,' said Cooper, 'and this gives another dimension to the dive. Compared with the North Sea this is quite different.'

For some divers work in the North Sea was often repetitious, sometimes even boring. Many realised that at 800 feet they would not be able to move at the speed they could at shallower depths. Some had been made apprehensive by the constant references to the depth and to the added danger of icy-cold water. Worldwide public interest had also brought a certain strain to the work ahead. 'But when you get on the bottom,' thought Geoff Reudavey, 'and you leave the bell you're going to be free from all top-side interference. You will be the man.'

Several divers took six months off each year to recover from the pressures of deep-sea diving. 'When you come back you ask yourself whether you can still do it,' said Cooper. 'But as soon as you get out from that little black hole at the bottom of the bell you know you can.'

One diver expressed fears about *Stephaniturm*'s DP (dynamic positioning) equipment, the thrusters which would keep the ship hovering carefully above the wreck. 'Being at 800 feet on DP and being in the wreck at the same time hasn't been done before,' he said quietly. 'The thought that the DP could take off, with the diver well inside the wreck, is always going to be in your mind.' Most agreed that if they considered every problem they might face on the sea-bed they would probably refuse to go down. There was a 'calculated risk' that only the sight of the gold would help to alleviate.

At 10.35 a.m. on 3 September, *Stephaniturm* drew closer to 72°04′ North 35°01′ West, the established position of the sunken warship. On board there was an air of expectancy only slightly dulled by fears that the wreck would not be located a second time. By midday, with the ship's powerful thrusters down, Ronnie Götz began searching for *Edinburgh*.

Ninety minutes later Andy North of Racal Decca found that two of the pingers left behind during the *Dammtor* expedition were dead. But then he succeeded inactivating the remaining Aquafix beacon which had been left behind when the wreck had first been found in May. So in a southerly Force 4 to 5 wind *Edinburgh* was found once more. The time had now come for Keith Jessop and his divers to find out what cargo might rest inside her.

8

The Dive Begins

In the early hours of Friday morning, 4 September, one of the large video cameras, welded to a conical steel frame, was lowered 803 feet to the sea-bed. But a fault developed and it was soon replaced by the pan-and-tilt camera. Soon the ghostly images of *Edinburgh* could be viewed on monitors in the control shack and the recreation room. Men gathered around the TV screens to examine what appeared to be one of the holes made by the German torpedoes that sank the cruiser.

Even now some expressed doubts that the *Dammtor* really had found *Edinburgh* in May. In London, Department of Trade officials were told that Jessop Marine may simply have located HMS *Trinidad*, another cruiser which had sunk in May 1942. But the warship, which Admiral Bonham-Carter had made his flagship after *Edinburgh* had been sent to the bottom, went down 200 miles away. Several men on board, including members of the German crew, wondered if they were hovering over the *Hermann Schoemann*.

Such an ironic possibility was not lost on Keith Jessop and other anxious officials on board. Soon they would know if they were on the right wreck or not. In the first compression chamber three divers prepared for the first bell run. Nearby the day-shift life-support team under Cyclops talked over their headphones to the three men. Already they spoke with the distinctive so-called 'Donald Duck' squeak which characterises divers' voices pressurised at depth.

Putting three divers in the bell, rather than two, was a controversial decision. Some felt that even with two divers the bell would be cramped; three might prove impossible. But the divers had agreed to try. With three men on the sea-bed, two of them could work around the wreck while the third would remain as an observer inside the bell.

By 4 a.m., the three waiting divers had clambered into the half-ton diving-bell, and six minutes later the space-age module was in the water. But 'Banjo' West, Legs Diamond and Brian Cutler soon had their attempt aborted. The diving superintendent, Mike O'Meara, explained that with three men plus their equipment the bell had proved to be too cramped. This, together with a slight build-up of CO_2, had made the men exhausted. The disappointed divers reappeared in the *Stephaniturm*'s moonpool, a hole in her bottom, and worried officials began taking stock of what had gone wrong.

After noting that the bell had reached 756 feet during the aborted dive, but without divers leaving the bell, Cyclops wrote 'exhaustion' in capital letters in the control shack log. John Clarke, who had at first agreed to keep Jessop's log, which every contractor is obliged to do, preferred to use the word 'fatigue' in his written account of the incident. For the divers themselves the experience had been more dramatic. 'With all that extra equipment we tried to do too much at one time,' explained West. 'The umbilicals for a start were longer, much longer, than we would use in any oilfield diving.'

What worried Mike Stewart was that the three divers had been trying too hard. In preparing for the operation they had become almost over-enthusiastic and had been told to take it easier. Energy had to be expended gradually or the divers would quickly become too exhausted to be useful. 'It probably was our fault on that first bell run,' conceded West. 'We were trying to work at the rate we normally would at any other depth. And, of course, it isn't any other working dive. This is a one-off.'

But feeling fatigued and cramped in the bell was by no means the only problem of Dive 1. In the control shack life-support team technicians had monitored a steady build-up of CO_2 gas, long before the divers were fully aware of the danger. 'We could have blacked out because we hadn't really noticed it,' said West. 'We were told afterwards that we could have just snuffed ... well, I won't say snuffed, but definitely blacked out.' If the men had become unconscious they would have been unable to employ the scrubbers which absorb the noxious gas. In fact, but for prompt action on the surface, the three divers, West, Diamond and Cutler, could have died.

Eight hours after the emergency the bell was back in the water, this time with only two divers inside. At 4.26 p.m. Geoff Reudavey, hot water circulating around his black rubber suit, looked out of the suspended bell now over the wreck. For two minutes he stood in respect for the men who had gone down with *Edinburgh*. It was, he said, a private gesture and nobody had suggested he make it. Over his headphones the Australian then said that he wanted more heat in his suit, and in the control shack on the surface a technician happily obliged. Dave Keene, wearing blue jeans and a special £9,000 gold Rolex, logged the first diver's progress as he moved across the sea-bed carrying his umbilical behind him. Reudavey was running a line from a beacon which would help *Stephaniturm*'s captain position the ship above the wreck with remarkable accuracy. 'Before I got back into the bell I had a look at the torpedo hole,' said Reudavey later. 'Wow, man, it's gigantic.'

Soon, Pete Summers had taken over from Reudavey, whose responsibility was now to monitor as best he could Summers' work near the towering wreck. Keene decided to lower the camera for a closer survey of the wreck's exterior. Summers had found several ammunition boxes, but nothing to identify them as British.

Close to the control shack Stewart and Clarke studied the TV monitor in a small cabin they had turned into a makeshift office. Ilin and Melodinsky, along with Jessop and other spectators, were asked to use the monitor in the recreation room; the office was too small for everybody to crowd in.

On the sea-bed, Summers was breathing noisily, a bubbling sound which could be distinctly heard at different squawk-box positions on the ship. Don Rodocker, the American who had provided the diving helmets, was irritated that Summers was using the 'open circuit' rather than the 'recovery circuit' facility on his helmet. 'Goddammit, we're losing precious gas whenever a man goes on open,' Rodocker complained to the day-shift team in the control shack. By recycling the 1,500,000 cubic feet of gas the expedition had loaded at Peterhead there might just be enough to last until the project was over. But some divers were uneasy using 'recovery circuit', claiming that 'open' gave them an 'extra lift' during their shift. 'That's baloney,' said Rodocker, 'and I know because I'm a diver.'

Rodocker would later explain at length just how safe his recovery system could prove in such a remote part of the world. For the moment he kept reminding the diving supervisors that the divers 'must' keep on recovery and 'save the goddam precious gas'. On Dive 3 Cyclops, wearing a bright orange boiler suit for his night-shift, took the point. The log-book that morning contained the entry: 'On the next bell run divers *must* go onto reclaim.'

If a slight squabble had broken out between one or two divers switching to open circuit breathing, louder rumblings were taking place elsewhere in the ship. Ilin and Melodinsky were demanding more information about what was happening around the wreck. On Dive 3 the pan-and-tilt camera had apparently become entan-gled with the bell's umbilical and the flow of pictures had ceased to arrive on the TV monitors.

David Keogh, the British government representative, who in addition had a watching brief for the Salvage Association and was the ship's padre, had the special task of seeing that the two Soviet officials were happy about the operation. Ilin and Melodinsky were becoming increasingly discontented. Officials on board would not allow them to have a copy of the control room log-book, although they could inspect it during their routine visits. Wrestling with the Russians' indifferent, though improving, grasp of English and the thorny problem of a different alphabet, the officials felt at a dis-advantage.

Moreover, one official – to Keogh's dismay – had taunted them in the mess with remarks about salt mines and Siberia; the strain between London and Moscow, in mirror image, began to reveal itself on the salvage ship. Keith Jessop tried vainly to patch over such seemingly inconsequential bad feelings, but on one occasion the matter came to a head. Jessop and Keogh seriously discussed the prospect of having the official in question removed from the ship, a move which was only partly designed to placate the ruffled tempers of the Russians.

Elsewhere others felt grievances, both real and imaginary. John Clarke, unhappy at times about pressmen being on board, discussed the publicity 'problem' with OSA headquarters in Bremen. In a telex message to Uli Reinecke in Germany Clarke said: 'I have instructed that no further press traffic be received or leave this vessel whilst it remains at sea on this operation. The press will also be given the option to leave the vessel on fishing vessel reported to be arriving tomorrow with various supplies.'

Exactly why some of the consortium's officials were nervous about press reports would emerge in the weeks that followed. At first Clarke kept to his ban on 'press traffic' leaving *Stephaniturm* but gradually he relented and allowed telex reports which had been painstakingly vetted, and on occasion censored, by the consortium officials and the British government representative. Only Ilin and Melodinsky showed no obvious concern about what the press might write about the operation.

In the meantime some wondered about the small, sprightly man with the wispy beard. Dr Sidney Alford, wearing a blue T-shirt with 'Université de Paris' in white letters across it, spent hours in his blue container-cum-room on the stern. In spite of now socialising in the recreation room at night, where he became the ship's Scrabble champion, the mystery figure refused to disclose why he was on board the *Stephaniturm*. In his charterer's cabin Jessop said he had no idea why Alford had joined the expedition. Keogh, who shared a cabin with Alford, also claimed he knew little about the man's work. 'I'm a chemist and interested in artifacts which might be found on HMS *Edinburgh*,' Alford would tell outsiders who questioned him. 'For the time being that is all I am going to say.'

Meanwhile, divers had begun cutting their route into the warship. Unfortunately an entrance could not be made through the vast torpedo hole, which was littered with débris. In London Stewart had taken divers on an inspection of *Edinburgh*'s sister ship, HMS *Belfast*, now moored permanently on the Thames. On *Stephaniturm*, armed with a blueprint of the cruiser's superstructure, Stewart had reminded people what they had learned from the *Belfast*. 'First of all we have got to establish exactly where we are on the wreck,' he said. 'We have got to measure our exact cutting position, which is below the armour plate, and cut a hole into the fuel tank there and find out what may be in there. It should be a void but it might not be and once we have cleared we can begin cutting and find out.'

On the other side of the bulkhead, or wall, where the divers would cut were bomb racks storing ammunition for *Edinburgh*'s Walrus aircraft. 'With bombs possibly there you could get a bloody great bang, and so it is very dangerous. We've got to find the best, and safest, place to begin cutting.' Down on the sea-bottom, more than 200 feet the height of London's Post Office Tower, men were having to translate surface theory into hard reality on the wreck.

'Banjo' West and Legs Diamond had recovered from their ordeal in the bell, and on Dive 5, on the night of 5 September, Diamond reported that the bomb-room bulkhead, behind which should lie the bullion, seemed to be intact. In poor visibility, and hampered by sludge and assorted débris from the wreck, no diver could be absolutely certain of what he had seen and reported to surface control.

But Diamond and West had established that they were working at Section 93 on *Edinburgh*'s port side. The control room log-book records their findings on their shift: 'Bulkhead number 93 intact. Compressor room. Deck has split and machinery is showing. Débris consists of pipe work . . . bomb-room bulkhead is exposed from w.t.b. [water-tight bulkhead] to torpedo damage in a strip approximately four feet deep.'

Such sea-bed-to-surface reports meant clearly that this operation was not going to be a simple walk into the wreck and a rapid exit with the bullion, should it be found. In spite of the cruiser's remarkably solid outside appearance her innards amidships had been gravely shattered by the first torpedo. The divers were going to be in for a long haul on their inch-by-inch path to the gold.

Reports of some of the divers' emotional reactions to working on *Edinburgh* were also being heard on *Stephaniturm*. 'Shock and the word incredible have been used too many times,' said West, when describing his first sight of the wreck. 'I really don't know another word to express the feeling. I stepped out on the bottom of the bell weight, with the lights on the ship's hull and, really, it was just massive . . . And the amazing thing that I noticed after being down for five, ten minutes: there are no fish, hardly any sea life. And the torpedo hole was big enough for a detached house to fit inside.'

So far the operation had been relatively fortunate with the weather. But nine days after leaving Peterhead the divers had to suspend work on the wreck because of a rising swell and rough seas. Although they were many days' work away from the bomb-room the divers were in need of a respite. Brian Cutler had reported a slight stomach upset and soon afterwards West and Diamond began to have severe headaches and to suffer from motion sickness.

When diving resumed the next day Keith Cooper and Jim Tucker slowly burned their way through the inch-thick armour plating. Despite the awesome prospect of cutting in almost pitch blackness, and the risk of unexploded shells, some divers offered to stay out from the bell for longer than their four-hour shifts demanded. 'I feel okay,' said Brian Cutler on Dive 10, 'so why not stay out a bit longer?'

Just after midday on Wednesday 9 September people gathered on *Stephaniturm*'s main deck in an impromptu ceremony to watch the first relic from *Edinburgh* being hauled from the freezing Arctic waters. There came no trace of the gold which Keith Jessop believed to be on board but a jagged-edged, oil-splashed, 3 ft by 2 ft 6-inch steel plate which the divers had just finished cutting from *Edinburgh*'s hull.

For all the attention, nostalgic comments and camera-clicking that symbolic slice of wreck evoked, it might have been made of solid gold. Once the crane had swung the metal plate on board, it was placed, not as a piece of scrap, but in the makeshift bullion room now awaiting the £45 million in gold.

If occasional Force 8 to 9 gales and moderate, sometimes heavy swells were hampering the painful but steady progress it was really the warship that was providing the biggest obstacle to finding the treasure. *Edinburgh* was necessarily a steel fortress, and despite nearly thirty-nine years on the sea-bed she was proving a formidable challenge to the divers and their back-up team on the surface. *Stephaniturm* and the technology she carried were impressive, but the wreck was resisting her advances.

'You've got to remember we're working at a world record depth for a salvage operation,' Stewart would tell the Russian officials, anxious to press ahead. 'Inside the wreck there is often no visibility because of the sediment kicked up by the divers and cutting equipment. We've not only got to cut our way in laboriously, inch by inch in some parts, but we've also got to ensure we can get out again.'

Forgetting the often heavy weather on the surface and the odd technical hitch with the cutting gear and the cameras, the project planners were delighted that they had correctly pinpointed the position on the wreck's hull to start cutting with their burners. 'By using the cruiser's original construction drawings,' said John Clarke, 'we've been able to measure up from the bilge keel to the armour-plating point we were seeking, to plus or minus an inch accuracy. Whatever diversions we may have to make en route to the bomb-room, we're confident we're in the right place.'

Morale on board appeared to rise and fall rapidly, just as the ship's barometer on the bridge had done during the past seven days. The divers were working their two-man, eight-hour shifts and were still being carefully watched on the TV monitors, when the cameras were working on the sea-bed, and were loudly cat-called or cajoled whenever they put a rubber fin wrong. Once they completed a dive the supervisors would analyse their achievements as if they were professional footballers after an important game.

Although the divers were among the most experienced and talented in the world, a few, mainly for medical reasons, were slowly running into problems which would need the skills of a doctor rather than a paramedic. The divers' curse, ear bacteria, and the strain of working long hours at such a depth were beginning to take their toll.

West, Diamond and Cutler were told to take a premature rest in their compression chamber. There, the life-support teams could try to cure the ear infection which had struck West and Diamond and to treat Cutler's burst eardrum as best they could. Because the men were in saturation and it would take some ten days to bring them out, medical attention had to be given over headphones and the TV monitors.

Stewart realised that the expedition would need a doctor. A helicopter was not really feasible because of the range and the uncertain weather conditions. On the radio telephone link to Wharton-Williams in Aberdeen Stewart outlined the dilemma. He also mentioned that they were short of ear-drops and drugs which would help West and Diamond and reduce the danger of the infection spreading to other divers. The ear bacteria are highly contagious as well as being extremely painful; a break-out of the problem could ruin the operation before it had even reached the bomb-room.

Exactly who had forgotten to pack enough drugs on board nobody was prepared to say. In Aberdeen Malcolm Williams promised to send out a special consignment of ear drug; hopefully they could find it in Aberdeen, if not, they would have it collected in London. The need was now becoming urgent, particularly as other divers might catch the infection. Sidney Alford, the mysterious chemist who hinted darkly of Ministry of Defence connections, volunteered to try and make the drug on board *Stephaniturm*. Alford had brought no test tubes with him, perhaps unusually for a chemist, and he was forced to make several crude tubes out of some glass rods he had found.

David Keogh discussed the problem with Ilin and Melodinsky. In a radio call to John Jackson at the Salvage Association in London, the MoD official asked if the Soviet Air Force might be able to help. Jackson agreed to speak with the Russian representative at the Soviet-owned Black Sea and Baltic Company. Hopefully the Red Air Force would oblige with medical supplies and drop them by parachute close to the salvage vessel.

Fortunately, Stewart had other divers who could take the place of the three sick men. On Thursday, 10 September, Dougald Mathison from Scotland and John Rossier from Zimbabwe prepared for their first trip to the Arctic sea-bed.

In the meantime there had been another minor incident. Pete Summers, who had been burning with his torch at Section 87 of the warship, suffered a 'blow-back' of oxygen, a familiar enough occurrence for many North Sea divers. Summers was particularly grateful for his space-style helmet, which took part of the blow. But although the diver had experienced a nasty thump on his chest and a smashed welding visor, he was not injured sufficiently to stop diving on subsequent shifts. Nobody bothered to record the matter in Jessop's log and neither did the technicians keeping the control shack log.

On 7 September Malcolm Williams was alarmed that a newspaper report in the *Sunday Times* had mentioned experiencing problems on the sea-bed. In particular he was concerned about a reference to one diver suffering a 'blow back' while he was cutting into the *Edinburgh*'s hull. In a telex to the *Stephaniturm* he said: 'Re:

Sunday Times article – we will obviously continue to have minor
diving problems and they make dramatic reading for the public.
Please arrange to remove similar references to diving problems in
any future despatches.' Whatever the reality might be on board the
salvage ship, 2Ws were not always anxious for the public to read
about it.

While Stewart waited for medical supplies that would take days
to arrive and Alford made up stop-gap potions that proved inadequate, the operation settled back to work. Every diver now knew
that they were the first salvors on the *Edinburgh*, for nobody else
had attempted to cut a route towards the bomb-room.

But were they working on the right warship? During one dive a
dinner fork was found along with a tea-pot and some oil-stained
papers. When the bell returned to the moonpool on *Stephaniturm*
men in the control shack were able to examine the artifacts which
had been uncovered inside the wreck. One former diver, who had
served in the Royal Navy for twenty years, examined the fork carefully. 'Typical Royal Navy issue,' he told his colleagues in the control shack. 'God, that brings back memories, I can tell you.'

Another man turned the fork over and noticed a tiny crest on the
back. In the middle of the engraving was a Nazi swastika; the fork
was German. For a few seconds it appeared to people standing
nearby that the salvage ship could be hovering over the wrong
location. 'We're on the *Hermann Schoemann* and not the *Edinburgh*,'
commented Rolf Nommensen, the wireless operator, who was passing by. Others joined in the light-hearted speculation.

Keith Jessop, who had shown a certain anxiety at the news about
the fork, began laughing broadly. Divers had also spotted and recovered a pad of Royal Navy message forms which had survived in
the deep water. So too had a Navy-issue tin of Brasso. 'There's no
doubt the lads are on the *Edinburgh*,' said Jessop, still smiling. 'At
this stage in time we've got to expect the divers will find all kinds of
unusual things.'

The fork with the Nazi swastika was probably taken from a gun-
boat which the *Edinburgh* had captured several months before she
sank. Sidney Alford, now describing himself as the project's arch-
aeologist, began restoring the message forms which had been found.
In his cabin he diligently separated the thin brown sheets in a

hand-basin with the affection of a scholar examining the Dead Sea scrolls.

Alford's cabin companion, David Keogh, was not altogether happy about *Edinburgh* artifacts being hauled to the surface. The MoD official also represented the War Graves Commission, along with his numerous other roles, and it was his responsibility to see that the wreck was treated with respect.

Inexplicably for some, David Keogh had not been given permission to keep various artifacts on board. A message from the MoD's naval law division instructed him to return each item hauled to the surface, except, of course, for the gold. Between dumping shells and bombs from a rubber dinghy, Sidney Alford helped others throw back some of the ship's trollies, chunks of the *Edinburgh*'s hull and other less romantic mementoes taken from the cruiser.

To underline the point Peter Blaker, Minister of State at the MoD, sent a telex to the *Stephaniturm*. 'I should explain . . . that it is not the MoD policy to allow any interference with a war grave,' he said, 'and I regret that no artifacts/memorabilia from HMS *Edinburgh* may be brought back.' But like the odd naval order in wartime, the MoD's instruction was deftly ignored and one or two 250 lb bombs, some pom-pom shells, gold boxes and trollies were quietly smuggled back home. And why not? After all, for some of those who would not be taking back a gold bar an *Edinburgh* souvenir was the next best thing. 'I've done my best to stop it,' said Keogh wearily, aware that his charges on board were not always as obedient as he might wish.

Keogh was also worried about the security aspect of artifacts which might come to light. With two Soviet officials on board he did not want Royal Navy message pads falling into Russian hands. When he demanded to vet a *Sunday Times* despatch, which mentioned artifacts, he wrote neatly in green ink against the reference to the message pads: '*Definitely Not*'. 'Once the Russians know there are message pads down there they might try and recover them,' he explained. He did not want a reference to them in any newspaper. Luckily for the reporter, perhaps even for Moscow, other officials on board were not particularly concerned about message pads, many of them dated 1941 and oil-stained and all of them blank, falling into Communist hands.

In their compression chamber, 'Banjo' West and the two other sick divers returned to the sedentary existence of life in a narrow tube. West likened the experience to being locked for weeks on end in a small bathroom. Naturally the men were disappointed that ear problems had forced the diving superintendent to pull them off the job. Once they got out of saturation, and were fit, they would return to ordinary deck-hand work – and thereby lose money.

'We accepted, of course, that infections in the chamber could jeopardise the whole operation,' said West back on the surface. 'If this were to spread through the chamber the whole operation could be called off within a couple of weeks. But the pain increased and we had to stop. I've worked on the *Edinburgh*'s hull but I am disappointed I've not actually had the chance of picking up a gold bar myself. But this is the type of thing which happens in the diving game. All the divers have worked together before and they all understand. They are the only people that I need account for and I don't have to stand up and prove anything to anybody else.' But if he recovered in time, would he go back again on the wreck? 'Without a doubt,' replied West unhesitatingly. 'Marvellous. Once in a lifetime, or maybe twice. Who knows?'

With medical problems and technical hitches affecting some of the diving equipment a few discordant voices raised doubts about the project's ultimate success. After more than a fortnight on the salvage vessel some believed that Keith Jessop would never recover those elusive tons of Russian gold. Many more were equally vocal and still convinced the bullion would be found.

'Think positive,' said Jim Lingetwood from Aberdeen. 'We'll do it, you'll see, but in our own time. This was never going to be a forty-eight-hour job. The divers are worth more every time than the cargo we're after. We'll bring them both back to the surface safely, you'll see.' The deck-hand, who wore a black Thomas More hat in bad weather, to lend an unexpected Renaissance touch to the scene, brought a lump to the throat of those who heard his firm confidence in the mission's outcome.

By Dive 18 Mathison and Rossier were finding more shells and bombs near to the bomb-room bulkhead. The day before, Keith Cooper had reported that he was looking into the bomb-room through a split in the thick metal wall. Gradually the diver had worked himself inside to take a closer look. 'It was just like a cellar, an old cellar full of rubbish,' he explained. 'But if you touched anything, then the visibility disappeared because of the sediment. So literally all I did was go in and find my way and then wait and let the dust settle. Then I could see part of the bomb-room.'

On the surface Stewart and Clarke waited anxiously to hear whether the bulkhead was still intact, and then if there were any 'great rips' in the deckhead on the starboard side bulkhead. Fortunately the evidence which divers were finding suggested there were no great rips, only the one large hole on the starboard bulkhead through which divers could pass.

When Cooper worked on the wreck he constantly reminded himself about the possibility of the ship suddenly going off DP (dynamic positioning). 'We were thinking about the job, but we were also thinking about the umbilical because there's a lot of junk in there. But you're sometimes wondering about what it'll be like when you get home. What's happening on the surface. What's for dinner.' Cooper had done many hours cutting the large hole through which the divers now entered the wreck. In effect they had burned a massive entrance, far larger than most castle doors. A Royal Navy-trained diver, Cooper knew he had to cut gently because of the unexploded ordnance lying about. Close to the bomb-room was the small-arms ammunition room; shells and bombs were everywhere.

'Obviously, if you're cutting through a piece of ordnance with a small thermal lance you're going to make it go bang,' said Cooper. 'You must keep an eye on where you're going and what you're doing. Instead of making a big cut, make an observation port and feel around for shells and bombs because you're breaking into a bomb-room.' Nobody was certain if the gold had been stored in a bomb-room packed with explosives. Now they knew it was. 'We basically thought it was going to be a lot easier than it turned out to be,' admitted the Liverpool diver. 'And it was turning out to be very difficult.'

When the divers first crawled through the hull and into a fuel tank some were shocked by the débris they discovered in front of them. Apart from the oil sludge and the thick sediment there were the added hazards of jagged pieces of machinery, tangled pipes and even a massive generator. With each minute came the risk that a piece of metal, even the hanging generator, might crash down upon them while they worked.

'Removing the generator and the other débris was a slow and painful process,' said Cooper. 'Partly because of the depth and the fact you get tired so quickly we were finding progress frustratingly slow. You can't really move a box, like you would on the surface, by just picking it up. You have to pick it up and put it into another box for the surface crane eventually to lift it out and dump it away from the wreck.'

Every diver was reporting similar difficulties to the supervisors back in the control shack. Whatever they said was taped on a recorder, just as a pilot's voice is recorded on an aircraft's black box. Sometimes, however, the machine was not picking up the diver's strange 'Mickie Duck' squeak, a fact which startled documentary cameraman Paul Berrif who discovered the fault. If there were an accident on the sea-bed, perhaps even a fatality, inspectors would have no doubt expressed disquiet about the silent and broken tape-recorder.

'Anybody who says they're not frightened when they go into a hole at 800 feet on a DP vessel is not telling you the exact truth,' Cooper continued. 'I don't mean a diver is terrified, just aware of the risks that exist. We were down there for hour after hour, day after day. In fact, I think we cut through three layers of steel before we even got to the bomb-room and we'd had to remove débris before we even got to the layers of plates to cut. When you have no visibility, it's not the easiest thing in the world to do.'

In spite of the difficulties of forcing their way closer to where the gold had been stacked thirty-nine years before, the divers were making progress. Often they were not fully aware if they were always working in the right spot. Fresh divers on the sea-bed, like Mathison and Rossier, had to orientate themselves just as their colleagues had done several days before them.

Mathison was struck by the sight of *Edinburgh* lying like a giant fortress on the bottom. Behind him the suspended bell, which housed Rossier, appeared like a brightly-lit toy. 'I was amazed at its size,' said Mathison after his first dive. 'I was astounded at the damage that was on the wreck. There were buckled plates, and the torpedo hole must have been at least thirty feet across. I suddenly realised why it had sunk.'

Soon the Scot was cutting and pulling at débris with his hands. 'We were singling each piece individually,' he said. 'I always remember one piece, the generator which I think was the biggest piece that did come out. It was quite spectacular to watch it coming out, although at first as it began to come up on the crane the straps started straining and one of them broke.'

When Mathison examined the fallen generator he became aware of its sheer size. Before, the engine had been partly buried in the débris and its real size hidden. Now the diver was not surprised that a crane strap had broken. 'Once it was clear of the hole we had the job of getting rid of it,' he added. 'So the salvage ship was moved and the generator was eventually dropped on *Edinburgh*'s starboard side.'

Yet the diver had not seen the last of the vast engine. 'Each time that we laid it down, it just toppled over the edge,' he said, 'and I couldn't get the strap off it. So we picked it back up again and took it forward of the *Edinburgh* and finally dropped it into the hole where the torpedo had gone.'

By removing the generator the divers had slightly loosened the débris and created more space in which to work. Yet mistakes were still inadvertently made. On two bell runs divers found afterwards that they had been cutting on a deckhead instead of a bulkhead; the discovery was frustrating and time wasting.   When they found their way again divers like Mathison and Rossier began burrowing a path into the bomb-room. 'Piece by piece, that was the way,' Mathison said. 'Just chucking away very small pieces at a time.'

Often *Stephaniturm*'s thirty-ton bright-yellow crane would lift a rectangular metal cage to the surface. The cage would be packed with débris, much of it saturated with oil. A diver would not necessarily know what he was putting into it, only that he wanted the débris out of the way. 'We found, when we were clearing débris to get into the bomb-room, some human remains,' said Mathison. 'Those remains brought the suffering of the men who had died on *Edinburgh* back to light. We were grumping and groaning a bit, silly things like hot water burns and how we were suffering on the job. But it wasn't half the suffering, it wasn't any of the suffering compared with what those men went through when the ship sank. I doubt, had we not discovered any remains at all, we would have thought about it. But actually seeing them and realising what had happened, well, that brought it all to light.'

Mathison's wholly innocent uncovering of human remains on the wreck led soon afterwards to an unfortunate and controversial incident on deck. When one of the metal cages reached the surface, Sidney Alford spotted human bones; so too did *Sunday Times* photographer Ian Yeomans, who has specialised in medical subjects.

Before the expedition left Peterhead officials said that they did not expect to find any human remains in the wreck. Some believed that any bones would have decalcified after thirty-nine years; others argued that as nobody would have been in the bomb-room when the ship was torpedoed no remains could exist alongside the gold bullion.

But on video film sent from the sea-bed and seen on the ship's TV monitors, a femur had been seen floating with other débris. And now divers had accidentally sent bones to the surface. In an incident witnessed by Yeomans and several other people standing on the stern, human remains, including a femur, were tossed somewhat casually into the sea without any ceremony.

Remarkably, Dr Alford was the person treating the bones of *Edinburgh* victims with apparent indifference. By coincidence Yeomans and cameraman Paul Berrif had been filming at the time, and horrified officials wondered if such unseemly behaviour had been recorded on film. After all, the Anglo-Soviet salvage contract had been awarded on the strict understanding and with a contractual clause to the effect that the official war grave should be treated with 'as little disturbance as possible' and with the greatest respect. The Alford incident could endanger the whole operation; indeed London or Moscow could call it off at any time if clauses in the contract were broken during the recovery attempt.

David Keogh, the War Grave Commission's representative, debated with officials about what he should do in the circumstances. At first he thought the matter best forgotten, but it could lead to complications later. Keogh was well aware that several people had witnessed the incident, including members of the German crew carrying cameras. There was a possibility that the news could get out and cause, said Keogh, 'most unfortunate publicity'.

After pressure from other people on board, the incident was officially noted in Keogh's log-book and a service conducted on the stern by the MoD official acting in his role as ship's padre. Remains were placed on a wooden board, covered by a Union Jack, and then slowly despatched into the chilling Arctic waters. 'One had to put matters right,' explained Keogh.

In the meantime the scientist had apologised profusely for his actions. 'I don't know why I behaved in such a silly way,' Alford explained. He added that his scientific work gave him a view of human remains which he now admitted others might well consider coldly callous and offensive.

Keogh had earlier claimed that he had not expected the press to be present during the venture, and before sailing from Peterhead, Department of Trade official Stanley Holness and Salvage Association spokesman John Jackson expressed surprise that the *Sunday Times* wished to report the operation week by week. They understood that articles would only be written if and when the cargo was recovered. And they wanted articles vetted.

After lengthy discussions on board *Stephaniturm*, Clarke and Stewart had, somewhat reluctantly, agreed that articles 'strictly vetted' could leave the vessel, a demand strongly endorsed by the MoD official. The two Soviet officials who learned that press reports leaving the ship were subject to censorship expressed little concern. But others on board were surprised that the right to report freely from the ship was being denied, even by the MoD official with the green ink in his fountain pen.

For the remainder of the voyage articles were censored, and on one occasion an article was banned by John Clarke from leaving the vessel. This dealt with the unfortunate and unseemly way some human remains on the wreck had been treated, including the fact that a religious service had been held to balance what had happened on board.

Logically there was little way that the news would not eventually leak to the press. Some people, disturbed at what had taken place, were determined to report what had occurred when they returned to Scotland. For the time being the secret would remain on board.

However controversial the human remains incident had been on deck, it had not stopped the work on the wreck for a single minute. But after a fortnight in saturation the divers were tiring fast. When they reached the bomb-room their problems had been compounded by the discovery of 250 lb bombs, shells and other ammunition. Mixed with the heavy ordnance boxes were metal trollies, tons of oil, slime and sediment, and other hefty machinery.

Some of the ordnance found on the *Edinburgh* was brought to the surface to be defused by Sidney Alford, who now shyly admitted not only to Ministry of Defence connections but also to a 'certain knowledge' of explosives. 'That ordnance which had not been affected by sea water,' he explained, 'must be regarded as sensitive as when it was first issued forty years ago. Naturally I treat all such material with caution and so do the divers, I trust.'

Alford was using his converted container on the stern of *Stephaniturm* to stack Second World War Oerlikon shells, .303 ammunition and assorted bomb-ware, like goods laid out neatly in a village hardware store. The Whitehall expert, who played a penny whistle at night, spoke Japanese fluently and was still the ship's Scrabble champion, remained an enigmatic figure. But he had defused a steady stream of potentially dangerous bombs and shells and for that some were grateful. From time to time he would leave the salvage vessel on a rubber dinghy to dump explosives well away from the wreck. The scientist appeared almost grateful that he had found something of a role in the operation, although few were convinced it was the only explanation for his presence. Certainly his patient restoration of Admiralty message pads, which he handed out as souvenirs, hardly justified a berth on an expedition in which there was not even enough space for a medical practitioner.

'The greatest potential danger in the way of bombs are any down there that contain white phosphor and some of the large anti-submarine bombs which the divers have reported seeing on the *Edinburgh* wreck. They're thin-skinned bombs and more liable to corrosion. In fact, they're best left 800 feet down at the bottom,' Alford said.

Although the two Russian observers and Keith Jessop said they still had no idea why Alford was on board, David Keogh admitted that he had been briefed before leaving Peterhead. So too, of course, had divers working on the wreck below. Ironically, a *Sunday Times* report on 4 October, which mentioned Second World War explosives, led to Sidney Alford's real function being revealed. Insurers at Lloyds in London were alarmed to read that explosives were being brought to the surface to be defused by the capable West Country scientist. For the salvage ship was not insured to carry explosives of any kind, even Second World War ordnance which had been in the water for almost forty years.

'That article caused a storm at Lloyds,' explained Jessop's lawyer David Bona. Aptly the *Sunday Times* feature had been headlined: 'Storm halts a golden harvest.' The headline-writers were thinking exclusively about the weather in the Barents Sea at the time. Behind the scenes, underwriters were trying to establish exactly what was on board *Stephaniturm*. Bona was in constant touch with Wharton-Williams and eventually discovered that the diving contractors had hired Alford, a well-known explosives expert in the North Sea, and helped purchase a quantity of modern explosives.

'We were perplexed as to the reason why 2Ws had apparently loaded explosives on the salvage ship,' said James Ringrose, Jessop Marine's operations director back in Britain. 'Our contract was quite clear about the war grave issue and explosives would not, and could not, be employed on the wreck. So why, we asked ourselves, were they on *Stephaniturm*?'

Ringrose had every reason to be concerned about an explosives expert being on board, along with a quantity of explosives. In time crew members had disclosed that if the divers could not cut their way into the bomb-room Alford would help them blast a quicker route into the wreck. Such a plan appeared to be in direct contradiction with the spirit and the clauses of the Anglo-Russian contract. Using explosives, however carefully, on an official war grave must risk offending the *Edinburgh* Survivors' Association and others who had already alleged that the recovery operation was 'sheer desecration'.

'Let me tell you that if we don't get into the bomb-room soon we have enough explosives to break that ship apart,' said a senior member of the diving team. 'Make no mistake, there's so much gold in prospect, and so much money invested, that explosive charges will open up the *Edinburgh*, section by section.'

Faced with such unofficial disclosures, Sidney Alford began to

speak more openly about his real purpose on board. Divers agreed
that they had been instructed in the use of explosive charges before
the salvage ship had left Peterhead. Dr Alford, who had arrived in
Aberdeen covered with a coat on the back seat of a car, was the
expert who would be directing the clandestine operation should the
need arise. And it was the scientist with the wispy beard who had
given divers the confidential briefing at dawn on 28 August, a few
hours before *Stephaniturm* left for the Barents Sea. Dr Alford's secret
mission, or at least part of it, was becoming known.

From inquiries made on the ship and later on shore, it appeared
that Wharton-Williams might also be anxious that observers on
board did not become aware that the *Stephaniturm was* carrying explosives and that these were for possible use on the wreck. Moreover,
from subsequent discussions with the diving team it emerged that
'everybody knew Sidney' in the North Sea, whilst Alford himself
claimed that he worked for the Ministry of Defence, sometimes
through a security company in Belgravia, London.

The scientist eventually admitted that he had bought £2,000-
worth of explosives a few days before the *Stephaniturm* left Scotland.
'I was told the job was very secret and that my presence was not to
be known until we had left Peterhead. Even other members of the
consortium on board, like Keith Jessop, did not necessarily know
who I was or why I was there.'

On board the *Stephaniturm* Keogh, who had helped Alford prepare
several explosive charges, said: 'The charges were prepared because
it was discovered that there were bombs near where the bullion was
stacked. There could have been a build-up of gas and that could
have led to divers being killed. Getting into the bomb-room with
shaped charges would have been safer than cutting. In fact none
was used.'

The fact remained that 2Ws appeared to have flouted the basic
principle upon which the contract had been awarded to Jessop
Marine. And outsiders, including Lloyds of London, were asking
why Keogh, who represented the British government, one of the
principals in the Anglo-Soviet agreement, was actively helping to
prime powerful explosive charges which might be used on an official
war grave. The enigma would not be answered until later in the
voyage when the use of explosives was actually attempted.

For the moment Bona and Ringrose were content to tackle the first part of the controversy surrounding explosives being on board. From Aberdeen, Ringrose commented: 'We were absolutely horrified to learn that explosives had been taken on board the salvage vessel, along with an expert who had been employed to place them on the wreck should the need have arisen. In my view this was not only dangerous but could have affected the outcome of the venture.' In fact Jessop Marine's lawyer confirmed later that they had written assurances from Wharton-Williams that no attempt would be made to use explosives.

The entire salvage operation had become somewhat obsessed with conspiratorial schemes, so much so that three parties in the consortium (the exception being Racal Decca) were not keeping each other fully informed of their activities. In the lust for secrecy it was Keith Jessop who probably had the most to lose.

Wharton-Williams would survive to work on in the North Sea; Bona and Ringrose would soon find fresh professional work, and OSA's *Stephaniturm* would be offered new challenges somewhere in the world. Only Keith Jessop really faced possible ruin and calamitous loss of face.

Nowhere in the world, in September 1981, were there so many hopes of overnight riches pinned on one's man's simple dream of finding gold on a remote ocean sea-bed. Jessop was poised to gain more than a king's ransom and, in the event of failure, to lose nothing more than his reputation and future as a salvor. Wharton-Williams and OSA would make a very considerable fortune and so, too, would other speculators who, far more privately, had invested their money in the Barents Sea gamble. Even some of the divers stood to take home about £30,000 apiece if they successfully re-covered the bullion.

By Dive 27 on Wednesday, 16 September, it was considered safe enough for men to work in the bomb-room. There, where the gold was believed to lie in rectangular deal boxes marked in Cyrillic, John Rossier, a twenty-eight-year-old Mexican-moustached diver from Zimbabwe, was loading a metal basket. By 10.30 a.m. *Stephaniturm* moved four metres starboard to allow its thirty-ton crane to bring the basket to the surface. Seven minutes later diving supervisor Dave Keene in the control shack told the bridge to move the ship four metres to port.

The day before, at 4 a.m., the Norwegian trawler *Lars Christiansen* from Vardo arrived at *Stephaniturm*'s location with much-needed medical supplies, back-dated newspapers and the first direct contact with the outside world for almost three weeks. But the ear-drops and other medication for the divers were wrong and another diver, this time the experienced Keith Cooper, was having severe ear-ache. It appeared likely that he too had caught the sea-bed infection bacteria.

Before the trawler began its twelve-hour journey through choppy waters to Vardo, press cameramen handed over the film they had taken of the operation so far. On Wednesday Clarke and Stewart sent an urgent telex to Malcolm Williams in Aberdeen: 'Suspect article for [*Sunday*] *Times* could have been got through . . . which may not be to our advantage,' began the message. 'Could this be checked?' In fact the trawler had taken off only film, and fears that the press had smuggled off uncensored reports about what was happening on board *Stephaniturm* were groundless. But such a curious message reflected the suspicion which increasingly bedevilled some individual members in the consortium.

Often doubts about what others were doing on board reflected the setbacks which the divers occasionally experienced on the wreck. During dives leading up to Dive 27 there were a number of niggling problems reported. Jim Tucker had experienced hot water problems with his suit and on one dive had had to return to the bell less than an hour after locking out. But as the contractor's log recorded. '[Tucker] reports can see boxes, diver describes boxes seen. Correct description of boxes containing gold!'

Dougald Mathison was already suffering from hot water scalds on his feet, making work particularly painful. The diver knew exactly what had gone wrong and why the hot water had reached his skin. 'Because of the depth of the water we were working in, the hot water had to be very finely set,' he explained philoso-phically. 'There are two heaters in the bell which took three or four degrees off the top of the hot water. When I burnt my feet, I was out of the bell and on the job. Suddenly the heaters in the bell had been switched off by the other diver and the temperature had gone up two or three degrees, which was enough to scald my feet.'

The water has to be hot in the bell to keep the diver warm in the freezing Arctic conditions. Normally it should be 'nice and comfortable' and allow the diver to survive at such depth. When the body becomes cold the diver has to switch on the heat to restore the warmth. 'But when the rest of the body is heating up, your feet are getting scalded,' said Mathison. 'So you just have to grin and bear it until you get back to the bell and get the water sorted out.'

Stephaniturm, which had behaved impeccably since leaving Peterhead, developed 'Number Two' thruster problems just before midday on what would prove to be an eventful Wednesday. Divers, too, were finding that they were still getting the odd snag with their cutting torches; and the water jet which was helping to shift sediment in the bomb-room had a tendency to entangle itself around the diving bell's umbilical.

Mike Stewart now knew more precisely what the bomb-room itself looked like. Vivid descriptions from successive bell runs added greater detail to the information already on the surface ship. Eventually the two diving supervisors, Dave Keene and Cyclops, were sketching rough diagrams of the bomb-room in their control shack log-book.

Then, suddenly, over the 'squawk box' linked to the control room, John Rossier's 'Donald Duck' voice could be heard screaming: 'I've found the gold! I've found the gold!'

9

Discovery

Rossier had been lifting small pieces of metal into an empty basket when his hand felt the heavy slab of gold. The control room log recorded the time as 10.48 p.m. and the larger-than-usual scrawl: 'FOUND ONE BAR OF GOLD.'

Dive 27, which had left the surface at 8.48 p.m. on Wednesday, would prove the first of several celebrated dives during the operation. Jessop's log entry was very similar: '22.48 FIRST GOLD BAR FOUND!!!'

In the control shack duty supervisor Dave Keene called Cyclops, his night-shift counterpart, and told him the news. A roar went around the ship as the first rumour about Rossier's gold bar spread throughout *Stephaniturm*.

While the diver closed his rubber gloves around the smooth bar of heavy metal, weighing 28 lbs, and lifted the ingot slowly up to the level of his helmet's face plate, Keith Jessop slept on in his cabin. A crew member went up to the charterer's cabin to rouse him from a deep sleep. He had been told to tell Jessop nothing about the first gold bar being found. The salvor slowly pulled on some clothes and prepared to go down the two flights of steps before reaching the control shack. Frankly, he said later, he thought another problem had erupted on board, but he was feeling too drowsy to wonder what it might be this time.

With visibility almost nil at 800 feet beneath the surface of the Barents Sea and inside the hull of a sunken ship strewn with débris, where the silt floated thicker than dust in the water, one bit of metal feels very much like another. But gold is different. As Rossier peered at the object he held in his hands he could see clearly from the lights set up outside the bomb-room that what he was holding was not just another piece of wreckage. 'I've found the gold! I've found the gold!' he kept on shouting over the intercom linking him with the diving control room and a growing group of excited by-standers. Melodinsky and Ilin arrived in the tiny room, and their worried frowns turned instantly to smiles. 'People in Moscow will be pleased,' said Ilin formally. Melodinsky nodded.

The first comments were not, perhaps, quite as romantic as the famous cry, 'Wonderful things!', uttered by Howard Carter on first peering into Tutankhamun's tomb. But to men on the *Stephaniturm*, for whom the three previous weeks had been a period of nail-biting tension, the moment was every bit as thrilling.

David Keene was still talking hard into the intercom trying to make himself heard over Rossier's joyful shouts from the sea-bed. 'What is it? What is it? John, you're screaming like hell at me. Christ, my hands are shaking. What are you going to do with it?' Listening to Rossier, who seemed to be executing a slow-motion dance of joy in his diver's suit on the ocean-bed, he added, shaking his head: 'He's flying down there like a doll. Flying like a doll.'

Soon everybody was listening to the commentary, as if it were the opening seconds of a classic Wembley Cup Final report. Everyone, that is, except the man whose dream and concept had been directed for several years towards this one moment and whose company, Jessop Marine, now stood to take £45 million from the *Edinburgh* below.

Jessop had stumbled into the control shack and now began hearing the excited exchanges between the surface and the sea-bed diving team. He simply stood, smiling broadly, saying nothing.

By now the first gold bar had been identified as number KP0620 and checked against the official list which Captain Hugh Faulkner of the *Edinburgh* had carried on its last fatal voyage in May 1942. At 11.05 p.m. Rossier placed the bar in a specially constructed metal cage and watched dimly as a crane on the salvage vessel began to winch it slowly upwards.

Men began leaning over the side of the *Stephaniturm* as the cage, twenty minutes later, broke the surface of a calm sea that clear Wednesday night. In the light of the powerful ship's arc-lamps could be seen KP0620, all £100,000-worth of it, nestling on the bottom of the cage among the débris cleared from the bomb-room.

The cage was swung on to the deck and opened up. Diving superintendent Mike O'Meara reached in and passed the bar in silence to Keith Jessop, who held it lovingly in his hands. Some of the *Edinburgh*'s survivors had described the metal bars they had loaded in Murmansk as looking more silvery than yellow. But now, after thirty-nine years in the icy seas, KP0620 at least was looking decidedly yellow. Surprisingly too, it was clean and turned out to have only minor scratches from the German torpedo explosions which had so damaged the cruiser amidships.

The one group unable to share fully in the excitement were those off-duty divers on the ship who had to stay in their compression chambers on deck so that their bodies, already acclimatised to working at 800 feet, were not exposed to the dangerous atmosphere on the surface. If anybody had opened the circular door to the chambers their bodies would quite simply have exploded.

In the wild excitement which had broken out on board Jessop carried the bar round the chambers to let the divers see what had been found on Dive 27. He held it up so that they could see it through their tiny portholes, and then handed it through the locking hatch so that the delighted divers could pass it around between them.

Minutes later everybody was crowding into the *Stephaniturm*'s mess-room where each member of the crew, including the Germans, was photographed on a Polaroid camera, holding the precious bar. Finally KP0620 was scrubbed down in a bucket inside a makeshift bullion room and was entered as 'Number One' in an inventory agreed beforehand by Jessop and the British and Soviet representatives on board the ship. All of them were now hoping that by the end of the operation, as the *Edinburgh* delivered up the last of its treasure, the inventory would finally number up to at least 465 ingots. Jessop, ever-optimistic, hoped the final tally would be more than double that figure.

Ilin and Melodinsky were particularly interested in the first bar. It was, after all, their gold in the first place, and, after Jessop had taken his share, 45% of it, they would claim two-thirds of the remainder, with the British government locking the final share away in the vaults of the Bank of England. Hopefully, the divers would now find more gold bars where KP0620 had been uncovered.

Two days before the first gold bar was found two Soviet vessels had joined the salvage ship at its remote position in the Barents Sea. One ship, the *Elton*, a converted trawler sprouting antennae which failed to respond to *Stephaniturm*'s calls, was one of the few strangers to have been seen in the area. Its Russian companion, the *Murena*, which the two Soviet officials on board described as a fishing protection vessel, was soon in radio conversation with Captain Ronnie Götz. In the contractor's log the two ships were welcomed: 'We were joined by two Soviet ships this morning, the fishing vessel *Murena*, also vessel *Elton*; nice to have company!'

At first the *Elton*, which was immediately dubbed 'John' by *Stephaniturm*'s crew, spent the whole of Monday morning monotonously circling the salvage ship. It was difficult to see how anybody observing the operation would have seen anything of real interest. The bell was 800 feet below and far from the eyes of Soviet sailors on the two observation vessels.

Occasionally twisted steel plates would be hauled to the surface and dumped unceremoniously on deck. Then there followed a collection of metal trollies which had been found on the *Edinburgh*, three of them still working and with grease thick around their wheels.

Although the *Murena* behaved well enough after she arrived, finding herself a convenient parking spot about a mile astern, the *Elton* began to venture too close for Captain Götz's comfort on board *Stephaniturm*. *Elton*'s inquisitive manoeuvring began to present a real danger to the German ship's dynamic positioning equipment. Because the vessel's position was kept steady above the wreck by computers on board, ensuring that the diving bell did not move close to the sea-bed, there was a danger that a sudden movement by the ship could tear a diver away from his position inside *Edinburgh*'s bomb-room.

Alarmed by the movements of the *Elton*, which sometimes drew less than a hundred yards astern, *Stephaniturm*'s captain threatened to report her to the authorities in Murmansk. 'I don't know if you understand English or German,' said one ship's officer on his radio

on the bridge. 'But you could be responsible for a nasty accident.'
For a moment the diving operation was interrupted.

Fortunately, however, *Elton's* captain decided to move slowly
away, although he resolutely refused to speak to Ilin or Melodinsky
on the radio telephone. Such manoeuvres, with their hint of international intrigue, even possible confrontation, were a welcome relief
for many on board, who were well aware that the operation was far
from over.

But the discovery of the first gold bar raised morale to a new
level altogether. 'I told you we'd get there,' said Jessop, somewhat
minimising the fact that he had only found £100,000 so far. 'You
see, the two Red Navy ships arrived at just about the right time.'
On 15 September, just after supper in the mess, Igor Ilin tried to
reach the Soviet ship *Elton* on the ship's radio but even in Russian
he got no response whatsoever. Even if *Elton's* Russian captain did
not invite the crew over for sundowners, however, there was now
much on board *Stephaniturm* which did give Jessop a constant glow.
But would he find any other bars on the sea-bed?

10

Gold Fever

Early on Thursday morning, 17 September, David Keogh called Jessop Marine's lawyer from *Stephaniturm*'s bridge to tell him the dramatic news about the recovery of the first gold bar. Believing that the salvage vessel was a potential terrorist target the consortium had devised a code which precluded would-be hijackers understanding what was being said on radio and telephone and telex links from ship to shore.

Operation Greyhound's anti-bugging code cipher was based on *Roget's Thesaurus* because David Bona had thought it 'more interesting and complicated' than simply using a standard English dictionary. Keogh's code-name was Henry, his pedigree red setter's name, while Jessop's was Sam, after his Jack Russell terrier. Bona in Manchester would be called Kennel and his secretary, Brenda, Kennelmaid.

'Gold bars would get Christian names depending on how many had been found on the wreck,' explained Bona. 'And each message would begin with the call sign Keeper and end with the signing-off word Collar. In this way we knew nobody else was trying to use our cypher.'

With KP0620 safely locked away in the bullion room on board, Keogh waited for the Norwegian radio station to put his vital call through to Bona in Manchester. Within minutes the link from *Stephaniturm* to Manchester was established.

'Who is that please?' asked Kennelmaid in Manchester. 'This is Sam here,' began Keogh rather hesitantly. 'Correction, this is Henry here speaking from *Stephaniturm*. Over.'

'It's David Keogh for you,' Kennelmaid was heard to say rather indiscreetly as she passed the telephone to Bona. 'Hello,' said the lawyer calmly.

'Hello, good morning, is that Kennel? Over,' asked Henry, adjusting his service tie. 'Kennel speaking,' answered Bona. 'Kennel, this is Keeper,' continued the MoD official from the middle of the Barents Sea. 'Greyhound, Henry, Zero One. Foxtrot, Collar. Over.' Bona repeated Henry's message, but made no comment.

Keogh sounded disappointed that Bona had not reacted to the remarkable news. 'I have one other message for you,' he told Bona. 'I hope you didn't mind being called too early?' The British representative wondered if Keeper in Manchester had properly understood his important message. Or had he not reached for *Roget's Thesaurus* to decipher the Greyhound code?

After a pause Bona replied: 'Congratulations. Over.' Keeper had got the message.

In the meantime Keith Jessop, after carrying KP0620 around the ship like a footballer who had won the Cup Final, had been snatching some sleep. His initial reaction had been rather uncharacteristically subdued, almost shy. 'Happy?' he had asked. 'Who wouldn't be! What can I say?'

In the morning the Yorkshire salvor had got into a mood that verged on gold fever. When he examined the log-book just before breakfast he could see that he was on the way to becoming more than a mere millionaire. Dive 27 had found five gold bars, £500,000-worth of bullion in all, and these were now safely on the shelf on the stern. Although John Rossier had returned to the bell early that morning, saying that he felt sick from a stomach upset, Dougald Mathison had locked out of the bell and over three hours later uncovered four more slabs of gold.

By midday a steady stream of the stuff had been brought to the surface. One of the Russians pointed out the characteristics of Stalin's gold bar. 'You see the marks,' he said. 'Moscow, the number, and the colour, and 999: the very best Soviet gold.'

Just how seriously the Russians took their interest in the bullion was underlined by the two Soviet vessels which had anchored a short distance away from the *Stephaniturm* that remarkable Thursday morning. Whether or not they could tell that the gold had been found nobody on *Stephaniturm* could establish, because they continued to ignore Captain Götz's calls from the bridge. The two ships had been described by the Russians on board as fishing protection vessels. 'Auxiliary intelligence gatherers, AIGs,' said ex-Navy diver Mike O'Meara. 'We know what they are.'

Meanwhile gold bars were becoming commonplace in the El Dorado-like atmosphere in the bomb-room. Before Dive 27 had finished Mathison had been finding gold wherever he looked or felt. At one stage of his shift the log-book read: '04.20: diver back down in the bomb-room. 04.28: diver has one gold bar. 04.29: diver has two gold bars. 04.32: diver has four gold bars. 04.40: diver has five gold bars.' And so it had continued with, on one occasion, £4 million in bullion coming up in the metal cage.

The routine that was established resembled a primitive production line in a factory. Gold bars, once found in the bomb-room, were lifted into the rectangular metal cage. The ship's crane would then take some twenty minutes to bring the cage to the surface. Outside the bullion room, Keith Jessop and David Keogh cleaned and checked every bar. Inside Keogh and Clarke, along with Ilin and Melodinsky, noted each bar's serial number and added it to the growing inventory.

It might be thought that a procession of gold bars appearing on board one after the other might have become a prosaic sight. But somehow the awesome realisation of the wealth they represented never quite wore off. Holding one of the bars in his hand, Dave Keene sighed and said: 'I've got £100,000 in my hand. It looks heavy but it just feels beautiful.'

'Banjo' West, Legs Diamond and Brian Cutler had at last been 'blown back' to the surface and had left their compression chamber. Now they could watch gold coming on the deck and photograph colleagues using them as body-building weights or playing with them like toy bricks.

'The whole scene looks quite bizarre,' said Keith Roberts, one of the life-support technicians. 'It's a bloody miracle,' repeated Keith Jessop as he had his picture taken for the umpteenth time. As he cleaned oil from the bars he would add: 'At this stage in time I don't know how rich I am.' The man with the dream and the £100 company, which had never salvaged a wreck in its short life, had apparently hit the jackpot.

For the divers, however, the work was by no means over. Progress in the bomb-room was relatively slow and there were lengthy periods when no gold was found among the treacherous débris. '*Edinburgh* is a tough ship,' said Jessop. 'The divers are still having to work amid tangled steel wreckage, unexploded ordnance and thick oily sediment.'

But the divers were the real heroes and the operation meant more than just the gold. 'It's not only the money,' said one, 'we also like the record for the world's deepest and richest manned salvage.'

Slowly they were notching up the value of the recovery and turning *Stephaniturm* into a floating Fort Knox. Although the world diving record was more than 2,000 feet, that was achieved in a dry chamber. There was nothing artificial about conditions in the bomb-room. By breathing the special mixture of helium and oxygen the divers could operate at the crushing pressures of around 350 lb per square foot and could now claim that much-prized world record for a saturation salvage operation.

Once John Rossier had found the first bar a new spirit took hold of the salvage vessel. Much had rested on the expedition finding gold; if the divers had found nothing they would have ended with nothing in their pockets, for 'no cure, no pay' was Operation Greyhound's maxim.

Although there were bouts of fevered success on the sea-bed, with bars being found thick and fast, the work was still painfully slow. Gold bars had been found still packed in the wooden boxes where they had first been sorted in Russia. Progress would have been faster if the gold could have been hoisted up in the boxes themselves, but this proved impossible. 'The boxes have sea-worm in them,' explained Mike O'Meara. 'Each box weighs about 130 lbs. and they disintegrate when they're moved with the gold inside them.'

Broken panels from the deal boxes were brought to the surface with the gold bars. Many had the red rivulets on them which one *Edinburgh* survivor, Reg Levick, had told his commanding officer was a bad omen 'and the blood of Russian gold'.

In spite of the consortium's success they were facing worsening weather and other man-made problems related to the project. A

few hours after KP0620 was fished on deck David Keogh had had
to put in an urgent call to John Jackson at the Salvage Association
in London. The two Soviet officials, he said, were becoming 'rather
tiresome' and he wanted help.

'We have a little problem which I would like you to sort out
with Moscow,' the MoD official told Jackson at his office. According
to Paragraph 2J of the Anglo-Soviet contract, a colour photograph
had to be taken on board and given to Ilin and Melodinsky. Photographs were being taken after the gold bars had been cleaned, but
there were no facilities on *Stephaniturm* to develop the pictures.

In their cabin nearby the two Russians, by now the ship's un-
disputed chess masters, waited for Keogh to sort out what for them
seeemed to be a major stumbling block in the operation. Jackson
agreed to help as best he could. After all, he was particularly keen
that Operation Greyhound should succeed. Since Jessop came to
the Salvage Association it had been his responsibility as senior
manager to look after the *Edinburgh* project. Eventually the Russians
on board, with the approval of their superiors in Moscow, agreed
to their getting colour slides of each bar of gold at a much later
date. The problem was trivial but the implications were not;
Moscow could stop the project at any moment it chose.

Meanwhile, just over twelve hours after the gold was first found
in the bomb-room, television reporter Michael Cole was broadcast-
ing the dramatic news over the BBC. Behind Cole's scoop was a
disclosure which was eventually traced back to Wharton-Williams
in Aberdeen. In London, Lloyds, the insurance underwriters for
the bullion, expressed concern at what they described as a leak.

On *Stephaniturm* John Clarke had intended that once the gold
was found it would be kept a tightly-held secret. Operation Greyhound, he and other officials argued, could be of great interest to
criminals and international terrorists. In spite of Red Air Force
planes flying overhead from time to time and the protection of the
Soviet 'fishing' vessel parked close to the salvage ship, Clarke had
been told to take no chances.

On the radio telephone to his employers in Germany Clarke expressed disappointment that the news about the gold had leaked
out to the world. But in such circumstances, he said, he would have
to allow 'so-called controlled publicity' to continue leaving the ship.

'We will vet the outgoing [press] information but we will not reveal the amount of cargo recovered,' said Clarke. In Bremen an OSA director enthusiastically agreed to press vetting and the news black-out on how much gold had been recovered.

In the control shack Dave Keene was talking over his headset to Dougald Mathison, who was just completing the first shift of Dive 30. The supervisor now talked about bullion with all the polished aplomb of a Bank of England official who handled gold every day of his life. 'Dougie, we need another ten bars which will bring us up to around £5 million,' said Keene laconically. 'That will make it a million quid an hour. Is that OK? They're complaining up here that you've only got £4 million in the box.'

The humour was not lost on the quiet Scot on the sea-bed below. In fact, the metal cage could only carry £4 million, or forty bars, on each lift. An extra million would have to wait for the next run before Keith Jessop could begin scrubbing it with petrol and soapy water from a yellow bucket.

In Aberdeen Ric Wharton heard the welcome news that half-a-ton had been landed on deck in one load. He wondered if the bars could be brought up in their original boxes, but Stewart, his project manager, told him it was impossible. The boxes were too flimsy and the débris too tightly packed. Wharton, who has an impressive array of artifacts and other treasures which have been partly collec-ted from the sea-bed, asked if he could have a Russian gold box for his collection. The box would look well in his castle in Scotland. 'If you can get enough pieces of the wood to get us a box I'd very much appreciate it,' said Wharton. 'You know I want to achieve a small collection of [*Edinburgh*] stuff in this place. I want a souvenir after the yellow stuff has gone.' Although Wharton and Williams were supposed to be using a code in their conversations with Stewart, the diving contractors in Scotland had temporarily mislaid their code-book. The men chatted openly on the radio link for anybody – amateur ham or otherwise – to hear.

Stewart mentioned that the subject of souvenirs was a sensitive issue with David Keogh in his function as the War Grave Commis-sion representative. There were other 'trinkets' but the project manager stressed that he had to be 'very diplomatic' about artifacts coming on board. 'I'm sure you can force the issue and make sure enough of that is tucked away,' said Wharton, who added he was aware that the matter was delicate. 'By the way, bring us back some of those trollies, would you? Presumably they were moving the aircraft stuff.'

Wharton was full of praise for the expedition. 'You have the world's congratulations. Frankly to get in to there in thirteen days and start getting it was bloody good. Tell the guys we're watching them close and give them our best wishes.'

The following day Malcolm Williams learned that Mathison had been injured on the wreck. The diver had been taking his helmet off in the bell when he slipped off the ladder in the bell's trap. 'I fell down and landed on my shoulder,' the Scot explained. 'I realised what I'd done right away because I'd done it before. It's not actually dislocated my shoulder, but it's pushed a bone wrong in my shoulder.' With his scalded feet and injured shoulder Mathison was in need of skilled medical advice. But, of course, he was still in saturation and could not be brought out for several days.

Over the radio telephone Williams heard that a doctor might have to be sent out to the salvage ship. Stewart began cataloguing the growing medical problems on board. He had no swab on board to check the ears of the four divers who had been forced to come out of saturation. Now there was the distinct danger that the project would run out of divers before all the gold had been recovered. And the weather was steadily worsening.

'My concern is that as the year is advancing and the season moving on, and now the first big gales starting to come through, well, my big worry is that you're going to get a series of big gales and heavily interrupted diving. I'm afraid you might lose the rhythm you've got into,' added Williams. 'And after almost thirty days divers are getting pretty exhausted and coming to the end of their run. That, plus gas starting to run down, we are running into a situation where we are facing a long hard drag to finish.'

On the bridge Stewart needed no reminding of the major snags which could hinder a relatively smooth-running operation. 'In no way do I want to leave site out here,' said the project manager, 'and I think the vessel owners will probably go along with that.'

But there was a depression coming in fast from the West and a doctor was now necessary to treat Mathison, who was lying in considerable pain in his compression chamber. For the moment Williams thought a doctor would not help. After all, Mathison was still in saturation and a doctor would need to examine the injured shoulder.

Williams had other problems to consider. Gas and fuel supplies on board would need replenishing in seven days' time. There was also considerable media interest in the operation, he said, but 2Ws was not getting sufficient credit. 'It looks like a one-company operation at the moment with references to "Jessop's divers",' Williams said ruefully. 'Maybe you can correct that when the divers in due course are being interviewed.' Later there were to be recriminations about who had performed which task on the operation. Parties within the consortium felt their contribution had been undervalued. But few doubted that James Ringrose had – along with David Bona – probably played the major roles in getting the venture past the slipway stage. The dream might belong to Keith Jessop, but many of the day-to-day headaches had had to be handled by them.

By now the media die was cast and Keith Jessop was being portrayed as the man behind the *Edinburgh* project. Williams might now want appreciation for the fortune and expertise which his company had invested in the salvage plan, but it was rather late to want publicity. In Peterhead the contractor had stressed that his company wanted to keep in the background quietly until they knew the mission's outcome.

But with the expedition experiencing 45-knot winds and Force 8 gales Williams had other tasks to combat from his vantage-point in Aberdeen. There was the fluctuating price of gold on the world's market which affected many people on board. Over the radio telephone Williams reported that in dollars the price had been about $456 to $458 on the day KP0620 had been found. 'The trend has been steadily up,' he said.

For Jessop, gold had also brought a few attendant problems on board. Over the radio telephone he told Bona on 23 September: 'I'd be obliged if you could keep your coded telexes a little shorter because we're working virtually round the clock and your telex this morning took about two-and-a-half hours to decipher. I got the gist of the telex, although I didn't fully understand all of it.'

Bona asked Jessop if he now wanted to order 'certain equipment' which had been mentioned to him by Graham Jessop. With gold arriving on deck hour after hour Jessop Marine had been able to borrow more than £600,000 from Rothschilds, the bankers. Jessop was rapidly becoming rich. In their coded exchanges Bona wondered if his managing director still wished him to order a silver Porsche, a gift which Jessop had always promised himself if he found the gold. Unfortunately for the moment Jessop did not understand what his lawyer had been saying in code and the necessary gobbledegook of the radio telephone.

While Jessop was being asked if he wanted to order his sports car, the operation was facing further problems. Mathison's shoulder seemed to be worsening, along with the weather. 2Ws now decided that they would send a doctor out to the salvage ship. They were also considering the possibility of despatching fresh divers from Aberdeen. But these could not be hired on a 'no cure, no pay' basis now that the gold had been found.

Over the radio, Stewart explained to Williams on 23 September that the divers were becoming exhausted. 'The original divers are definitely showing signs of fatigue,' reported the project manager, 'but no signs of mental fatigue or flagging enthusiasm and I emphasise that. They want to see the job through but it's quite apparent that they are falling off quicker just through straightforward physical fatigue.'

That Saturday afternoon Stewart had established that the divers had removed 1,300 cubic feet of débris. 'The cubic capacity of the bomb-room is 2,300 cubic feet, which leaves 1,000 feet to go,' he said. 'We've approximately over 50 per cent of the cargo on board and that leaves forty-five boxes to go.'

In Aberdeen Malcolm Williams considered the calculations carefully. 'Perhaps there was greater tonnage after all,' he told his project manager. If they did find more than five tons Jessop would be proved right. Coupled with the rise in the world price of gold the consortium would have struck an even greater bonanza than anybody had dared hope.

Remarkably there were men on board the salvage ship who would still endanger the full success of the operation. One of them was Dr Sidney Alford, the mysterious explosives expert. Now the scientist, who had been partly to blame for the incident over the human remains brought on board, was turning his mind to an underwater experiment which had little if anything to do with the aims of the expedition. At the same one diver in the bomb-room was hatching another ruse which would badly backfire and endanger the whole *Edinburgh* venture.

When David Bona learned that explosives had been stored aboard the survey vessel for possible use on an official war grave there followed a series of heated exchanges with Wharton and Williams. The lawyer alleged that bringing Sidney Alford and a substantial quantity of explosives on the *Stephaniturm* was a breach of the Anglo-Soviet contract which Jessop Marine had signed. Moreover, a secret cache of dangerous material put at risk the insurance policy he had taken out with Lloyds and threw doubts on his company's integrity. 'And it gravely affected our credibility with the British and Soviet principals. Either party could have taken us to task over explosives being brought along,' said Bona, who had to sort out the mess from Manchester while the operation continued in the Barents Sea.

Before *Stephaniturm* left Peterhead Bona had received a telex from Mike Stewart confirming that no explosives would be carried on the vessel. 'It is verified that it is not our intention to use explosives to penetrate the wreck but to use conventional cutting techniques which have always been the proposed prime mode of entry.' Stewart went on: 'It is still our plan to proceed as originally planned.'

In July 1981 2Ws gave further assurances that no 'bulk explosives' would be carried on the expedition. But in a telex sent to Bona that same month the company commented: 'But there is no reason why OSA should not carry a selection of shaped charges if they so wish.'

Wharton-Williams apparently saw nothing wrong with employing shaped charges on the *Edinburgh*, although they recognised that if the news leaked out it might prove controversial. Whether they would be used, the telex went on, would be decided 'on site'. 'Sadly to the uninitiated "explosives" generate an emotive reaction,' volunteered 2Ws, adding: 'You have our assurance that explosives will not be used without approval.'

Bona was not reassured and reminded Malcolm Williams that there would be British and Soviet representatives on board. 'The very mention of any proposed use of explosives will undoubtedly cause them to terminate the salvage agreement of the 5th May,' replied Bona in his telex. In the lawyer's view 2Ws were ready to use a 'blast and take' technique which was fundamentally the same as 'blast and grab'.

The summer's discussion about explosives had suddenly turned into an acrimonious autumn row before the gold had even been taken off the *Edinburgh*. When Lloyds heard that unexploded 250 lb bombs, anti-aircraft shells and other ordnance were being hauled on deck and defused immediately above the room where the gold was stored, they reacted sharply. When they then learned there were also modern explosives on board they declared the policy was gravely at risk. But how much did Keith Jessop know about there being explosives on board? As chairman of Jessop Marine he did not know about the devices being stowed on *Stephaniturm*, but he did eventually become aware during the voyage that explosives were locked away on the stern.

While the shaped explosive charges which Alford had prepared in secret no longer looked as if they would be used on the wreck, Bona tried to soothe the rumpled nerves of the insurance under-writers. He could not deny that a quantity of explosives was on board the *Stephaniturm*; eventually it was agreed that the scientist would dispose of the charges, in the same way that he had been dumping Second World War ordnance.

Alford was disappointed that his skills had not been employed. 'I hate to see £2,000 of good-quality explosive get chucked over the side,' he said, staring sadly out at sea. In a radio telephone call with a retired British Army officer, who ran a 'security equipment' company in Belgravia, the scientist again expressed his sadness at not being able to use his explosives. 'I still haven't so far used *the method*,' Alford told the retired brigadier in London. 'I see,' the officer had replied crisply.

In the deliberately cryptic conversation over the radio Alford said he hoped to bring back 'the material' to Scotland, a veiled reference to the explosives he had on board. 'But can you?' asked the brigadier. 'I thought we were disposing of it.' Alford said he still was not quite sure what was going to happen to it.

Clearly the scientist was still keen to try out his explosives, although he was careful not to mention this over the radio. And still only a handful of officials knew exactly what his purpose was on board even at this late stage in the operation. But Alford's secret would soon spill out in a remarkably zany incident involving the two Soviet officials who had eyed him increasingly with perplexed and cautious interest.

For the moment attention turned to the arrival of the doctor who had undertaken the lengthy journey by air and boat to join the *Stephaniturm*. Mike Childs, from Aberdeen, arrived feeling badly sea-sick but soon began to examine the injured divers who had already come out of the compression chambers. 'The special problems of this expedition are because it has been particularly long and a particularly deep dive,' said Childs. 'We're seeing here the standard diving illnesses.'

After strapping Mathison's shoulder and dressing his scalded feet, the doctor began examining the four divers who had caught the ear infection known as pyarhsienius. 'The ear canal can become infected on the surface, but in pressure chambers with an atmosphere of helium and oxygen and with a high humidity, this organism, suomonis, finds the conditions particularly pleasant.' Childs added: 'And the organism can cause infections in the external canal of the ear which it wouldn't normally do on the surface.'

Gradually, by using the one antibiotic which can treat the complaint, Childs observed the sick divers recovering rapidly. Apart from Mathison, the three divers almost immediately began working on deck at a critical moment in the operation.

On the sea-bed men were showing distinct signs of fatigue. Around the ship strain was beginning to show itself more markedly. Dave Keene, the diving supervisor, no longer disguised his concern. 'They're exhausted,' said Keene. 'They've been working throughout at record depths in terrible conditions. They need fresh air to bring them back to their peak, and rest. But we're running out of time.'

The operation was also running out of fit divers, but none were aboard the supply ship *Hafentor* when it arrived from Bremen. The supply ship brought out fuel, water, provisions and stand-by gas for the divers, in case the expedition went much further into October.

At the beginning of the sixth week of the project, Keith Jessop was strongly hoping that, with a little luck from the elements, he could complete the recovery within seven days. But progress on board the *Stephaniturm* was beginning to slow down everywhere.

Derrick Hesketh, the diving supervisor who had been doing twelve-hour shifts day after day, began encouraging the tired divers on the bottom: 'Keep plodding, just keep going with clearing that débris and we'll find more gold.' Fortunately for people's flagging spirits, he was proved right. Only hours before a violent storm, gold was struck again and another forty bars, worth £4 million, were brought laboriously on deck. Mike O'Meara had changed the rectangular metal cage for a canvas bag, which could be handled more easily by the divers negotiating their way inside the wreck.

By the beginning of October, exactly one month after the *Stephaniturm* had begun operations, a Force-11 storm had pushed the ship from its fixed position in the Barents Sea. For forty-eight hours the expedition had to ride out the storm before the divers could return to search for the seventy-nine missing bars.

Already the makeshift bullion room contained nearly £40 million. But with exhausted divers, deteriorating weather and tons of débris still to be cleared, the prospect of recovering every last bar began to fade.

So too, finally, did the hope that the operation would avoid further controversy over the sensitive war grave issue and the human remains already found on the *Edinburgh*. Among a tiny circle of people on the *Stephaniturm* an occasional wry comment had been made about the 'bank managers' which had been uncovered in the bomb-room. Once a reference to human remains had been made in the detailed log-book, only to be scrubbed out soon afterwards. Divers finding human limbs and skulls properly reported the fact to their supervisors over the intercom system. The salvage contract had laid down the procedure to be followed in the case of human remains being found.

But in one incident in the bomb-room, remains – including skulls, one with a large hole at the back of the cranium – were arranged, some with chemical lights in them, to startle the next diver down. This macabre and tasteless 'joke' had offended the vast majority of the divers. One of them, who was being interviewed for the television documentary being produced on board, said: 'The vast torpedo hole can only make one remember how these poor men died. Several of us are pretty disgusted at what happened. It has tarnished a highly successful operation.'

After complaints David Keogh conducted a hasty service and said he would include the matter in his official report. 'I was horrified at what happened,' he said. 'All along we have been trying to avoid upsetting relatives of the men who died. We thought the chances of finding remains were negligible, but we were proved wrong. If we had known there were three corpses in the bomb-room we would never have allowed anybody in. What happened was in bad taste. The divers had been told and told and told to avoid such behaviour.' When a report about the incidents appeared in the *Sunday Times* later in October government officials announced that they would investigate why human remains had been brought to the surface and why there had been unseemly behaviour in the bomb-room.

David Bona later pressed 2Ws on why such behaviour had occurred in the way human remains had been treated on the wreck and on *Stephaniturm*. Williams denied that light-sticks had been placed in skulls and added that whether human bones had been treated 'with reverence or not is a question of opinion, and I cannot comment further on this point'. As to explosives being on board – apparently in breach of the contract – Williams said: 'It is correct that a two-part explosive device and a qualified technician were on board the vessel . . . The contract to carry out this work would not have become effective until such time as a need was required and it was never intended, under any circumstance, that such a device would be used without reference to the principals.'

Oddly, a few weeks before the *Stephaniturm* left Peterhead, a party from 2Ws, including Mike Stewart, had visited Dr Alford's quarry near Pickwick in Somerset, a test-range where explosives could be demonstrated. In spite of the Anglo-Soviet contract ruling out the use of explosives on the war grave, the Ministry of Defence had also visited the test range.

Exactly why Sidney Alford had been attempting to set off an explosive device in Soviet waters used by their nuclear submarines has not been satisfactorily answered. Alford had his own company which specialised in explosives, but a Belgravia company, S & D

(Equipment), appeared to represent the mysterious scientist. On 21 October 1981 Lt. Colonel J. M. Gaff, GM, told David Bona in a letter: 'Dr Alford is . . . specialising in explosive and chemical substances and reactions. He has been employed at various stages by certain private companies and also by the Ministry of Defence. Dr Alford was on board the *Stephaniturm* due to his qualifications and expertise in the construction and use of two-part low-level explosive charges . . . Having regard to the statement that the *Stephaniturm* was stopped at sea during its return journey we can confirm that such action was taken but only with the consent of the contract Principals.'

On board the *Stephaniturm* some saw Alford's attempt to make a loud bang on the sea-bed as roughly equivalent to the Russians – with two British Ministry of Defence officials on board – sailing towards Portsmouth and letting off an explosive device in the Solent. Others speculated that the experiment was some secret MoD mission to register Soviet responses on their sea-bed sonar devices, a claim dismissed by some as arrant nonsense.

By Dive 66 on 5 October, divers were back on the wreck and still finding gold bars. In fact, twenty-five bars, worth over £2¼ million, were brought to the surface just before dawn that morning. But the weather was worsening again. The Russians were formally told that the operation would not go on much longer; gold bars would be left on the sea-bed for another diving season.

On Wednesday, 7 October, Jessop and the consortium decided everybody had had enough. He had recovered 431 ingots valued then at between £43 and £44 million, and it had been a truly remarkable performance. Jessop beamed as he spoke each day to his wife Mildred in Keighley. Over the radio he told her the salvage ship would soon be leaving for Murmansk, 200 miles away. The Russians, he said, were waiting for their portion of the gold, some £16 million-worth.

Before *Stephaniturm* sailed away from the location which had been their home for over a month, Keogh, as ship's padre, held another service for the men who had died on the *Edinburgh*. After the Royal Navy service had been read to a small crowd of British and German crew members, including the two Soviet officials, a plastic wreath was thrown into the choppy grey waters below. 'Banjo' West and

Keith Cooper had been chosen from the divers to throw the wreath over the spot where they too had risked their lives.

The violent storms in the Barents Sea, and the sheer exhaustion of the divers, had prevented the expedition from recovering every last bar of gold on the sunken warship. But 431 out of 465 bars known to be on board the wreck represented a formidable achievement in some of the most difficult deep-sea diving conditions in the world.

Jessop, the newly-fledged millionaire from Yorkshire, was already saying that he would be back the following year to 'pick up' the other thirty-four bars, still worth at current gold prices a cosy £3½ million. 'You never know, there might still be three-and-a-half, or even five, tons more on her,' said the salvor. 'But I'll be back, and there are hundreds of other wrecks I want to do around the world.'

Yet Jessop and his consortium were still not finished with some of the problems which had blemished the *Edinburgh* operation. For it was on the way to Murmansk that the two Russians discovered Sidney Alford's cache of hidden explosives.

Again the circumstances of their chance find were in keeping with other bizarre incidents during the voyage. On the evening of 7 October, the day the *Stephaniturm* had moved away from the wreck, John Clarke had ordered the vessel to stop. Klaus Schlarbaum on the bridge asked Clarke if the captain knew about the unscheduled stop-over? Clarke replied irritably that the captain had been told earlier that night.

The decision to stop the 1,400-ton *Stephaniturm* in an area well within Soviet territorial waters seemed a curious one, but the first officer obeyed the instruction he had had from OSA's representative on board. Clarke disappeared to his cabin and some ninety minutes later the salvage vessel shuddered noisily to a halt. Outside it was cold and snowing lightly and there was a heavy swell.

Clarke had ordered the *Stephaniturm* to stop at night to allow Sidney Alford to try an experiment with one of his underwater explosive devices. At 10.20 p.m. many of the ship's company were asleep in their cabins; the operation was almost over, or so they thought. On deck, wearing yellow oilskins, Alford began preparations for his unique experiment. Alongside him were two deck-hands laying out some 800 feet of cable. When anybody appeared on the stern, and few did that cold night, the scientist immediately stopped what he was doing.

In an area not far from the Kola Inlet, frequented by Soviet submarines and other Red Navy warships, Alford and the deck-hands began lowering a blue rectangular plastic package over a hoist and into the sea. The explosives expert had attached a deton-ator and explosive to a piece of steel and had lowered it to a depth of 600 feet. But Leonid Melodinsky, who had been in his cabin, had noticed that *Stephaniturm* had stopped moving. He had strolled on deck, wearing his heavy anorak and Lenin cap, and watched the Englishman lowering cable into the water. For a few seconds Alford did not notice he was being observed; then Melodinsky hurried back to his cabin. Minutes later both Soviet officials were back on deck and demanding to know what the scientist was playing with at the end of his cable.

Other officials, learning about the rumpus, also came on deck. Alford was now trying to explain to the baffled Russians that he wanted to detonate one of the charges to see how his device 'behaved' at depth. 'We don't have such deep waters around the British Isles,' he told Ilin and Melodinsky, somewhat coyly. 'I thought being out in these parts it would be ideal for trying an experiment.'

The Russians said they would lodge an official complaint and report the matter to the appropriate authorities in Moscow. After their complaint to Keogh, the experiment was aborted. The Rus-sians also pointed out firmly that explosives should not be on board. The contract made that perfectly plain, one of them explained angrily.

Keogh said: 'I was in bed feeling unwell. When I heard what had happened I ran on deck and told Dr Alford, "Stop it, Sidney! The Russians don't want it. It's bloody stupid."' The MoD official, who had helped Alford prepare his shaped charges at the beginning of the expedition the month before, tried to placate the upset tem-pers and feelings of the Russians.

Despite the bizarre appearance of explosives on deck, *after* most of the gold had been recovered, a strong force of Soviet officials, obviously pleased at the operation's success, greeted the *Ste-phaniturm*'s arrival on the quayside at Number 11 berth at Murmansk. Nearby, a number of soldiers in green and khaki uniforms and bright red epaulettes looked out from a green railway carriage, worthy in its appearance to stand comparison with the Orient Express.

The carriage was in a siding alongside the quay where the *Stephaniturm* had berthed that Thursday afternoon, 8 October. The soldiers peeping from behind curtained windows were watching for the gold to be transferred from the ship. From the time *Stephaniturm* arrived until late Friday morning, the soldiers waited patiently before the gold bars destined for the Moscow State Bank were handed over to their care.

Nearby, other uniformed Soviet guards, with semi-automatic rifles, guarded the train and the salvage ship, which, even after the Russians took their £16 million portion on the Friday morning, would still contain a very considerable fortune. On an old-fashioned diving vessel in the harbour frogmen and armed sailors stared constantly at the bullion room on the stern, often using binoculars.

While the large group of Soviet officials waited for their first glimpse of the gold, Ilin and Melodinsky looked on anxiously. David Keogh, along with two officials from the British embassy in Moscow, stepped forward to unlock the bullion room. The key would not turn in the lock. Gradually Keogh's smile disappeared. The stiff-looking Soviet party looked uneasy. Above the scene stood a group of laughing divers, their cameras clicking. One of them had squeezed superglue into the key-hole, and Keogh and the Russians were prevented from reaching the gold for almost half-an-hour.

Meanwhile, there were still twelve divers in saturation. Soviet border guards had even taken the precaution of peering through the compression chamber portholes and checking faces against individual passports. Those divers not in their saturation chambers, and their back-up team on the ship, were allowed into Murmansk on the Thursday night. At the Seamen's Mission in Murmansk, a bleak-looking town dominated by a massive concrete Red Army soldier perched on a hill, divers and ship's crew were able to buy vodka and beer and play ping-pong and chess.

They were also provided with female interpreters and invited to watch a film about Moscow and a cartoon. Later they could choose free books and pamphlets about Russian Communism. 'It was very interesting,' said one diver. 'Like a sedate night out in Tunbridge Wells with the Sally Army.'

Others in the party, including Keith Jessop who now wore a collar and tie and sports jacket, were taken to the town's main hotel for foreigners, the Sever, a rather down-at-heel place, not noted for its cuisine. There Jessop and other consortium officials, and one or two divers, were given a traditional Soviet welcome: endless speeches, followed by endless toasts in vodka and a dry Soviet champagne.

Memories of the last war were recalled during an evening which at times appeared a trifle sentimental. The chief Soviet representative from Moscow and his team of officials said that the divers had recovered a 'noble metal' which had 'not fallen into enemy hands during the last war'. The divers had brought 'a benefit' for both the Russian and the British peoples.

Outside in the colourless streets, with very few cars about, drably dressed people bought *Pravda* and *Isvestia* and read the Soviet press's account of the *Edinburgh* operation. Grandiloquent phrases about the war and the successful Anglo-Soviet project made only the slightest reference to Keith Jessop who had begun it all with a dream. And Murmansk television, while reporting the gold recovery, said nothing about the real story of the Yorkshire salvor who with next-to-nothing in his pockets had found well over £40 million on the Arctic sea-bed: nor the fact that he had carefully arranged to keep for himself a goodly chunk of the bullion and need never work again.

'Oh, I'm not retiring,' Jessop told his hosts at the official celebrations in Murmansk. 'I'd like to do other wrecks, some of them in Soviet waters.' Russian officials murmured approval and expressed repeatedly their 'deep satisfaction and pleasure' at the way the mission had been carried out. Publicly at least Ilin and Melodinsky made no mention of the bizarre incident the night before on the approach waters to the Kola Inlet. But Sidney Alford had not been invited to the Sever Hotel's formalities; he had had to make do with the Seamen's Mission.

But, like Cinderella, the official party and the visitors at the Mission had to return to the *Stephaniturm*. For foreigners, even those bearing gifts of gold, are not permitted to wander around

Murmansk after midnight. So the salvage vessel sailed for Britain the following afternoon, still carrying millions in bullion, and with the two Soviet observers, Ilin and Melodinsky, still on board. 'We must inspect the compression chambers once the divers come out of saturation,' explained one rather shamefacedly. 'Only a formality.' In fact, it was in case any of the divers had kept back a gold bar.

Back in relative normality, and with the operation a stunning triumph, the divers and their back-up team celebrated with a ribald vengeance. The two reserved Soviet officials, still uncertain about Western ways, stared in disbelief as the British government representative was filmed being debagged and having beer poured all over him. But even such stolid citizens as Ilin and Melodinsky were forced to join the lads in the seemingly endless parties which took place on the voyage home. 'Oh, the lads like letting their hair down when the job is over,' said a beaming Keith Jessop. Mysteriously, Jessop's diaries – upon which he hoped to base his autobiography – went missing on board the *Stephaniturm*. Confidential documents and other material about the operation had simply vanished from his cabin, a loss he could not replace or explain.

Every expedition has to have a sour point. Some of the divers felt their achievement had not been sufficiently acknowledged by the British government. So far there had been no official telegram of congratulations or thanks from the Bank of England, which was about to take possession of a sizeable amount of free gold bullion. Although there was talk in Whitehall, behind closed doors, of the divers being offered medals for the courage they had shown and the feat they had pulled off, the matter had been dropped for the moment.

On board *Stephaniturm* Keith Jessop, now used to handling his freshly-recovered gold bars and to feeling what it was like to be a millionaire, was asked how he would spend his money. Some of it, he explained, would be spent on salvaging new, untouched wrecks around the world.

And what about Jessop Marine's charity, the impressive trust established to benefit the relatives of men who had died on the *Edinburgh*? And the other charities – including the *Mary Rose* Trust – which had been promised donations? 'What bloody charity?' said

Jessop with a trace of annoyance. 'Where I come from charity begins at home. I don't know what my fellow directors may have agreed but I didn't set up any charity.'

Jessop's decision to dissociate himself from the company's charitable aims surprised and disappointed Bona and Ringrose. But the lawyer had already established a fund into which more than £100,000 had been placed. In January 1982 Jessop asked for the money to be transferred to a new account which he later set up at a solicitor's office in Leeds. He would examine the question of any charity and where any money might be donated. For the moment Jessop's *Edinburgh* fund, the London hospice and the Royal Navy association – along with Prince Charles and the *Mary Rose* Trust – would have to wait.

Meanwhile, as *Stephaniturm* headed back to Britain, officials on board at first maintained strict radio silence as a precaution against marine hijackers. Not even Keith Jessop knew precisely where the gold would be unloaded. He wanted to sail up the Thames, the ship's horn blaring, in a final lap of honour. In the event he would have to settle for the austere granite charms of Peterhead in Scotland. But Stalin's gold was gradually getting closer to the West.

On Wednesday afternoon, 13 October, six contented divers clambered from their peaceful compression chambers into a happy semblance of the outside world. Applauded like conquering heroes, the divers joined in the exuberant mood on board, a party mood that occasionally made mayhem seem respectable.

Overnight *Stephaniturm* had come to resemble a luxury liner during a particularly riotous New Year's Eve get-together. Some of the men, who had just returned safely from the deep, could now afford to behave like Californian gold-diggers who had made a gigantic lucky strike in the Yukon. For on *Stephaniturm*'s triumphant voyage home gold fever and high spirits broke out in a continuous party of back-slapping and self-congratulations. Vodka and beer were mixed together like campari and soda and drunk as effortlessly at breakfast as they were at midday or in the afternoon.

Feverish card games for high stakes sometimes turned into funny bouts of Indian arm-wrestling. Igor Ilin, the slim Russian, battled magnificently for many minutes with Gunter, the burly German crane driver. Dr Sidney Alford played on his penny whistle while

John Clarke reflected contentedly on the warm fact that he was now a wealthy man.

Some of the divers would pick up £30,000 apiece for the risks they had taken on the *Edinburgh*. Mindful that wives would be waiting on the quayside, men began buying gold necklaces from a diver who produced jewellery from his suitcase like a conjurer picking silk flags from a top hat.

The 431 gold bars had been divided at Murmansk in the agreed proportions of 55 per cent to the principals (37.22 per cent to the Russian government, 17.78 per cent to the British government) and 45 per cent to the salvor, Jessop's personal share being 4.5 per cent, 2Ws 16.6 per cent, Racal Decca 1.12 per cent and OSA 22.68 per cent.

Edinburgh bullion had made several men rich, but it was Keith Jessop who had most reason to feel gold fever. Only yards from his cabin were neatly-stacked ingots, a goodly number belonging to him. KP0620, the first gold bar, he would keep for himself. 'At this moment I'm a very happy man,' he would tell people who wanted to know how he felt about his sudden riches. 'What else can I say?'

For 48-year-old Keith Jessop, with a little help from his friends, really had shown the world how to turn £100 into over £40 million. On the quayside his shining silver Porsche was waiting, along with a large Brinks-Mat security truck and a million memories of HMS *Edinburgh*. The impecunious salvor, with the simple dream, had returned.

Index

Aid to Russia Fund 63
Alford, Sidney 154, 160, 173, 177, 178, 184–5, 215, 217–18; explosives work 186–8, 205–8, 210–13
Amazon 15, 19
Anglo-Russian Protocol 55, 57–8
Archangel 68
Argus 57
Austin, William 4, 11

Ballet 12
Bank of England 143–4
Banister, Capt. John 114–15
Bannister, Dicky 11
Barents Sea, military importance of 121
Beagle 15, 19
Beaverbrook, Lord 53, 57
Belfast 104, 173
Berrif, Paul 182, 184
Bettridge, P.O. Harry 16, 17, 29, 31, 34, 39, 41
Bevan, Rear-Admiral 43, 65, 68
Beverley 15, 19
Black Prince 71
Blaker, Peter 179
blast and grab technique 76–7, 111, 113, 207
Bollard, Wilfrid 82
Bona, David 94, 96, 107–8, 115,

152, 187, 197–8, 204, 210, 217; possession of gold and 154–5; publicity and 126–7
Bonham-Carter, Rear Admiral Stuart 5, 14, 20, 21–2, 25, 27, 31, 33, 34, 39, 71–2; reports by 75, 133; transferred to *Trinidad* 43, 46
Britain: relations with Russia 50–72
British Government 33 *see also* Ministry of Defence
Brown, David 85
Bulldog 15, 19
Butt, Simon 164
Byrne, Austin 12

Cairo 70–71
charity 109–10, 216–17
Charlie (NY) 12–13
Childs, Mike 208
Chulmleigh 88
Churchill 71
Churchill, Clementine 62–3
Churchill, Winston 50–72 *passim*
Clarke, John 103, 127, 130, 148, 155, 166, 170, 171, 172, 212, 218
Cockroft, Barry 125, 126
coded messages 105–6, 197–8, 204
Cole, Michael 201
Colville, Sir John 52
compression 147, 149, 162, 164
convoys xi, 57–72; losses 70; PQ13

convoys—*contd*
  60; PQ14 60; PQ16 45, 60; PQ17
  xi, 61–2; QP9 71; QP11 xi, 5, 17,
  19, 20, 26, 60–61; RA57 71
Cooper, Keith 'Scouse' 151, 160,
  161, 165, 167, 175, 181, 182, 212
Cosser, Norman 41, 49
Cripps, Stafford 51, 53, 55
Cutler, Brian 170–71, 175, 176, 199

Daily Express 134, 139
Daly, Bill 127, 139
Dammtor 124–33 *passim*, 168
Daniels, George 49
decompression *see* compression
Dennerly, Edwin 36, 44
Department of Trade 87, 110, 143–4
Diamond, Legs 170–71, 175, 175,
  176, 199
divers 149; briefing 159–62; cele-
  bration 216–18; control room
  156–7; fatigue 205, 208; helmets
  171–2; life support team 149, 162,
  169; number of 146; recruitment
  of 149–51; supervisor 156–7; tape
  recorded 182
diving bell 147–8
diving techniques 81–2; hot water in
  suits 165, 190–91; Russian 123;
  saturation 146–7, 165, 200
Doyle, James 34, 48
Droxford 97
Duke of York 69–70

ear infections 162, 176–7, 208
Eden, Anthony 52, 53, 69
Edinburgh: abandoned 28–31; armaments 3; attacked by destroyers
  21–5; attacked by U-boats 6–14;
  casualties 22–3, 34, 38, 39–40, 49–
  50; convoy protection experience
  3; gold loaded onto ix–xi; listing
  14–15, 18, 22; Russian inquiry
  into loss of 64; sunk 31–4, 72;
  towed 18–19
Edinburgh wreck: artifacts from 175,

178–9, 202–3; cost of salvage 100;
  debris inside 181–2, 200; designated a war grave 77–8, 85,
  110, 112, 121, 127, 139–40, 179,
  209; discovery of 127–33; divers'
  reaction to 174, 183–4; entered by
  divers 173–6; generator removed
  from 183; human remains on
  129–40, 183–5, 209–10; information about, available 84; initial
  failures to locate 89–91; position
  kept secret 149; relocated 168;
  researched by Jessop 83–4; Russian records of 128–9
Edinburgh Survivors' Association
  85, 121, 127
Elton 195–6, 198–9
Empire Lawrence 45, 61
Entwhistle, Clive 125, 126
explosives: Alford's experiments
  205–8; carried on *Stephaniturm*
  187–9; danger of inside *Edinburgh*
  150, 151, 159, 174, 181; defused
  by Alford 186–7; insurance and
  187, 188–9, 201, 206–7; not to be
  used by Jessop 111, 139, 189, 206–
  7; purchased by 2W 187, 210
Express Newspapers 127, 134

Faulkner, Capt. Hugh ix, 5, 33, 36,
  39, 71, 72; U-boat attack and 7,
  11
Foresight 15, 17–19, 20, 26, 34–5, 37,
  47; sinks *Edinburgh* 32
Forester 15, 17–19, 20, 26, 34–5, 47
Fowells, Lt-Cmdr Joseph 31, 34,
  35–6, 37, 42

Gaff, Lt-Col. J. M. 211
Galewsky, Hermann 19, 21, 22, 24,
  28, 35, 39
Gamvik 131
George, Cmdr Eric 13, 24, 32, 39–
  40
Germany 50–72 *passim*
Gernhard, Viktor 32

Giddings, James 9, 28, 36

Götz, Capt. Ronnie 155, 195, 199

gold bullion: boxes 200, 202; discovered 191–6; first bar 193–4; governments' share of 104, 121; insurance 39; Jessop Marine's share of 143–5; landed at Murmansk 213–14; loading ix–xi; loading on *Stephaniturm* 199; photographs of 201; quantity of 67, 100, 205, 211; Russians' view of loss 66–7; security of 153, 201–2; sunk 33, 39; VAT and 144; value of 204, 208

Golovko, Arseni 64, 66–7

Gossamer 16, 20, 22, 26–8

Gremyaschi 8, 15, 128; returns to harbour 18, 21, 37, 65–6

Grenfell, Cmdr Eric 45–6, 48, 61

Hafentor 208

Hampshire 75, 84

Harrier 16, 20, 22, 26–8, 32, 35, 37, 104; navigational reports 129–30

Harriman, Averell 57, 59

Hay, Flt-Lt 61

Hember, Alner 30

Hermann Schoemann 16, 17, 169; hit by *Edinburgh* 23, 26, 28, 35

Hesketh, Derrick 150, 162, 169, 191, 209

Higgins, Alan 4, 8, 14, 24–5, 29, 31, 32, 33

Hinds, Fergus 112–13, 117

Hinton, Cmdr Eric 27, 35, 39

Hodges, Frank 38

Hodson, Capt. 111

Holness, Stanley 118, 138, 185

Holt, Neville 4, 9

hospitals 44–5, 68

Howe, Lt-Cmdr 16, 21, 23, 24, 25–6

Hughes, Pat x, 4, 24, 38

Hussar 16, 20, 21, 22, 26–8, 37

Hyderabad 61

Ilin, Igor 129, 132, 155, 165, 171, 172, 177, 185, 193, 196, 199, 201, 214, 216, 217

Induna 12

Ingrams, Colin 119

international waters, salvage in 78, 86

Jackson, John 83, 87, 97, 107, 111–12, 118, 154, 177, 201

Jarrett, Cyril 10, 25, 29

Jefford, Percy 45

Jeffries, Cmdr ix

Jessop, Graham 107, 126, 205

Jessop, Keith 171, 199; complaints about 136–8; diary 162–3, 216; discovery of the gold and 193; diving work for 2W 80–81, 123, 126, 136, 137; first salvage work 79–80; knowledge of explosives on board 207; money problems 96, 116, 122–3, 126; Moscow negotiations and 118–24, 136–7; possession of gold dispute and 153–5; publicity and 125–6, 172–3; spending plans 145, 216, 218; Stolt-Nielsen and 94; survey permission 97–8; 2W and 98–102; U-boat 570 and 78–9; YTV and 125–6

Jessop consortium: British approval of 114; disputes within 153; formed 107; in Russia 213–16; information on competitors sent to 109, 112–14, 137–8, 163–4; investigated by Bannister 114–15; Russian approval of 114–24; share of the gold 143–5; supported by Salvage Association 111–12; tax problems 143–4

Jessop Marine Recoveries Ltd 95; contract with 2W 100–102; financial problems 124, 135; further ambitions of 120; joint venture proposal 103–7; loan from Rothschilds 205

Keene, David 161, 171, 189, 191, 192, 193, 202, 208
Keller, Hannes 82
Kenya 71
Keogh, David 154, 158, 172, 177, 179, 186, 188, 197–8, 199, 201, 213, 214; human remains buried by 184–5, 210, 211–12
Kola Inlet 8, 67–8 *see also* Murmansk
Krumin, Miraslav 114

Lars Christiansen 190
lend-lease 54–5, 58–9
Levick, C.P.O. Reg ix, x, xi, 9–10, 25, 31, 200
Lewis, C.P.O. 30
Lewis, Edward 42
Lillie, Douglas 23
Lingetwood, Jim 180
Lloyd, Harold 4, 11
Lord Middleton 19, 28

McIntyre, P.O. 4
Mathison, Dougald 177, 180, 182–3, 190, 198, 202; injured 203–4
Matthews, Peter 4–5, 8, 28–9, 43
Melodinsky, Leonid 155, 171, 172, 177, 185, 193, 199, 201, 213, 214, 216
Miles, Bill x–xi
Miles, Rear-Admiral Geoffrey 53
Ministry of Defence 84–7, 89, 104, 127, 210
Molotov, Vyacheslav 69
Moore, Cyril x, 6, 43
Moore, David 27, 32
Morrice, David 97, 111
Murena 195, 198–9
Murmansk 41–50; convoys to 54; gold landed at 213–16

Newman, C.P.O. Lawrence 4, 21, 29–30, 31, 22, 41
Niagara 77
Niger 16, 20, 21, 37

Nommensen, Rolf 178
North, Andy 168
North Sea oil diving 81–3, 148

OSA 102, 107, 110, 124, 151, 155, 166, 202
Ogden, Cmdr Graeme 43
O'Meara, Mike 159–60, 162, 165, 200, 209
Operation Dervish 57
Operation Greyhound 145; all-British claim for 167; secrets 154
Otranco 80

Peters, Cmdr 24
Pickford, Tom 76, 77, 118
Polyarnoe 42, 43, 44, 56–7, 68, 69
press, the: interest in operation 158; reports from *Stephaniturm* 172–3, 185, 190, 202
Prince Charles 109–10
publicity 125–6, 172–3
Punch, Kip 129, 131

Queen Elizabeth 13
Quinn, colour-sergeant x

Racal Decca 102, 103, 107, 124
Reudavey, Geoff 150, 168, 171
Richmond, Cmdr 20
Ringrose, James 83, 84–96 *passim*, 107, 109–10, 113–14, 125, 140, 144, 152, 204, 217; possession of gold and 154–5; publicity and 126–7, 134–7; wreck's location and 128–35 *passim*
Risdon Beazley 75–8, 81, 86, 87, 89, 94, 125; closure of 117–18; Salvage Association and 111, 112; salvage proposal 108, 112–14; survey of wreck 96–7, 117
Roberts, Keith 161, 199
Rodocker, Don 151–2, 167, 171–2
Roosevelt, President 51–2, 54
Rossier, John 177, 180, 182, 189, 191–3

Rubin 16, 20–21, 28, 37

Russia 213–16; receives share of gold 213–14; relations with Britain 50–72; searchs for *Edinburgh* 89–90; seizure of gold by, feared 104; ships guarding *Stephaniturm* 195–6, 198–9

Salter, Jocelyn 18, 26, 72

Saltzwedel, Fregattenkapitan 19, 23, 25

salvage: depth and 76, 78, 81–2; secrecy and 79, 106

Salvage Association 83, 86, 127 *see also* Jackson, John

Scharnhorst 69

Schlarbaum, Klaus 212

Schulze-Hinrichs, Capt. 23

Sea Hawk 89

search technology, underwater 130–31

Second Front 56, 58, 68

security 106–7; for the gold 153–5, 201–2; messages from ship 157–8

Seibicke, Kapitänleutnant 5

Sheffield 33

Snowflake 19

Sokrushitelni 8, 15, 128; returns to harbour 18, 21, 37, 65–6

Stalin, J. 50–72 *passim*

Star Off-Shore 97

Stephaniturm 102–3, 110, 145–6; accommodation on 155–6; capability 146, 148, 168; dynamic positioning 181, 191; Soviet protection of 120–21, 195–6, 198–9; supplies for 151

Stewart, Mike 124, 146, 148, 150, 152, 157, 166–7, 171, 203, 206

Stolt-Nielsen 87–9, 163–4; failure to find *Edinburgh* 90–91, 128; leaves Jessop 92, 94; Salvage Association and 111; salvage proposal 108, 112–14

Suffolk 70

Summers, Pete 171, 177–8

Sunday Times 139, 140, 143, 154, 157, 158, 177–8, 179, 184, 186–7, 190, 210

Sutherland, Sam 161

2W 84, 98–102, 124, 134–5, 149, 187, 201, 210; contract with Jessop Marine 100–102; credit for 204; joint venture proposal to 103–7; legal possession of gold and 153–5

Teichert, Kapitänleutnant 5–6, 7, 14

Tirpitz 62, 68

Trinidad 33, 43–4, 46, 47, 60, 169

Tucker, Jim

U-boat 436 5, 18

U-boat 456 5, 14, 16, 18

Vaenga 42, 43, 45, 46, 49, 68

Vardo 131

Vian, Rear-Admiral Philip 56

War Graves Commission 77, 179

Waziristen 88

weather problems 146, 165–6, 174–5, 203, 209, 212

West, Barry 'Banjo' 151, 159, 170–71, 174, 175, 177, 180, 199, 211–12

Wharton, Ric 84, 98–102, 133, 202–3

Whitehead, Charles 4, 9, 17–18, 23, 25, 42, 44

Williams, Malcolm 84, 98–102, 133–4, 156, 177–8, 205, 210

Wookey, George 82

Yates, James 71

Yeomans, Ian 184

Yorkshire Television 125–6

Z 24 and 25 (destroyers) 16, 17, 19, 23–4, 26, 35

Zetterstrom, Arne 82

Zlobin, L. 119